Britain's
BEER
REVOLUTION

Behind the scenes with the people, breweries and beers inspiring a nation

Roger Protz & Adrian Tierney-Jones

BOOKS

Published by the Campaign for Real Ale Ltd.

230 Hatfield Road
St Albans
Hertfordshire AL1 4LW
www.camra.org.uk/books

First published 2014

© Campaign for Real Ale Ltd.

ISBN 978-1-85249-321-9

A CIP catalogue record for this book is available from the British Library

Printed and bound in Slovenia by Latitude Press Ltd

Type set in Chaparral, Myriad Pro, Sketch Block, Bullpen and Palatino

Head of Publishing: Simon Hall
Project Manager: Katie Button
Editorial Assistance: Emma Haines, Julie Hudson
Design & Typography: Hannah Moore
Design Assistance: Keith Holmes, Thames Street Studio
Senior Marketing Manager: Chris Lewis

DISCLAIMER

PUBLISHER'S THANKS

The publisher would like to thank everyone who has helped to make this book possible – brewers, publicans, producers, beer writers and many others. The publisher would also like to thank the CAMRA branches and members who contributed with suggestions for the book, and Martin Ellis and Colin Valentine for contributing to the North East and Scotland regions.

PICTURE CREDITS

FOREWORD

In *Britain's Beer Revolution*, leading beer writers Roger Protz and Adrian Tierney-Jones set out to explore Britain's flourishing contemporary beer scene and capture the mood of these exciting and inspiring times.

Divided into regional chapters (as illustrated below), the book looks at evolving beer culture and traditions across the country with in-depth features highlighting some of Britain's most innovative breweries – from massive to micro – that best exemplify the brewing revolution. With close to 1,300 breweries now operating in Britain, the authors have hand-picked those that best highlight the enormous changes that have taken place in recent years. In region after region they show how new artisan breweries have started up, embracing ideas from across the globe, while older family-owned companies have been inspired to join the revolution.

Britain was once famous for having just two beer styles – mild and bitter – but now offers a vast range of styles, from golden ales through India Pale Ales, porters, stouts, old ales, barley wines, fruit beers and sour beers to ales aged in whisky and wine barrels. Innovation goes hand-in-hand with reviving older styles that have been culled from brewers' logs in the 18th and 19th centuries.

The book profiles some of the key people in modern brewing, including not only brewers but also specialist barley farmers, maltsters and hop growers. Also included are must-visit regional beer and pub destinations; special features on key trends in British beer and brewing; plus personal insights from producers, brewers, publicans, beer critics and others.

Pour yourself a beer and enjoy this fascinating look behind the scenes...

HOW THE BOOK WORKS

Regions The book is divided into ten regions, covering the whole of Britain. Regional maps identify the location of the featured breweries and beer destinations

Brewery entries Breweries are ordered alphabetically by region

Beers to try Roger and Adrian suggest some of the best examples of each brewery's beer to seek out

Beer destinations A selection of the best pubs, bars, brewery taps and visitor centres in the region, chosen for their beer range and commitment to stocking examples of the best British beers

Features Articles expand on some of the most interesting trends in British brewing, exploring ingredients and current developments in how beer is brewed, served and enjoyed

CONTENTS

INTRODUCTION

Roger Protz

Two press releases, received just as this book was nearing completion, underscore our main theme: that exhilarating change has shaken up a once staid and hidebound brewing industry. The first release was from Pauls Malt, a major supplier of grain to brewers, who reported a substantial increase in sales and income due to the rise of microbreweries 'who use a higher proportion of malt in their grist'. It's perfectly possible – and legal – to produce something called beer made with rice, cornstarch and liquid caramel, with the process speeded along with the addition of industrial enzymes, but that's not the style of the brewers featured in these pages. They are driven by flavour and know that good beer, whether it's the colour of golden dawn or midnight black, gets its flavour from the finest raw materials.

The second release came from the Suffolk brewer Adnams, which asked drinkers to send them any hops they found in gardens and hedgerows to be used in a Wild Hop beer they planned for the autumn. Brewing has come a long way from the early 1970s when producers not only guarded their recipes as though they were state secrets but also refused to declare the alcoholic strengths of their brews. Today brewers welcome the participation of beer lovers: Windsor & Eton, for example, asked home brewers to work with them to fashion a Magna Carta Ale while Stewart brewery near Edinburgh invited students from Heriot-Watt University to come along and brew on their plant.

As Adrian points out, the most amazing range of beers is now produced in Britain. I doubt that members of my family who resided in Bermondsey in south-east London would have expected to drink a Berliner Weisse produced by a small brewery, Kernel, under a local railway bridge. Their tipple, years ago, would have been either mild or bitter.

And long live mild and bitter. But now there's a beer for all seasons and all occasions, brewed by 1,300 breweries: some new, some ancient and rejuvenated.

As the lady said: Rejoice!

Adrian Tierney-Jones

'This is a great time to be a brewer.'

I've had these words said to me several times over the past 12 months when sitting down with brewers, tasting and talking about their beers, and trying to find out what makes the men and women who stand by the mash tun tick and turn over their lives to the making of beer.

Despite the issues facing the pub trade, there is a genuine sense of excitement among the brewing community at the opportunities and revelations that beer drinkers want and expect these days – there is a sense of exploration, a sense of freedom. If a brewer wants to make a Limoncello-flavoured IPA, as is the case with Ryan Witter-Merithew of Siren brewery, then he will; or maybe a brewer wants to weave a strain of Belgian yeast into the midst of their beer while letting a big punch of rye muscle its way into the mash tun - how about Bristol Beer Factory's sensuously spicy Belgian Rye?

Breweries are trying their hands at making Gose [sour wheat beer], wheat wine, barley wine, session IPAs (and all manner of IPAs); they are also reinvigorating mild (and looking back to the fog-shrouded city streets of Victorian England for stronger versions). They are punching up the hop ratio on bitter and carefully crafting porters and stout. And this activity does not just involve new breweries – traditional family firms such as Brains and Adnams are discovering what it's like to move outside their old comfort zones and take a look at brewing from a new and exciting angle.

This is certainly a great time to be a brewer and it's also a great time to be a beer drinker, as I hope that this book that Roger Protz and I have written together, will demonstrate in the brightest and boldest way.

Cheers!

ALL ABOUT BEER

WHAT IS GOOD BEER?

The world of brewing is riven by a growing chasm between two contrasting visions of what constitutes beer. Global producers, dominated by their accountants and marketing departments, concentrate on selling industrial beer made as cheaply and as quickly as possible. International giants such as AB InBev, SABMiller, Molson Coors, Carlsberg and Heineken make drinks that may be legally definable as beer but which are a long way removed from the notion that it should be made with such time-honoured ingredients as malted grain and hops.

As the label on a bottle of Budweiser, the 'Great American Lager' – the world's single biggest beer brand – makes clear, rice accounts for a substantial proportion of the grain bill. Other brewers of industrial beer use maize and starch to dilute the malt content. The fleeting acquaintance such beers have with the hop comes often in the form of hop extract: the cone of the plant is pulverised and its juices extracted to create a green liquid that leaves a sharp and often unpleasant aftertaste. Industrial enzymes are used to speed up the brewing process while fermentation is as brief as science and nature will allow.

PUTTING TASTE FIRST

There is a growing counter culture. It's driven by consumers concerned with how food and drink is made and provenance – a desire to drink beer made from traceable, often locally-grown ingredients. The demand has been met by brewers who combine a love of their craft with a passionate desire to create beers packed with natural aromas and flavours. To stress their radically different approach to beer-making, the brewers of the counter culture are variously described as artisan or craft producers. They do not set out to challenge the power of the global producers but instead offer a concept of beer that enshrines taste at its heart.

It would be a mistake to assume that all craft brewers are newcomers to the trade. Far from it: there are many family brewers with long pedigrees that are as passionate about beer and modern brewing practice as their younger rivals. As Stuart Bateman of Batemans brewery in Wainfleet, Lincolnshire, says: 'Don't tell me I'm not a craft brewer because the company's been around for 140 years'.

THE GROWTH OF CRAFT

British breweries both ancient and modern have a shared commitment to creating good beer, using the finest raw materials, for today's discriminating and rightfully demanding audience. Beer drinking is in decline in Britain, most notably mass-marketed lagers and 'smooth flow' keg ales. But craft brewers, who give drinkers a wide portfolio of styles, and an extraordinary variety of exciting flavours, have seen growth in both their sales and their numbers. The days when brewers offered just mild, bitter and a stronger brew for Christmas are long-gone. Today, pubs offer a vast and growing range that includes faithful recreations of such historic styles as porter, stout and India Pale Ale along with new interpretations: the diversity of beers available in Britain has never been greater.

Stuart Bateman says 'Don't tell me I'm not a craft brewer because the company's been around for 140 years'

Despite the emergence of new types of beer such as 'craft keg' it is cask beer (real ale) that is the real driving force behind Britain's beer revolution

BREWERS PROUD OF THEIR INGREDIENTS

As their choice at the bar increases, consumers demand and are given more and more information about the brands they drink. Forty years ago brewers blanched at the notion of sharing information with their customers – even the strength of beer was treated as though it were a state secret. Today, the measure of alcohol in beer is clearly stated on pump clips and labels, and brewers have gone the extra mile and routinely inform consumers of the malts and hops they use. They are proud of the provenance of their ingredients, and drinkers are becoming increasingly knowledgeable about the role that malt and hops play in their favourite beers. A remark in the 1990s by a brewer in Yorkshire, Sean Franklin, that 'hops are the grapes of brewing' has become widespread and encapsulates the important role hops play in beer. Drinkers are now aware of the great variety of hops available and the distinctive character each gives to the finished product. English hops are renowned for their resinous, spicy, peppery and restrained fruit notes while varieties from the United States and New Zealand add a profound citrus trait. Drinkers are now well-informed about the characteristics of Cascades, Citra, Fuggles, Goldings and Nelson Sauvin as wine drinkers discussing the merits of Cabernet and Merlot grapes.

A QUEST FOR THE NEW

The story of British beer in the 21st century is one of innovation and dynamism, a quest for new and exciting flavours to satisfy a demanding audience. 'Craft beer', increasingly, is the expression used to distinguish the products of independent brewers from the industrial beers of the global giants. A number of independents have developed a new type of keg beer, often called 'craft keg', that is radically different to the derided kegs beers of the 1970s and 80s. CAMRA believes in choice for drinkers and is relaxed about the emergence of modern keg. But the Campaign is rooted in the belief that real ale, naturally conditioned, unfiltered and served without applied gas pressure, offers the fullest flavours and finest drinking experience for beer lovers.

FROM FIELD TO GLASS: HOW BEER IS BREWED

'Beer', said Julius Caesar, encountering it for the first time as he marched across northern Europe to the British Isles, 'is a high and mighty liquor'. A few centuries later, in 1158, the English priest Thomas à Becket took two chariot-loads of ale with him on a diplomatic mission to France 'as a gift for the French who wondered at such an invention – a drink most wholesome, clear of all dregs, rivalling wine in colour and surpassing it in savour'.

The Romans and the Normans, who drank wine and cider at home, found that the dogged British preferred a grain-based alcohol, a preference eventually passed on to the invaders as well. They realised that ale and beer are not inferior drinks to fruit-based ones and that it requires skill to make them. If you squeeze grapes and ferment the juice, you get wine. If you crush apples and ferment the juice, you get cider. But crush an ear of barley and you will get dust on your hands.

MALT: BEER'S BACKBONE

Long before the brewer can start to make beer, the essential raw material – grain – has to undergo an exhaustive transformation. The journey that ends with the glass in your hand begins not in a brewery but in a maltings. There the grain – usually barley – is turned into malt, which has the essential sugars needed for fermentation. Barley is the preferred grain: it makes inferior bread but it delivers the biscuit character needed by an artisan brewer. Other grains used to make good beer include wheat, oats and occasionally rye. But even 'wheat beers' are a blend of barley and wheat malts.

Only the best barley is used for brewing. Many brewers consider that maritime barley, grown near the coast in dark, alluvial soil – as is the case in Norfolk in Eastern England – is best for brewing. There are many varieties of barley, some more delicate ones grown in the spring, more hardy types in the autumn, but the overwhelming choice for British brewers looking for a rich malt loaf/cracker biscuit character is Maris Otter.

In the maltings the grain is thoroughly washed then warmed to allow it to germinate or sprout, which starts the process that turns starch in each ear of grain into fermentable sugar. When germination is underway, the grain is loaded into an oven called a kiln. The temperature is adjusted to produce the type of malt needed by the brewer. All beer – even jet black stouts

Left: Barley is the key ingredient in beer **Right:** Hops provide much of the flavour and aroma

– are made predominantly from pale malt as it has the highest level of enzymes – proteins that complete the conversion of starch to sugar in the brewery.

The temperature in the kiln is raised to produce such darker malts as amber, black, brown and chocolate, which add notes of coffee, chocolate, liquorice, molasses, and raisin and sultana fruit to the finished beer. Roasted barley is not malted but is often used in dark beers, porter and stout in particular, to give a vinous, slightly acrid and burnt fruit note.

A specialist family of stewed malts comes under the heading of caramel malts. They are made in a similar fashion to toffee and add – as the name suggests – a caramel/toffee/butterscotch note to the beer, sometimes with a strong hint of cobnuts. Crystal is the main type of stewed malt used in British ale brewing.

The first stage in the journey is over. Now the malt is ready to meet its partners in the brewing process.

HOPS: PEPPER AND SPICE

Hops famously make beer bitter but a greater understanding has developed that recognises the remarkable flavours and aromas hops also bring to beer-making. Hops grow in both the northern and southern hemispheres with the leading producers based in North America, England, Germany, the Czech Republic, Australia and New Zealand. Slovenia is another major producer while Poland and other Central and Eastern European countries grow excellent hops, as does Japan. China is coming up fast on the rails.

The character of the water used in brewing plays an essential part

Hops thrive in well-drained loamy or sandy soil and need both sunshine and rain to grow. The plants are trained to climb trellises to gain as much sunshine as possible and also to make them easy to pick by hand or machine. While brewers of mass-market global brands essentially want just bitterness from hops, craft brewers seek out the finest aroma hops to add spice, pepper, grass, orange, lemon, grapefruit, peach, melon, pine and cedar wood to their beers. Many beers use more than one hop; blending together two or more varieties that offer both aroma and bitterness.

Brewers now offer far greater information about the hops they use. As a result, drinkers are aware that English varieties give peppery and spicy notes along with orange, lemon and lime fruit while American hops have a more robust citrus character, with grapefruit to the fore. German hops, grown predominantly for lager beer, have a restrained floral and grassy note while the Czech Žatec, better known by its German name of Saaz, has a piny, floral and resinous character. Australian hops are bold and brassy while those from New Zealand are highly prized. The Nelson Sauvin in particular is widely exported, its tropical fruit character similar to that of the Sauvignon grape.

WATER: THE ESSENTIAL LIQUOR

Water in a brewery is not just for cleaning. Brewing water – always known as 'liquor' – plays a critical role in the character of beer. It may come from a spring or bore hole on the site of the brewery or from the public supply but its mineral content – whether naturally occurring or provided by added salts – brings out the full flavours of malt and hops.

In England, water helped reshape brewing in the 19th century when the mineral-rich waters of the Trent Valley enabled brewers in Burton to fashion the world's first pale beer, India Pale Ale. Trent water is rich in gypsum and magnesium sulphates. The salts are flavour enhancers and drinkers were suddenly offered a new style of beer that blossomed with rich malt and hop character. Today brewers throughout the world talk of 'Burtonising their liquor' to create a true pale ale.

The mineral-rich waters in Edinburgh and Alloa enabled Scottish brewers to develop their interpretation of IPA known as Export. Burtonising water is not necessary where dark beer production is concerned: at the start of the industrial age, when London was a great producer of mild, porter and stout, it was the calcium carbonate in London water that enhanced the soft, creamy and vinous character of the beers.

In classic lager brewing, water is low in mineral content. In Pilsen in the Czech Republic, home of the first golden lager, the water is almost free of minerals.

YEAST: FUNGUS WITH ATTITUDE

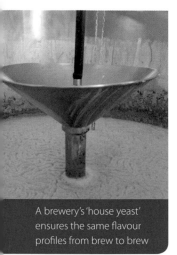

A brewery's 'house yeast' ensures the same flavour profiles from brew to brew

Yeast is the catalyst that turns a sugar-rich liquid into beer. It's a type of fungus: a single cell plant that greedily attacks malt sugars and creates alcohol and carbon dioxide. But it also has a critical role to play in the flavour of beer. It picks up and retains the character of a particular brew and passes on that character to successive brews. During fermentation it creates esters, compounds similar to such fruits as apple and pineapple as well as fresh tobacco. Brewers talk of the 'house character' of their yeast and guard it carefully, refrigerating their supply. They also deposit a sample of their yeast at a special laboratory: the National Collection of Yeast Cultures. If a brewer gets a yeast infection he or she can quickly obtain a fresh sample from the lab.

Ale yeast works at a furious pace and builds a thick protein-rich head on top of the fermenting liquid. Its work is done within seven days. Lager yeast works at a lower temperature, creates less head and takes longer to finish its work, which continues in the lager cellar. In real ale, yeast continues to work in the cask in the pub cellar.

A third type of beer is made by 'wild' or spontaneous fermentation. The beer is called lambic and is confined to a small area around Brussels in Belgium. Instead of cultured yeasts, brewers open the windows and allow passing yeasts in the atmosphere to start fermentation. Brewers in Britain and the United States who replicate lambic with 'sour beer' inoculate their worts with a yeast called *Brettanomyces*, the main strain used in lambic production.

LET THERE BE BEER

Beer is racked into casks, where it undergoes a secondary fermentation

The cast of characters has been assembled and now the drama can begin. No two breweries are identical but all follow a similar path. Brewing starts in a mash tun, much like a giant teapot. Instead of tea leaves, grain is mixed with hot liquor (brewing water) and left to stand while the enzymes in the malt convert the last remaining starches into sugar. After a few hours, when the brewer is satisfied that full starch conversion has been achieved, the sweet extract, called wort, is run from the tun to a copper where it's vigorously boiled with hops.

Hops are usually added in three stages: at the start of the boil, halfway through and just before the end. The aim is to extract as much of the oils and from the plants as possible for aroma and flavour in the finished beer. The boil lasts for between 1½ and two hours.

The 'hopped wort' is cooled and pumped to fermenting vessels. Fermenters can be open, closed, round, square and built with one or two storeys but whatever the shape everything is now left to nature as yeast creates alcohol. When fermentation is complete, the 'green' or unfinished beer rests in conditioning tanks for a few days to purge itself of unwanted rough flavours. It then goes in different directions. Real ale is racked or run into casks, often primed with malt sugar to encourage further fermentation, with the addition of extra hops. It's delivered to pubs in an unfinished state and enjoys a second fermentation in cask. Keg beer is filtered and often pasteurised and run into sealed containers and delivered to the bar by applied gas pressure. Most bottled beers are filtered and pasteurised but bottle-conditioned beers contain live yeast in order to gain maturity and flavour.

BEER STYLES

Brewers have a fantastic range of ingredients to play with – all of which can be combined in the brewery in multiple ways to produce beer. The history of brewing in Britain has led to some iconic beer styles, while new beer styles, with golden ales leading the charge, have flooded into pubs in recent years.

BITTER

Bitter has close links to pale ale and developed from the major changes in brewing practice in England in the Victorian period that enabled paler beers to be produced. The result was India Pale Ale – at first an export beer – and its lower-strength offshoot, pale ale. They were beers that were stored or 'vatted' for some time to reach maturity. When brewers built estates of pubs late in the 19th century they moved away from vatted ales to what they called 'running beers' – today's cask-conditioned real ales.

To give what brewers call 'mouthfeel', a new type of malt known as crystal – made in a similar way to toffee – was blended with pale malt to give a rich butterscotch note. Hops were generously used and it was their uncompromising contribution that led to the beer being dubbed bitter by drinkers.

As sales of both mild ale and IPA declined, bitter became the dominant style. There is a considerable crossover between bitter and pale ale. While most bitters are copper coloured, due to the use of crystal or other slightly darker malts, some bitters are extremely pale

– the much-missed Boddingtons Bitter is a case in point. Most brewers today reserve the term pale ale for bottled versions of their bitter.

If that's confusing, then so is the dividing line between bitter and best bitter. It should be 4% – above that level, the style becomes best bitter but a number of brewers call their ordinary bitters 'best'. Special bitters and extra special bitters are a stronger breed, 5% and upwards.

What to look for: While there are some pale bitters, in general the style is marked by a copper or deep bronze colour. There's a juicy and biscuit malt note overlaid by a big peppery, spicy and fruity hop character. The finish is dry with continuing rich malt and fruit but with an intense bitterness. Best bitters have a great malt character but are balanced by generous hopping. Special and extra special bitters are marked by a distinct fruitiness – Fuller's ESB has been likened to 'liquid marmalade' – but malt and fruit flavours are balanced by big hop resins.

MILD ALE

Mild ale was once the main beer drunk in England and was designed for industrial and agricultural workers who wanted to restore lost energy with a beer sweeter and less heavily hopped than bitter. As work in factories and on the land declined after World War Two, sales of mild fell away, though it remained popular in parts of the West Midlands, Wales and Merseyside. It has shown a welcome return in recent years as brewers prove that the style doesn't have to be low in strength: several new wave milds are 4% or more.

What to look for: Most milds are dark – russet, amber or black – due to the use of substantial amounts of crystal and darker malts. Roasted barley is occasionally used. Aromas and flavours tend to be dominated by coffee, chocolate, caramel or vinous characteristics. Bitterness is low but there are good earthy, spicy notes from traditional English varieties. A few light milds exist, such as Taylor's Golden Best or McMullen's AK, similar to bitter in colour but with a maltier character.

INDIA PALE ALE

India Pale Ale is the buzz beer of the moment. It's a style that went into rapid decline at the end of the 19th century but has been brought back to life by scores of brewers in both Britain and the US. It was first brewed with high levels of alcohol and hops which helped before to keep it in good condition on long sea journeys to India. Some modern interpretations of the style are too dark: it was a genuinely pale beer, made with just pale malt and brewing sugar. Hop rates were high as the plant acts as a preservative but the rates were lowered considerably when the style was refashioned for domestic drinking and called pale ale. Strength should be 5.5% or higher: Thornbridge Jaipur IPA at 5.9% is a benchmark and 'IPAs' of 3.6 or 4% don't deserve the label.

What to look for: A pale bronze colour with a big hit of hops, tart fruit and juicy malt on aroma and palate, with a long, quenching finish that ends dry, hoppy and with an almost quinine-like bitterness.

PORTER AND STOUT

Porter and stout date from the early 18th century when a strong ale, blended from pale, brown and old ales, became popular with porters working the markets and docks in London. It was given the nickname of porter as a result and the strongest version was called stout porter, later shortened to just stout. Restrictions on the use of dark malt in Britain during World War One led to porter and stout becoming Irish specialities but they are once again being made with relish by many British brewers. The colour comes from the use of darker malts – black, brown and crystal – with roasted barley often added. Unlike mild, porters and stouts should have a good solid backbone of hop bitterness to balance the rich grain.

What to look for: Black in colour with a ruby edge and a rich vinous, slightly acidic aroma with strong hints of espresso coffee and bitter chocolate. Dark grain on the palate and the finish often has a burnt fruit – raisin and sultana – note alongside coffee and chocolate. The finish may start bittersweet but coffee, chocolate and spicy hops lead to a dry, fruity and hoppy end.

GOLDEN ALE

The revival of porter and stout proves that modern drinkers are not deterred by dark beer. But in sharp contrast, golden ale is without doubt the success story of recent years. It was first brewed in the early 1990s by a handful of brewers – Exmoor, Hop Back and Kelham Island – to wean younger drinkers away from lager. Golden ale may look like lager but as a result of the ale system of brewing has a rich biscuit and honey malt character overlain by powerful fruity hops. Many brewers used imported hops from North America and New Zealand to give a citrus balance to the malt. Almost without exception, British brewers now offer a golden ale as part of their portfolios and the beers are often served cold – at around 8°C – to satisfy modern palates.

What to look for: A pale straw colour with tangy and tart citrus fruit on nose and palate, balanced by a juicy and honey malt note. The finish is bittersweet with continuing citrus fruit and honey malt, though some golden ales, such as the award-winning Crouch Vale Brewers Gold, can be more bitter and hoppy.

OLD ALE AND BARLEY WINE

Old ale and barley wine are styles that have survived from the 18th and 19th centuries. Old ale's name came from its long period of ageing in wooden vats where it picked up some lactic character from wild yeasts. It was nicknamed 'stale' as a result and was one of the beers used in the early blended porters. Barley wine, as the name suggests, was a strong beer that rivalled wine and was drunk by the patriotic English when the country was at war with France. It was aged for long periods and had a strength of around 12%. In contrast, old ale does not have to be especially strong: its best known versions are Theakston's Old Peculier and Gale's Prize Old Ale. In the barley wine category, Fuller's Vintage Ale at 8.5% is a true flag-waver for the historic style.

What to look for: Neither style needs to be dark, and paler versions will have luscious malt and strong peppery hop notes. Whether pale or dark, expect pear drop fruit and peppery hops, with fresh tobacco and polished leather. There can be a touch of acidity, as in Gale's Prize Old Ale. Both styles tend to mature in bottle rather than vats these days.

WHEAT BEER

Wheat beer is a recent addition to British beer styles, brewed in response to the popularity of Belgian and Bavarian versions. In spite of the name, wheat beers are a blend of malted barley and wheat but the latter grain gives a distinctive creamy note and – if a proper wheat beer yeast culture is used – a banana and bubblegum flavour. The Belgian influence encourages brewers to add spice and fruit, such as orange peel, coriander and cloves.

What to look for: Hazy when unfiltered – *mit hefe* or 'with yeast' as the Bavarians say – wheat beer is usually pale, though there are darker versions. Creamy malt and sweet fruit dominate aroma and palate and there's only a light hop character. Fruit and spice will make for a more pungent and complex beer in the Belgian interpretations.

SCOTTISH BEERS

Traditional Scottish beers have been overshadowed in recent years by the rise of paler, English-style ales. But the likes of Fyne, Stewart and Orkney are keeping the flag flying for lights and heavies – the Scottish equivalent of mild and bitter. And Scottish brewers have been at the forefront of ageing beer in whisky casks. As a result of a climate that doesn't encourage hop growing, traditional beers tend to be rich and malty, with lower levels of bitterness than in beers south of the border. They may be labelled 60, 70 and 80 shilling beers from a Victorian method of invoicing beer based on strength. Scottish stouts are distinctive, often with the addition of oats that give a creamy appeal.

What to look for: Beers range in colour from pale copper to deep russet. Aromas offer roasted grain and burnt fruit with hints of chocolate and caramel. Stronger beers have a biscuit malt/cracker wheat character and more balance from peppery English hops.

REGIONAL VARIATIONS

Beer is to Britain as wine is to France: it's the regional variations in both countries that make drinking both pleasurable and fascinating. Beer styles are rooted in history and tradition but – just as with wine's *terroir* – geography, climate, soil and water play crucial roles in brewing and in the character of the finished product.

Scientific advances in how water, yeast, grain and hops are used have to be married to time-honoured consumer preference. Tell a Yorkshire drinker there's too much 'head' or foam on the beer and at best you will get a withering look and a shake of the head that regrets your lack of knowledge about the way beer is made in God's Own County.

YORKSHIRE AND THE NORTH WEST

Beer character in Yorkshire was determined to a large extent by a fermentation system known as 'the Yorkshire Square'. It was introduced to tackle the problem of Yorkshire yeast, which works slowly and needs to be roused by the brewer and reinvigorated on a regular basis. This is achieved by using a vessel with two chambers, linked by a manhole in the centre. Every few hours, the fermenting wort is pumped from the bottom chamber into the top via the manhole where it's sprayed with more liquid and yeast. This aerates the wort and encourages a powerful fermentation when it runs back into the bottom chamber, leaving unwanted yeast cells behind. The result is a beer with that famous 'Yorkshire head' and a pronounced hop aroma, an almost vinous fruit note and creamy malt. Samuel Smith of Tadcaster and Black Sheep in Masham still maintain Yorkshire Squares.

On the other side of the Pennines, where water is soft even in mountainous Cumbria, beer has a rich creamy malt character. Dark milds were once highly prized in Lancashire, Manchester and Merseyside, and porters and stouts have made a return to popularity in recent years. But the region is better known today for its pale and golden ales in which honeyed malt is well balanced by generous hop notes.

THE MIDLANDS

Beers in the Midlands reflect the history of a region that for centuries was the industrial heartbeat of the country: it was factory chimneys pouring forth smoke and dust that gave the area around Wolverhampton the nickname of the 'Black Country'. With prodigious thirsts to slake, Birmingham and the Black Country were synonymous with dark mild, a rich, malty and lightly-hopped brew with some unfermented sugar to restore lost energy. Bathams and Holdens still maintain that tradition with their luscious, slightly vinous milds. Even the bitters of the area have a bittersweet character.

Further east, brewing styles reflect the powerful influence of Burton upon Trent, once the most important brewing town in the world and now enjoying a welcome renaissance. Burton's position of influence is based on the waters of the Trent Valley, rich in mineral salts that act as flavour-enhancers, and the 'Burton Union' system of fermentation. The unions, in common with Yorkshire Squares, remove yeast from fermenting beer with an elaborate collection of large oak casks, pipes and troughs. The end result is a delicate yet robust pale ale, a superb balance of juicy malt and pungent hop resins, with a sulphury note from the water. Marston's, the major brewer in the town, still uses and cossets its Union Rooms.

Marston's historic Union Room is known as the 'Cathedral of Brewing'

THE SOUTH

The southern area of Britain, which includes the West Country, is a soft water region and the resulting beers have a dry malt character balanced by floral hops. Vanilla, butterscotch and vinous fruit are other notable characteristics. Until brewers learned how to 'Burtonise' their water by adding mineral salts, London water, with a sodium chloride base, was best suited to producing dark, vinous beers. Porter, stout and mild once dominated the capital. The decline of dark London beer at the end of the 19th century led to the arrival of distinctive interpretations of bitter: the proximity of the Kent hop fields added an uncompromisingly tart, spicy and peppery note to such beers as Young's Bitter. Young's has gone but scores of new breweries wave the flag with challenging but rewarding and intensely hoppy offerings.

SCOTLAND AND NORTHERN ENGLAND

In Scotland, dark malts have been used for centuries to impart powerful influences on the flavour and character of beer. While Scottish pale and 'Export' ales have a high level of hopping, older styles such as heavy and stout, the latter made with the addition of oatmeal, survive with a rich malty and vinous character. South of the border, the Northeast – centred around Newcastle and Sunderland – has long been renowned for brown ales that are sharply different from the mild or brown beers further south. Northeast brown ales are higher in alcohol than southern milds, and have a pronounced fruity (pear drops and banana) note. The style has been undermined by the decision of the makers of the best-known version, Newcastle Brown, to move production to Yorkshire but Double Maxim from Sunderland remains a potent example.

The beer revolution has turned the spotlight onto styles that were in danger of extinction. The use of oak casks has enabled such styles as barley wine and old ale to reappear, beers that age for many months and pick up fascinating 'woody' flavours with a hint of lactic sourness. The use of wood has also enabled a growing number of brewers to produce beers aged in casks bought from whisky, Bourbon and wine makers, adding new depths of aroma and flavour.

Hoppy or creamy, dark or pale, British beers, whether new styles or recreations of older ones, offer a variety and diversity found in few other countries. Marvel and enjoy.

West Country beers often have a dry malt character balanced by floral hops

Brewers are experimenting with styles that were in danger of extinction, such as beers aged in oak casks

BRITAIN'S NEW BEER SCENE

Jim Makin, Bill Mellor, Michael Hardman and Graham Lees celebrate CAMRA's 10th birthday

HOW WE GOT HERE

When four young men launched the Campaign for the Revitalisation of Ale in 1971 they had no idea they were unleashing a mighty consumer revolt that would transform beer drinking and brewing in Britain and around the world. Quickly renamed the Campaign for Real Ale – on the grounds that 'revitalisation' is hard to handle after several pints – and known by its acronym CAMRA, Michael Hardman, Graham Lees, Bill Mellor and Jim Makin found there were thousands of kindred spirits anxious to save the country's beer tradition and heritage.

It was a heritage under attack by new national brewing groups that had gone on the rampage in the 1960s, taking over and closing down smaller breweries and their beers. Much-loved cask ales were being replaced by a poor apology for beer known as keg – filtered, pasteurised and served by gas pressure. The British were faced by a beery future dominated by such reviled keg beers as Watneys Red Barrel, Double Diamond and Worthington E.

FROM TINY ACORNS...

Three of the founding four – Hardman, Lees and Mellor – were journalists and they used their skills to garner media attention for their aims. Soon CAMRA had a national profile, drinkers rushed to join and within five years the campaign had 30,000 members and full-time staff. A beer festival held in London's Covent Garden attracted crowds that queued round the block to drink the ales on offer from the country's remaining regional brewers.

Beer festivals became the bedrock of the campaign's work, enabling brewers to present their beers to a public bamboozled by slick TV commercials for the new keg beers. The campaigning pressure worked: Red Barrel was withdrawn and Whitbread and the other big brewers were forced to rekindle an interest in cask beer.

A THORN IN THE SIDE OF BIG BREWERS

Scroll forward 43 years and CAMRA remains a potent force and permanent thorn in the side of big brewers and – a new phenomenon – giant pub companies. The Campaign today has 165,000 members and it faces opponents even more powerful than those of the 1970s. Big brewers are no longer national, they are global: the major producers of lager and 'cream flow' keg beers are AB InBev – an American/Belgian/Brazilian conglomerate – Carlsberg, Heineken and Molson Coors. As a result of changes brought in by the government in the late 1980s, big brewers were forced to sell thousands of pubs and they are now owned by pub companies or 'pubcos', the biggest of which restrict choice to heavily-discounted beers from the global brewers. The giant pubcos ruthlessly close and sell pubs to boost their profits.

CAMRA's work is more complex today. Its core aim remains the need to bolster the fortunes of cask beer but it has to fight on several other fronts. It has campaigned successfully to reduce the burden of excise duty on brewers and it has a fully worked-out strategy for saving pubs. It sees pubs as vital hubs of their communities and encourages local people to form co-operatives to buy and save pubs threatened with closure. It backs publicans calling for a better deal for landlords with fair rents and the right to buy beer 'free of the tie', which means going beyond the list imposed on them by their brewery or pub company. A government Bill in 2014 goes some way to meeting these demands.

Beer festivals remain central to the Campaign's work, crucial shop windows for the country's independent breweries. There are around a dozen festivals a month, the largest of which is the Great British Beer Festival in London in August. It has become one of the world's biggest celebrations of beer, attended by some 50,000 people.

NEW BREWERIES

The festivals pinpoint the greatest change in CAMRA's lifetime. The first *Good Beer Guide* published in 1974 listed around 40 breweries, producing mainly mild and bitter. Today there are more than 1,200 breweries and the choice facing drinkers is spectacular, ranging from new golden ales to revivals of porter, stout and IPA, and even beers aged in whisky casks.

The proliferation of new breweries is due to the determined and pugnacious work of SIBA, launched in 1980 as the Small Independent Brewers' Association and renamed the Society of Independent Brewers in 1995 to reflect its growing size and influence. In common with the founding fathers of CAMRA, the tiny group of microbrewers who started SIBA in 1980 could have had no idea they would grow to a membership of more than 800 and would have a profound impact on beer drinking by breaking out of the straitjacket of mild and bitter. Golden ale started with micros and they have been the pacesetters in developing new styles and recreating old ones.

SIBA's main demand has been for a tax break for smaller brewers and this was achieved under the last Labour government when it brought in Progressive Beer Duty that dramatically lowered excise rates for the micros. As a result, scores of brewers have entered the industry, adding to the pleasure and choice available for drinkers. Its Direct Delivery Scheme bypasses big wholesalers and pubcos and supplies beer direct to free trade pubs.

CAMRA and SIBA are bonded together as the champions of good beer. Their success has laid the foundations for Britain's beer revolution.

Beer festivals are enormously popular. CAMRA's Great British Beer Festival is attended by 50,000 visitors and showcases beers from over 400 UK breweries

THE CONTEMPORARY BEER SCENE

One of the hallmarks of Britain's beer revolution has to be the explosion of new beer styles suddenly available to beer-lovers. Golden ales were the first, but now brewers are throwing away the rulebook and style guidelines and experimenting with new flavour combinations. Black IPA is arguably the most contentious new beer style to have emerged in recent years. For a start there's the issue of the name. Critics (Roger Protz among them) ask how can you have an India Pale Ale that is also black? Other names have been suggested, but none has gained traction, so black IPA still remains on the bar top: a beer with the aromatic character of an IPA but the colour of the middle of the night.

IPA INNOVATION

The passion surrounding this highly drinkable beer style is indicative of the way people feel about beer, especially during the current boom of British artisanal brewing. There's another element to the debate about black IPA, though: this is that many modern brewers, taking their cues from across the Atlantic, are getting hold of beer styles and mutating or innovating them.

Black IPA isn't the only version of IPA to have received this treatment. Cumbrian brewery Hardknott have an 8% beer called Queboid. This is a Belgian IPA, where the malt and hops give the beer the characteristic of an IPA, while fermentation is with Belgian yeast.

Siren produces White Tips, a white IPA, where the brewery's love of hops comes up against the spritzy mouthfeel of a witbier. Furthermore, there are Rye IPAs, saison IPAs, sessions IPAs and someone somewhere is probably coming up with a non-alcoholic IPA.

During the summer of 2014, the Canadian beer writer Stephen Beaumont wrote that every beer was now an IPA; he might have been writing with his tongue firmly lodged in cheek, but on the other hand he has a point: for both new and established brewers the IPA has become the default beer style to have within their portfolio, whether it's hopped to hell, low in alcohol or zapped with Belgian yeast.

EXPERIMENTATION

It's not only in IPA that innovation can be seen. Other beer styles – whether British or from elsewhere – have been tinkered with. Stouts and porters have had fruit or spices added to them. Over at Burning Sky in Sussex brewer Mark Tranter had a dark beer slumbering away within a wine barrel. 'I used a stout recipe but added our house *Brettanomyces* and *Lacto* to it,' he said, 'then it spent eight months in a French oak barrel that had previously held Chianti. Our *Brett* is quite gentle so the result was a beer with gentle roast notes alongside equally gentle barnyard and red wine characteristics. I believe in pushing the boundaries of beer, but sensibly.' When we spoke he was getting ready to brew a porter, which would use local hops and be aged in the same Chianti barrel as the previous beer, again with added *Brettanomyces*.

LOOKING BACK

That grand old man of English beer, mild, has also seen its style perimeters pushed: there has been a version with pepper and ones with more hops than were thought decent. Back in 2009, Rudgate's Ruby Mild became the Champion Beer of Britain; according to a couple of letter writers to CAMRA's *What's Brewing* this was a hoppier mild than what they were used to. Strong versions of mild are also out there, but they have a history going back to the 19th century. The Sarah Hughes brewery has long produced one, but it's heartening to see newer breweries such as Partizan in London having a go at a Victorian one. The next step should be the resurrection of the much-neglected light-coloured mild, of which few breweries produce these days (Timothy Taylor in Keighley is one).

Over at Kernel Evin O'Riordain oversaw the production of a forgotten beer, Export India Porter, a dark beer that was sent over to India in the 19th century for the troops. Meanwhile, one Victorian style that doesn't seem to be on anyone's radar is the stock ale, which quite a few breweries of the late 19th century used to make. Some American breweries have done one but so far only one UK brewery – Teignworthy in Devon – produced one, but then stopped because the grain bill for such a strong beer was pretty expensive. No doubt some young brewer somewhere will take up the challenge as the mutation and rediscovery of beer styles continues to be part of Britain's beer revolution.

LOOKING ABROAD

Then there are the continental beer styles. Camden Town's Hells has a lot more hops than a traditional Bavarian Helles; Adnams has a dry-hopped lager. There is also Imperial Pilsner, a style imported from the USA, though cynics dub it simply a strong lager. No one as far as we know has produced a sour lager, though over in the USA Doug Odell of the eponymous brewery did have a go: 'We tried adding some *Brettanomyces* to some Double Pilsner for secondary fermentation, but it kind of overwhelmed the flavour.'

One of the more curious German beer styles is Gose, a sour wheat beer with coriander and salt in the mix. Both US and UK breweries have started to brew their own versions. Magic Rock produced Salty Kiss, to which they added gooseberries, sea buckthorn and rosehips; at the Jolly Butchers pub in London, it was served through an infuser filled with gooseberries.

No doubt, beer style tyrants on both sides of the Atlantic will frown at all this excessive redrawing of what constitutes a beer style. However is it such a bad thing? After all, beer styles change through time, they are fluid. New hop and barley varieties keep emerging on the market and the current state of British brewing with its sense of adventure means that brewers cannot stop themselves from experimenting and if that means a new beer style, a mutation or even a beer without a style home so be it. The excitement that surrounds craft beer at the moment also means that a lot of drinkers constantly crave something new from their favourites, and craft brewers are eager to provide it.

BREWING COLLABORATORS

Another trend that shows no sign of slowing is craft brewers getting together to share ideas and brew collaboratively. It could be argued that until about 10 years ago the majority of British brewers had a halfway house attitude when it came to collaboration: head brewers would share drinks at dinners and meetings (and occasionally exchange yeast strains if someone was in trouble), but they never met on the brewing floor, unless they changed jobs. Only a few micros bucked the trend.

It has all changed since then. These days, brewers' collaborations almost come as standard, and on any given week you will see collaborations declared on social media, usually between two breweries; though pubs, pop stars and beer writers are not averse to this special kind of beery bonding either. Meantime even collaborated with the great Bavarian maltsters Weyermann to make a fantastic smoked porter.

With all these superstars of brewing coming together, cynics might say that it has merely become a case of 'X brewery has smashed it with Y brewery and the result is Z beer'. Others just want to know if the beer is any good. The easy answer to that question is a lot of the beer is exemplary, however there's more to it than a glib publicity stunt – the reason why breweries are collaborating is that a lot of them enjoy hooking up with like-minded brewers and seeing what they can get out of their brewing kit.

Adnams' revered head brewer Fergus Fitzgerald, himself no stranger to collaborations, said of the beer South Town, which he brewed with Camden Town brewery: 'We were very excited to be working with Camden and together with their head brewer Alex Troncoso we created a recipe that plays to the brewing heritage and use of modern ingredients and flavours that both our breweries enjoy. Collaborations are great fun and we have also worked with several US craft brewers such as Alchemist, it's always entertaining and we get a great response from beer fans.'

This sense of fun is what causes brewers to spend time together formulating a recipe and seeing what might happen. It's also a great cultural exchange. Collaborative brewing is also a day out of the office and a day spent talking the lingua franca of beer along with a few glasses. Of course, there is certainly a commercial element to it, but then brewing is a business and no one does it for free. It is a chance for brewers from different countries to learn about their host's brewing traditions; American brewers seem fascinated by cask beer, while Brits go over there to learn about hopping rates. Danish 'gypsy brewer' Mikkeller does not own a plant but seems to spend its whole working life collaborating all over the world; British breweries that have worked with Mikkel Borg Bjergso have included BrewDog (naturally) and, more surprisingly, Jennings in Cumbria.

According to Tony Gartland, Saltaire's managing director, 'working with other brewers enables the fusion of ideas, talent and approaches, with the end result being the creation of unique and exciting beers for drinkers. The beer we created with Dark Star has already collected two awards.'

One of the most accomplished collaborations was between Fuller's head brewer John Keeling and Manchester's Marble (the city, incidentally, Keeling comes from). The end result was the incredible Old Manchester, a potent 7.3% dark amber ale with a spritzy mouthfeel, plenty of fruit on the palate and a long dry bitter finish. With that in mind, it's safe to say that collaboration has been an invigorating force in brewing.

DRINKING BEER

The restless search for beer innovation is not just restricted to what we drink, but is echoed in how we drink it. As if to mirror the changes that Britain's beer revolution have brought to brewing, where we drink great beer has also undergone a metamorphosis. Even though thousands have closed, the pub remains the place where fresh cask beer can be drunk and appreciated. Some pubs are content with a couple of hand pulls, while others have up to a dozen at the bar; providing a nightly beer festival. These are destination pubs, highlights on the apps and maps of the connoisseur.

CRAFT BEER BARS

The enduring popularity of the pub notwithstanding, it has its rivals for drinkers' custom. One of the most noticeable arrivals in this field in the past few years is the craft beer bar. North Bar in Leeds is often seen as the pioneer, a wine bar lookalike on first glance, but

North Bar in Leeds is seen as the pioneer of the new trend for craft beer bars

once safely inside it's a place that gleams with handpumps, stainless steel fonts and rows of bottles from some of the most highly sought after breweries in the UK and beyond. North Bar opened in the 1990s, and was an inspiration for a growing number of similar beery paradises, many in the north of England. Sheffield, Leeds, Huddersfield, York and Manchester now all vie for the title of best beer city in the country.

Not to be outdone, an anonymous-looking pub in London's Pimlico that was leased by its owner Greene King to entrepreneur Martin Hayes, became the Cask Pub and Kitchen where a veritable tsunami of beer swept over those that entered through the door. The irrepressible Hayes went on to found the Craft Beer Co that now has six pubs, five in London and one in Brighton.

The premise of a craft beer pub is simple. The interiors are modernist and stylish with a hint of retro and often celebrative in the approach to beer: on the walls there may be arty black-and-white photographs of brewers at work, framed beer posters for a range of breweries and even a wall signed by visiting brewers from around the world (as at the Rake in Borough Market). The beer offering is typically a mixture of cask and craft keg with plenty of bottles from around the world, some of which compare with a bottle of good wine in their price; critics often complain that it is not cheap to drink in craft beer bars, but champions counter-argue that these establishments are not pint swilling places, being centres of beer appreciation instead.

The Rake pub in London's Borough Market has a wall signed by visiting brewers

Beers are often available by the third of a pint: enabling beer explorers to range widely without being laid out by a host of boldly flavoured and often strong beers, and the clientele is more beer-savvy than your average pub-goer; beards and ironically worn flat caps are not obligatory but are often in attendance, while there is a healthy proportion of young men and women enjoying themselves studying the beers.

Another welcoming change that has swept the world of drinking has been the onset of tasters. Given there is so much choice out there it makes sense for bar staff to offer a small drop of an unfamiliar beer. For those who still find it hard to make up their minds, some pubs, usually brewpubs, offer flights of a selection of beers; sometimes accompanied by various foods.

Beer flights are a great way to try a selection of beers without drinking too much

BEER FESTIVALS

Beer festivals have equally undergone a change. CAMRA has been running beer festivals and showing people the light since the dark days of the 1970s. Today, it runs over 200 festivals across the country, from small village events to the famous Great British Beer Festival at Olympia, London. They show cask beer in all its glory and underscore the remarkable choice now available to beer lovers. But their success and the increasing popularity of real ale and other craft beers has seen newcomers join the party, often with their own unique twist. The Indy Beer Man Con in Manchester is an annual festival of cask, keg, street food and music that began in 2012 and is held in Victorian swimming baths. Other cities have been home to similarly inspired events such as the Birmingham Beer Bash, Craft Beer Rising and London Beer City.

Another addition to the promotion of beer has been the emergence of beer weeks and beer cities. Norwich, led by Philip Cutter and Dawn Leeder, can claim to be Britain's leading City of Ale. Over 10 days from late May, Norwich's pubs put on a show of beers and beer-related events that draws thousands to the city. There are no doubt plans on drawing boards in other cities up and down the land to emulate Norwich.

BEER IN THE PUBLIC EYE

What is it that has helped to drive the British beer revolution? America is perhaps the main influence: brewers have gone there and experienced all manner of epiphanies, while stay-at-homes will have had similar ructions within their beery souls by tasting beers from across the Atlantic. Then there has been the continual rollout of hops from the US as well as from the southern hemisphere; hop merchants have been proactive in letting brewers know of new arrivals, which sometimes have been greeted with unabashed acclaim (Oakham's John Bryan confesses to dancing around with strips of hop sack in his clothes when the first bags of Citra arrived). There are the UK breweries whose hop-forward beers have challenged and woken up a beer generation. Finally, and more prosaically, the arrival of Progressive Beer Duty for small brewers in 2002 enabled hundred of micros to spring up like mushrooms after the rain.

All these have their place but the one thing that has helped to bond all these factors together and drive British craft brewing is the advent of social media, whether Twitter, Facebook, Instagram, Untappd or the fathomless abyss of beer blogs. Brewers: keg, cask or both, disregard the use of social media at their own peril; in the past beer reputations spread by word of mouth, but that was then, this is now.

SOCIAL MEDIA

Twitter is awash with beer. Take this random snapshot of Twitter on a Friday afternoon:

'Who loves beer? We love beer! Do you love beer? And cider? On our pumps right now!'

'God bless Tim Martin, let the drinking begin!!'

'The lovely Golden Pride....as clear as the day is long! Not to mention the lovely malt flavour. #Getitwhileyoucan'.

There are positive effects: beer lovers can talk directly to brewers on Twitter and Facebook. Brewers get positive and immediate feedback on their beers (and egos are flattered and massaged); though often there are views that they might not always agree with. Brewers have also taken to social media with a vengeance. Not only do they engage with drinkers but they talk with fellow artisans, tell the world about the latest brew to meet its fate in the mash and sometimes post photographs about the more offbeat parts of life in a brewery, such as emptying out the mash tun or people at work in accounts. Not wanting to be left behind, pubs tweet news about what's on the bar or an upcoming festival.

Granted, some of this instant tweeting can be irritating (so and so has just got his badge for drinking so and so beer and he must tell the world about it on Twitter), but whatever the content it is about beer and getting beer out into the world. The offline world of print journalism and TV broadcasting is very adept in ignoring beer (unless of course it's a finger-wagging piece about binge drinking or the occasional business story).

BEER BLOGGING

Before social media changed the world, beer writing was very much confined to print. However, with the advent of the blog in the late 1990s, the following decade saw an explosion of beer blogs – first of all in the USA and Canada and then in the UK. This turned traditional beer writing on its head. One of the most popular UK blogs was Stonch's Beer Blog, written by lawyer-turned-publican Jeff Bell – this was opinionated, occasionally infuriating and incredibly popular; sometimes it was worth reading for the comments alone. Another perceptive blog was written by the late Simon Johnson, known as The Reluctant Scooper. At the same time, established beer writers also turned to blogs as adjuncts to their published work – the Roger Protz has a thoroughly informative blog, while Pete Brown is funny, enlightening and unafraid to tackle controversial subjects.

Brewers also started writing blogs. Brewing Reality by Sharp's head brewer Stuart Howe was one of the most enjoyable; at one stage it recorded his attempt to brew a different beer for every week of the year. These 52 brews include a stout made with offal, a Trappist IPA and ESB Barley Champagne; sadly due to pressure of work he did not get to brew the whole 52. Even though some of the pioneers of British beer blogging have stopped, there still remains a healthy tribe of bloggers eager to share their world view on beer. They even have their own weekend-long conference. Also let us not forget CAMRA's online forum where members can discuss various issues such a pub closures and important industry campaigns.

Some bloggers, such as Jessica Boak and Ray Bailey, have progressed to the world of print – the duo's 2014 book *Brew Britannia* is a fascinating overview of British beer from the 1960s onwards. Not all of this is jolly cheery beery stuff though. On occasions the 'beer blogosphere' can overheat as opinions become divided, for instance, on the merits of cask beer and craft keg. However, even this discord has its positives as it demonstrates the seriousness with which drinkers regard their chosen tipple.

Stuart Howe of Sharp's blogged his attempt to brew 52 different beers in a year

BEER WEBSITES

Alongside the blogging world, beer continues to remain in the public eye with a plethora of websites. The most recognised one is Ratebeer, which initially started in the USA but now girdles a global network of beer geeks, who comment on every beer they taste. It also has reviews of bars and pubs around the world, which is very useful if you are going to Lisbon and want to find a bar that sells something more than the local lager. For UK pub finding, CAMRA's WhatPub.com is a great resource, with entries for 36,000 pubs throughout the UK.

ADVERTISING

Advertising has always been a key part of communicating beer and brewing, going back to the 19th century when breweries began producing gaudily coloured posters and show-cards to encourage drinkers to taste their pale ales, stouts, dinner ales and IPAs. We've passed through the age of laddish beer adverts (Hofmeister's 'Follow the bear'), stylish mini movies (Stella Artois) and more surreal productions (Guinness), and now breweries such as Fuller's use celebrities (James May) while others have gone almost cartoonish in their ads (Hogs Back). A lot of craft breweries are too small to advertise – relying on social media – but the medium sized ones are increasingly eschewing placing adverts on billboards, opting instead for sponsorship of events: musical, sporting and cultural.

Whether it's a tweet, a photo of your pint uploaded onto Instagram, a blog post or even a comment on one, beer is increasingly in the public eye and long may it be so.

HOME COUNTIES

BERKSHIRE, BUCKINGHAMSHIRE, EAST SUSSEX, ESSEX, HAMPSHIRE, HERTFORDSHIRE, ISLE OF WIGHT, KENT, OXFORDSHIRE, WEST SUSSEX

The counties surrounding London have a long-standing reputation as the larder that supplies the capital. Kent, in particular, is known as the Garden of England. And as well as the foodstuffs grown for the capital, the Home Counties also grow the hops and barley that are the building-blocks of beer, with the Thames the ideal route to market.

The term Home Counties was first coined in the 17th century by people living close to London who considered they paid higher rates of tax as a result of their proximity to the capital. Later it took on a more derisory meaning, a reference to wealthy Londoners who had second homes in the surrounding countryside. Those wealthy Londoners included brewers, such as Samuel Whitbread, who made their fortunes in London and built large pub estates. They were dubbed 'the beerage' by cynical drinkers who enjoyed the products but not the wealth – an attitude that overlooked the jobs and incomes created by agriculture and its contribution to brewing and beer.

Chiltern: Aylesbury, Buckinghamshire

Siren: Finchampstead, Berkshire

Windsor & Eton: Windsor, Berkshire

BEER DESTINATIONS
> go to page 56

Shepherd Neame: Faversham, Kent

Ramsgate: Broadstairs, Kent

Hook Norton

Aylesbury

Aldworth

Finchampstead   **Windsor**

Faversham

Broadstairs

Crockham Hill

Ringwood

Partridge Green

Lewes

Brighton

Westerham: Crockham Hill, Kent

Harveys: Lewes, East Sussex

Dark Star: Partridge Green, West Sussex

The Thames and other rivers were conduits for farmers and maltsters delivering hops and grain to breweries in and around London and taking the finished product back to the capital. The Brakspear brewery in Henley-on-Thames was just one of scores of breweries that used the Thames artery to bring the essential raw materials to them and then send casks of ale back to the 'Great Wen'. Ware in Hertfordshire became a major malting town, using the River Lee to deliver grain to East London: Ware played a critical role in the rise of commercial brewing in the capital, created by the craze for porter and stout in the 18th and 19th centuries.

Agriculturally, there is a division between the northern and southern Home Counties that has influenced their brewers: the counties north of London are in close proximity to the 'grain basket' of East Anglia, while the southern counties, Kent in particular, are home to renowned hop-growing areas: traditional oast houses for drying hops are still prominent in the Kent countryside. As with

Terroir is critical: dark alluvial soil creates good grain, while loamy soil is essential for hop-growing

wine, terroir is critical: dark alluvial soil creates good grain while loamy soil that retains water is essential for hop-growing.

The finest malting barley is often associated with Norfolk, but Hertfordshire barley has a good reputation, which is celebrated in a village called Barley on the boundary with Cambridgeshire. Similarly, hop growing is not confined solely to Kent: Harveys brewery in Lewes buys hops from local Sussex farmers and the Hogs Back brewery near Farnham in Surrey restored hop growing in 2014 by planting several acres with the White Bine variety, a predecessor of the Golding, which had disappeared decades before.

FAMILY BREWERS

Harveys and Hogs Back represent the good health and diversity of brewing in the region. The former is one of several sturdy, family-owned breweries that survived the takeover-and-closure frenzy of the late 20th century and continue to make beers of great quality. Harveys, in common with Shepherd Neame in Faversham, Kent – Britain's oldest brewery, dating from 1698 – not only maintains a firm commitment to traditional beer styles but also reaches out to younger consumers with golden

Regional breweries such as Harveys (left) and Shepherd Neame (right) are reaching out to younger drinkers with new beer styles

ales and beers with more pronounced hop character. Proud of their roots, both have dug deep into ancient recipe books to bring back genuine IPAs and strong porters and stouts.

Hogs Back on the other hand is part of the modern 'micro' movement but has registeredsuch success with its beers, ranging from TEA – Traditional English Ale – to Hop Garden Gold, that it now enjoys regional status.

YOUNG BLOOD

Kent, as befits the major hop-producing county, has blossomed with new breweries, such as Eddie Gadd's Ramsgate brewery which produces a Green Hop beer in September made with freshly-picked local hops. The twin Sussex counties are similarly well-endowed with Dark Star providing further evidence of the astonishing growth of small breweries: it started life in a pub cellar in Brighton using souped-up home-brewing kit and is now looking for a new home having outgrown its 45-barrel plant where one of its main brands – Hophead – sums up its no-nonsense attitude to beer-making.

North of London, Hertfordshire, as befits a county with a rich barley and malt tradition, has seen a growth of new breweries but also retains the family-run McMullen's in the county town. Berkhamsted-based Red Squirrel has won plaudits for a range that includes a traditional mild, citrus-driven Hopfest, London Porter and an American IPA. Tring brewery is yet another brewery that has grown, moved out of its cramped first home to sizable premises on a farm and has a beer portfolio ranging from golden to jet-black. Its Tea Kettle Stout is based on the shape of the old county before it lost territory to the ever-encroaching Greater London. And new breweries continue to appear: the great novelist Graham Greene, a member of the Greene King brewing dynasty, would surely rejoice at the fact that Haresfoot restored brewing traditions in 2014 to his Berkhamsted birthplace.

Insider's view...

Tony Leonard
www.thesnowdropinn.com

The Home Counties have a proud, and in some cases, uninterrupted, brewing heritage, with stunning Victorian tower breweries owned by regional brewers such as Harveys here in Lewes, Sussex, which still delivers to local pubs by horse drawn dray. But the region is also home to some of the country's newest breweries, with over 40 in Sussex alone, according to Brighton & South Downs CAMRA Branch, and new additions almost weekly.

Leading the first new wave, Eddie Gadd at Ramsgate combined a refreshing approach to experimenting and collaboration while maintaining a steadfast loyalty to the hops of East Kent, while Dark Star grew rapidly from the cellar at the Evening Star in Brighton, to gain a national reputation for innovation.

Former Dark Star head brewer Mark Tranter and founder Rob Jones have recently both branched out on their own: Mark at Burning Sky is taking on European brewing traditions, including barrel-aging, and bringing inspiration and ingredients from the South Downs. Meanwhile, the fruits of Rob's new labour at the Duke of Wellington in Shoreham are eagerly awaited.

Tony Leonard is co-owner of the Snowdrop Inn in Lewes, East Sussex

Established: 1980

Founder: Richard Jenkinson

Beers: Cobblestones, Ale, Black, Foxtrot, Nut Brown Mild, Beechwood Bitter, Copper Beech, Glad Tidings, John Hampdens Ale, 300's Old Ale, Lord Lieutenant's Porter, Bodger's Barley Wine

Website: www.chilternbrewery.co.uk

CHILTERN

Aylesbury, Buckinghamshire

Chiltern is a fine example of how a brewery can be rejuvenated and made fighting fit for the 21st century in the hands of a new generation. George and Tom Jenkinson took over from their father Richard in 2005 and widened the beer range with such success that, in 2014, they started work on extending the site to cope with the growing clamour for their products. Getting planning permission was no easy matter, as the brewery stands on the site of a former farm on green-belt land, with the Chiltern Hills forming a rolling sylvan backdrop.

Richard Jenkinson was a great innovator in his own right. When he opened for business in 1980, it was the first new brewery in the county for decades. Richard was an engineer and a keen home-brewer and was well placed to design his own brewing equipment. He launched the brewery on the assumption he could get cask beer into local pubs but found it was, in his words, 'frontier territory – there were loads of free houses in the area but most of them were not free at all.' So he carved out a new road to market by opening a shop on site that sold beer in bottle and cask and also such specialities as

beer cheese, beer mustards and pickles along with beer bread made by a local craft baker.

FIGHTING BACK

Life became harder in the 1990s, when the national brewers were replaced with new pub companies. Richard found that the big 'pubcos' would only stock his beer if he accepted ruinous discounts, so he battened down the hatches and concentrated on bottled beer, much of it in naturally-conditioned form. The tide turned with Progressive Beer Duty, introduced by the government in 2002, which dramatically reduced the amount of excise duty smaller brewers had to pay. Suddenly, brewing became viable for Chiltern and scores of other small brewers who had been living on the margin.

Out of the blue, the National Trust asked the Jenkinsons if they would like to run the medieval King's Head in Aylesbury. Chiltern now had a major shop window for its draught beers. Richard decided it was time to take a back seat and allow Tom, with an engineering degree, to take over brewing while George became manager of the King's Head.

The beer range in cask and bottle has always been rich with the history of the area: 300's Old Ale commemorates a historic method of subdividing the county, and John Hampdens Ale and Lord Lieutenant's Porter celebrate a Member of Parliament who played a key role in the English Civil War. Tom has added a Battle of Britain Ale to mark the Second World War, a modern Gold, and has aged his Bodger's Barley Wine in Scotch whisky casks. With expansion under way, Chiltern will boost production while remaining true to its roots deep in the Buckinghamshire countryside.

Top: Tom, wife Charlotte, parents Richard and Lesley, and George Jenkinson. **Centre:** Tom Jenkinson has now taken over brewing from his father.

Beers to try ...

300's Old Ale, 4.9%
This beer recalls an old English custom of dividing counties into 'hundreds'. It has luscious nutty malt and tangy hop character.

Lord Lieutenant's Porter, 6%
Brewed to celebrate John Hampden, local MP and dignitary during the Civil War. Based on London porter, it is smoky and fruity with a delicious hint of chocolate, underscored by spicy hops.

Bodger's Barley Wine, 8.5%
Bottle conditioned beer, available seasonally in cask, and occasionally aged in whisky barrels. Rich, complex, fruity and hoppy: the perfect digestif.

Dark Star's acclaimed hoppy beers are brewed using modern kit in a plant just outside Horsham, East Sussex. **Bottom left:** One of the brewery's directors, James Cuthbertson

Established: 1994

Founder: Rob Jones

Beers: The Art of Darkness, Hophead, Partridge, Seville, Espresso, Hylder Blonde, Summer Solstice, American Pale Ale, Summer Meltdown, Sunburst, Festival, Original, Winter Metldown, Bock, Revelation, Victorian Ruby Mild, Six Hop

Website: darkstarbrewing.co.uk

DARK STAR

Partridge Green, West Sussex

The brewing team at Dark Star is rather fond of hops, a not particularly surprising state of affairs given that their most popular beer is Hophead, a pulsating and lustrous pale ale that bursts with grapefruit notes and has a stern bitter backbone keeping the fruitiness in check. This was one of Dark Star's first brews and features the US hop varieties Amarillo and Cascade – you could argue that it has helped define the American-influenced pale ales that a lot of British breweries now produce; it was a game-changer, a herald of what, for better or worse, British breweries would be putting in their beers. Under the guidance of founder Rob Jones (who now runs a brewpub in Shoreham) and former head brewer Mark Tranter (who left in 2013 and has set up Burning Sky in Firle) and continuing with the present team, Dark Star have an highly accomplished raft of beers that include Hophead, American Pale Ale and the hop bomb Revelation, which was launched in 2012. There's a lot to be proud of, especially given the rather compact beginnings of the brewery in 1994.

'The brewery has had a "Forest Gump" type of life, punctuated with luck and naivety,' says one of Dark Star's directors, James Cuthbertson. 'Before there was a brewery there was a brew-pub, the Evening Star, Brighton, with a nanobrewery in its cellar providing enough beer to whet the appetite of the beer enthusiasts who drank there. Without any sales or employees or any commercial ideas at all, it was decided to incorporate the brewery as a separate business in 1995 because Rob Jones, the brewery designer and beer-nut, held the trademark to the name Dark Star and it was thought too much of a coincidence. So with three directors, no employees and no customers outside of the Evening Star, the business started.'

Prior to starting brewing in the Evening Star, Jones had been part of the London microbrewery Pitfield with fellow brewer Martin Kemp (who ran it until recently). One of the beers brewed was Dark Star (named after a song by the Grateful Dead) – it was a rich and dark beer with plenty of hop character and was voted CAMRA's Champion Beer

Dark Star's bold branding, like many of their beers, is influenced by the craft brewing revolution in the USA

"The aroma was unlike any beer I had made before — a circus of big bold tropical and citrus fruit flavours in the nose and mouth. I could only dream of the West Coast IPAs but this helped me!"

of Britain in 1987. After Jones left Pitfield, he took the recipe of the beer with him and it was brewed at the Evening Star; nowadays it's called Dark Star Original and still one of the brewery's regular beers.

UK AND US INSPIRATION

That was then, but now the brewery is based in the village of Partridge Green, just outside Horsham (in September 2014 Dark Star announced that it was looking for a new location as it had outgrown its current home); the town was once home to the family brewery King & Barnes and one of the brewery regulars is Festival, which is a tribute to the late and lamented K&B's classic Festive. The brewery has come along way since the Evening Star; the current set-up is a celebration of stainless steel vessels, where casks clang and the appetising aroma of the boil drifts about as beer is being made. Hophead is naturally on the rota, but other days it could be American Pale, Espresso Stout or Six Hop Ale, a ravishing IPA that was developed by Mark

Tranter in 2008. This beer was the idea of Matt and Karen Wickham, who then ran the Evening Star. According to Tranter, 'they had travelled to the US a fair bit and were in love with the big US style IPAs. I hadn't tried any at this point but could imagine... Also around this time, the hop merchants Charles Faram were bringing in a wider variety of American hops and I was keen to try them – this was a good chance. The aroma was unlike any beer I had made before – a circus of big bold tropical and citrus fruit flavours in the nose and mouth. I could only dream of the West Coast IPAs but this helped me!'

There are two Dark Star pubs, one the evergreen Evening Star, a few yards stroll from Brighton station, and the Partridge, which is very close to the brewery. This is an ideal place to study the beers of Dark Star, conscious of the great works that are going on just several minutes walk away.

'All our beers, past and present, can all be seen as copies or hybrids of the great beer styles from anywhere in the world,' says Cuthbertson. 'We argue

Espresso Stout, 4.2%
Mocha coffee milkiness on the nose, not dissimilar to what you'd get in a mild/stout hybrid; the mouthfeel is creamy with the coffee adding a jagged raspiness. The finish is dry and coffee grain bitter.

Revelation, 5.7%
Bracingly bitter American-style pale ale with a fruit bowl of aromatics, including sweet pineapple and lemon pith. In the mouth it's a big blast of tropical fruit, malt sweetness and a long finish with more fruit in it.

Six Hop, 6.8%
The nose is Cointreau-like orange with sweet tropical fruit notes in the background; on the palate more orange, some grapefruit and an appealing malt sweetness; the finish is long dry and bitter. A monthly special.

over our beers very much in the way like a family squabbling over who's got the telly remote. Putting the beer list together was once an annual event to decide the coming year's beers, however, under pressure from customers to become more business-like (heaven forbid) we now do battle monthly and try and assemble a rolling six-month list of new beers. So our influence and inspiration comes from pretty much every corner of the beer world, from the great Belgian brewers to the new breed of US and Antipodean brewers and not forgetting that in Britain we have a rich brewing past where whole encyclopaedias could be dedicated to creamy stouts, hard bitters and strong, dry IPAs.'

Harveys still brew their traditional ales at their red-brick Victorian tower brewery in Lewes, but they are are also innovating and experimenting with new styles

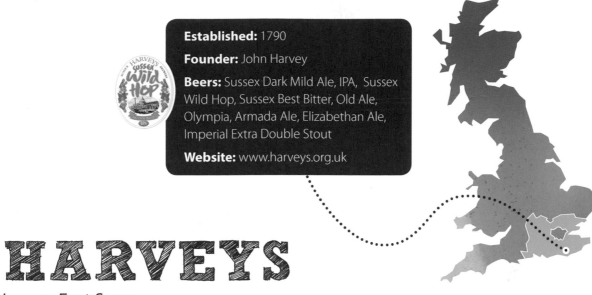

Established: 1790

Founder: John Harvey

Beers: Sussex Dark Mild Ale, IPA, Sussex Wild Hop, Sussex Best Bitter, Old Ale, Olympia, Armada Ale, Elizabethan Ale, Imperial Extra Double Stout

Website: www.harveys.org.uk

HARVEYS

Lewes, East Sussex

Harveys is a quiet but firm believer in traditional values amid the whirlwind of change in the beer world. Its main beer, Sussex Best Bitter, is an unsung hero: quite simply, one of the finest traditional ales to be found. But the family-owned company is content to supply its 50 pubs and free trade accounts, based mainly in south-east England, and resists siren songs to 'go national'. It's an achingly traditional brewery, opened in 1784 on the banks of the River Ouse, which on at least one occasion has burst its banks and flooded the buildings: visitors are shown tide marks on the wall indicating how high the water reached.

However, it would be a mistake to think the company is resting on its historic laurels. It has added a fashionable golden ale called Olympia, which celebrates Sussex Best winning its class in the Champion Beer of Britain competition staged at London Olympia, and has built a micro-brewing plant to make short-run special beers, several of which commemorate the history of the ancient town of Lewes. There is one especially deep and reverential bow in the direction of brewing history:

Harveys has painstakingly recreated a beer style from the 18th and 19th centuries, Imperial Stout, that was exported to Russia and the Baltic States and won approval from the royal court in St Petersburg.

BUILDING ON HISTORY

The spacious rooms in the brewery – brewhouse, copper room and fermenting area – are packed with superbly maintained vessels, with wood and burnished copper dominating. Parts of the building still have some Georgian artefacts but the brewery was rebuilt in 1880 in red-brick Victorian Gothic style. It's a 'tower brewery' designed by the celebrated architect William Bradford who also designed the Hook Norton brewery in Oxfordshire. The simplicity of the design means that the brewing process flows naturally from floor to floor, with malt store and water tanks at the top feeding mash tuns and coppers below.

The eighth generation of the Harvey family are still involved in the company. In the 20th century they were joined by the Jenners, who had run a

Harveys brewery is a wonder of Victorian engineering and, as such, tours must be pre-booked and currently have a two-year waiting list. **Centre:** Miles Jenner

brewery in south London since the 18th century before moving to Sussex. The head of production today is Miles Jenner who lives with his family just a few yards from the site in the brewer's house. He has a firm belief in using English raw materials and is keen to garner them as close to source as possible. In 2012 he brewed a strong, 7.5% Elizabethan Ale to mark the Queen's Jubilee, based on an identical beer made in 1953 at the time of the coronation. He used the same malts and hops and was even able to get Fuggles and Goldings from the farm in Kent that had supplied them in 1953. The bottle-conditioned beer is known locally, with a touch of *lèse majesté*, as 'Lizzie': Miles Jenner says bottles

Miles Jenner says bottles of the original beer – made in 1953 at the time of the coronation – are still 'drinking well' after 50 years, scotching suggestions that beer cannot age as well as wine

of the original beer are still 'drinking well' after 50 years, scotching suggestions that beer cannot age as well as wine. To prove his commitment to locally-sourced ingredients, Miles Jenner has added Sussex Wild Hop, a pale ale that uses hops first discovered growing wild in the Sussex countryside.

REDISCOVERING A CLASSIC

Harveys' interpretation of Imperial Stout is a horse of a different colour: 9% alcohol compared with Wild Hop's moderate 3.7%. By the middle of the 19th century, some 10 London breweries produced strong stouts for export to Russia and the Baltic states. One of the breweries was Barclay Perkins, which later merged with its Thames-side neighbour, Courage. A consignment of Barclays Russian Stout ended up on the seabed in 1869 when the ship containing it was wrecked. In 1974, divers who discovered the wreck brought to the surface bottles of beer bearing the enigmatic name A Le Coq. Research showed this was a Belgian, Albert Le Coq, who had exported London stout to Russia. The company had been granted a royal warrant by a grateful Russian court when it donated beer to soldiers wounded during the Crimean War: the

warrant allowed Barclays to call the beer 'Imperial Russian Stout'. Early in the 20th century, Le Coq's company built a brewery in Tartu, now in modern Estonia, to supply the region, but its success was short-lived as the brewery was nationalised following the Russian Revolution in 1917 and, from then, only pale lager was produced. In 1998, Miles Jenner negotiated with the descendants of Albert Le Coq to brew the beer once more. The brewery in Tartu was also happy to hand over its records. As a result, Jenner was able to design a recipe based on Maris Otter pale malt, with amber, brown and black malts and Fuggles and Goldings hops. The beer is bottle fermented and is matured in the brewery for a year before it is released. When it was first brewed, a wild yeast strain, similar to the Belgian *Brettanomyces* used to make lambic beer, infiltrated the maturation vessels, adding what brewers call a 'horse blanket' note to the aroma. This has been retained and adds to the complexity of the finished beer, which Harveys exports to the United States to great acclaim.

Beers to try ...

Sussex Best Bitter, 4%
Copper-coloured beer with grassy and spicy hops, biscuit malt and tangy fruit aroma and palate, with a dry, bitter and hoppy finish balanced by juicy malt and tart fruit.

Armada Ale, 4.5%
Amber best bitter with a big attack of spicy hop resins, tart fruit and biscuit malt on nose and palate, followed by a well-balanced finish offering bitter hops, rich malt and fruit.

Imperial Extra Double Stout, 9%
A bottle-fermented beer with vinous fruits, fresh leather, tobacco, smoky malt and peppery hops and a long warming finish packed with dark fruits, roasted grain, liquorice and spicy hops.

Ingredients...

WARMINSTER MALTINGS

Warminster Maltings sits in the heart of the malting barley growing area of Southern England, a place where great golden fields of grain wave in the wind and slowly ripen beneath the sun.

Warminster Maltings is one of just a handful of malt houses left in England that still uses the traditional floor malted method of production; it also has a special place in the history of malted barley – it was once owned by Edwin Sloper Beaven, who back in the 19th century bred Plumage Archer, the very first recognised malting barley.

Naturally, the Maltings is a major supplier of British breweries, but thanks to the dynamism of barley merchant, Maris Otter saviour and owner Robin Appel, Warminster Maltings has a Warranty of Origin scheme, which gives brewers the chance to tell drinkers where the malt in their beer originated – the grower, the farm, even the field it grew in. Furthermore, brewers can ensure than the barley used was grown in a farm close to their brewery, which helps to add to the local feel of a beer.

French wine has long had its terroir and appellations for wine buffs to slather over, but poor old beer and barley has always come off second best when it comes to origins, but the success of this scheme has meant another boon to brewers as they continue on their journey. 'The existence of this scheme essentially underlines the state of food now,' says Warminster's head maltster Chris Garrett, 'with food, beer and wine more people want to know what they are eating and drinking. The head brewers of the new craft breweries can now shout about ingredients and say my barley is in this field.'

Drying malt is turned by hand at Warminster, who still use the traditional method of floor malting

"A growing number of farmers are very interested in the end user of their barley"

Alasdair Large, founder and head brewer of Keystone brewery

We are based on a large farm in south Wiltshire 10 miles from Warminster. When we started brewing in 2006 we wanted to brew beer with local character: our water comes from a borehole on the farm and we sourced our malt through Warminster's Warranty of Origin scheme that guaranteed us Wiltshire-grown barley. All but one of the hops we use are UK grown. We can see the barley growing around the brewery and regularly shoot the breeze with the farmer. The barley is malted 10 miles away, the beer brewed back on the farm and we then sell locally (mostly within 35 miles) or deliver direct to our own pub in Tisbury (three miles from the brewery).

Chris Garrett, head maltster of Warminster Maltings

A growing number of farmers are very interested in the end user of their barley. If you look to add value to it you need to know the end use of your produce and that way you will get a better price. We work hard with farmers: for instance we have barley on the Windsor estate and it goes to Windsor & Eton brewery – though we did have an issue over the need to harvest once as the Queen was shooting that week.

Teddy Maufe, Maris Otter farmer at Branthill Farm in Norfolk

In an age when food and drink provenance is being taken more and more seriously as an important buying factor it makes great sense for smaller brewers to have a direct link with the farmer and thus the field where their malt is derived from. Often this also taps into the local food/drink mantra that has become prominent in recent years. As a farmer it helps elevate my malting barley from being just a commodity to a specialist, hopefully sought-after, brand. I have just sent a harvesting photo to the Norfolk brewers I supply of 'their field' being combined.

Established: 2002

Founder: Eddie Gadd

Beers: No 7, East Kent Pale Ale, Seasider, No 5, No 3, Dogbolter

Website: www.ramsgatebrewery.co.uk

RAMSGATE (GADDS)

Broadstairs, Kent

Eddie Gadd is passionate about the beer he makes, emotional even. Get him talking about Green Hop Ale, which he only makes once a year using freshly picked hops, and you can hear a quaver in his voice, a tremulous seesaw of emotion as he describes its inception. 'It's the beer that most expresses my brewing philosophy,' he says, 'fetching hops in the morning, connecting to the earth, talking to the grower and its all done on my doorstep in Kent. With this beer I'm trying to capture the soul of the county and then put it into the beer. It's proper provenance; magical.'

As for the beer itself, it's a crisp, soulful little number, packed full of hop resins and citrus notes, with a dry and bittersweet finish. In a world where everything can be devoured at any time of the year and throughout the whole day, it's equally magical that sometimes we have to wait for good things.

"I'm trying to capture the soul of the county and then put it into the beer. It's proper provenance; magical"

Not that the Gadds' beers available throughout the year are also-rans. No 3 is a self-proclaimed Kentish Pale Ale liberally doused with East Kent Goldings and, according to Gadd, 'is about and for Kent'. However, for a beer that aims to connect itself with Kent, the inspiration is many thousands of miles away, on the west coast of America. 'It [No 3] was supposed to be like Sierra Nevada Pale Ale,' he says, 'I've always adored that beer. It was the first beer we brewed and we were only going to do one, but people kept asking for more and since then I've done about 30 including five to six regulars.' These have included mild, rye pale ale, barley wine and imperial stout. Gadd is no stick in the mud.

INSPIRED BEERS

Gadd started building the brewery back in 2001 after being made redundant from the Firkin pub chain, where he was a brewer – 'I had to do it, not only because I needed an income but I suppose to prove myself, and what better way to do that than to build a brewery.' Ever since, this exuberant brewer has ploughed a dynamic if often lonely

Ramsgate's modern yet well-balanced English ales are racked by hand

furrow. The brewery's first home was at the back of a Ramsgate pub, which Gadd once described as being full of 'louts and ne'er-do-wells'. In 2006, it moved to its current home and since then the brewery has picked up plenty of awards for its beers.

'I make modern yet conservatively balanced English ales,' he says, which suggests a certain stasis, but then when asked on how he designs a new beer, the real Eddie Gadd emerges, a contemplative and creative brewer, a craft brewer even. 'The inspiration comes first, and can come from different places: other beers, other flavours, special occasions, special people. I find a hook, be it theme, style or flavour, and build on it in my mind's eye until I have something, then build a brew sheet, consult with my fantastic team, adjust and go.'

Is it any wonder that when asked what his brewing philosophy is, he replies, 'you can find Buddha or whoever you're looking for in the fermenter'.

Beers to try ...

Dogbolter, 5.6%
Gadd brewed the original Firkin Dogbolter. His own version is dark, rich, roasty and packed full of chocolate and coffee notes.

No 3, 5%
Gadds' debut beer – a bracingly bitter, temptingly tangy, modern remodel of an old school premium bitter using locally grown hops.

East Kent IPA, 6.5%
This is one of Gadds' seasonals and it's a roistering English-style IPA with a juicy mouthfeel and a hoppy swerve of citrus notes that leads straight into its bitter finish.

Richard Frost is head brewer at Shepherd Neame,
Britain's oldest brewery

Established: 1698

Founder: Richard Marsh

Beers: Canterbury Jack, Master Brew, Kent's Best, Whitstable Bay, Spitfire, Early Bird, Amber Ale, Late Red, Spooks Ale, Bishops Finger, Christmas Ale, Brilliant Ale, 1698

Website: www.shepherd-neame.co.uk

SHEPHERD NEAME

Faversham, Kent

When you are – indisputably – the oldest brewery in Britain, it would be tempting to opt for the easy life, concentrate on tried-and-trusted core brands served in a large estate of 350 pubs, many of them ancient, historic and white-boarded in the Kentish style. But there's a restless determination to innovate at the brewery: no laurels are rested on here. Led by chief executive Jonathan Neame, representing the fifth generation of the family to run the company, new beers have appeared and a special micro-plant, installed in 2007, develops short-run ales. These include beers from the 19th century based on original recipes written in secret code and deciphered with a dedication that would leave World War Two code breakers at Bletchley Park open-mouthed in admiration.

The brewery makes much use of 1698 as the year it was founded. But recent research by company historian John Owen suggests it may be even older. What is certain is that brewing has been conducted in Faversham, an important port as well as a market town, since the 12th century, when monks brewed at the local abbey. The brewery in Court Street came into the hands of the Shepherd family in 1732 and they joined forces with the Neames in 1859. While brewing today takes place in an ultra-modern brew house, the old site is a museum of brewing, with ancient oak vessels on show and steam engines that can be brought back into use in the event of power cuts. Brewing water is still pumped from an artesian well on the site.

LOOKING FORWARD

'Sheps', as the company is popularly known, has the good fortune to be surrounded by Kent's famous hop fields and brewers have been able for centuries to pluck the first and finest plants from the bines at harvest time, including the prized East Kent Golding. Goldings and Target varieties form the backbone of such stalwart brands as Master Brew, Bishops Finger and 1698 – the last named is a bottle-conditioned beer first brewed in 1998 to

Centre: Double Stout is one of the historic recipes unlocked by brewery historians **Right:** Brewer Chris Gregson adds fresh hops to the copper

The brewery maintains and financially supports the National Hop Collection in Kent, where every known hop from the county is grown

commemorate 300 years of brewing at Court Street. Looking forward rather than back, the brewery has had great success with Whitstable Bay, a beer that uses organic malts and hops, and Early Bird, a golden ale that celebrates the arrival of spring, using the Early Bird hop, a new variety cloned from East Kent Goldings. The brewery maintains and financially supports the National Hop Collection in Kent, where every known hop from the county is grown and cuttings are used to develop new varieties.

Sheps' main brand today is a premium bitter, Spitfire, introduced to mark the 50th anniversary of the Battle of Britain, when British fighter planes fought for supremacy over German Messerschmitts in the sky above Kent. The beer is now an international best-seller – but not in Germany.

UNLOCKING THE PAST

In 2012, Shepherd Neame unlocked the recipes to beers brewed in the 19th century that paint a fascinating picture of brewing practice and the almost comical attempts to keep recipes secret. Deep in the cellars beneath the brewery, historian John Owen found several large, dust-covered tomes that contained brewing logs from the early to the late 19th century. When he sat down with brewer Stewart Main, they found the recipes were written in code. In took them months of patient work to break the codes, with the help of Main's knowledge of the malt, hops and other ingredients used by the brewery during that period. Slowly, Owen and Main were able to piece together recipes for two beers, Double Stout and India Pale Ale, which were then brewed by Main in the pilot brewery.

Why would a brewer go to such lengths to hide his recipes? The answer is that competition for beer sales was fierce in the 19th century. The 'tied trade' – pubs owned by breweries – didn't exist. Every alehouse, tavern and inn was a free house run by

an individual owner who could pick and choose his suppliers. Shepherd Neame faced especially tough competition from a brewery called Rigdens, which opened across the street. So bitter was the rivalry between the two companies that the Neames and the Rigdens never socialised, except when 'riding to hounds' – a euphemism for fox hunting.

Double Stout was first brewed in 1868 and used pale malt and roasted grain with East Kent Goldings. The brewery never exported beer to India – 'it got as far as Sumatra', according to John Owen – but it launched an IPA in 1870 at the height of the style's popularity. It was brewed with pale malt, a touch of darker malt and Fuggles and Goldings.

The most fascinating revelation was Brilliant Ale, brewed between 1825 and 1855 with just pale malt and Goldings. The received wisdom is that the production of pale beer was concentrated in Burton upon Trent for most of the 19th century until brewers elsewhere learnt how to 'Burtonise' their water with the addition of sulphates. But Brilliant Ale proves that pale, even golden, ales were brewed more widely than previously thought. Shepherd Neame obtained samples of Burton-brewed pale ale for scientific analysis and the result was a beer that challenged the domination of darker beers – mild, porter and stout – in Kent.

The three beers form part of the brewery's Classic Collection. They are available in bottle all year round while cask versions are part of Sheps' seasonal programme.

Rigdens fared less well than its rival. It was bought by Fremlins of Maidstone, which was taken over by national giant Whitbread and it closed in 1990. Whether riding to hounds or brewing beer, Sheps had the last laugh.

Cheif executive Jonathan Neame is the fifth generation of his family to take the helm

Established: 2013

Founder: Darron Anley

Beers: Half Mast QIPA, Undercurrent Oatmeal Pale Ale, Sweet Dream, Soundwave IPA, Liquid Mistress Red IPA, Broken Dream Breakfast Stout, Limoncello IPA, Big Inflatable Cowboy Hat

Website: www.sirencraftbrew.com

SIREN

Finchampstead, Berkshire

Unit 1 is not the most inspiring address in the world, it's utilitarian and singular, suggestive of a lack of imagination, an industrial estate perhaps where stacks of stationery might be kept. However, drinkers wanting imaginative and inspirational beers have been known to set the sat-nav for the tap room of Unit 1 in the town of Finchampstead: Unit 1 is where Siren have been producing their exemplary beers since early 2013.

At this innocuous address, American brewer Ryan Witter-Merithew has been responsible for a raft of exciting and highly accomplished beers. As you might expect from his background, you find amongst Siren's portfolio a West Coast IPA (as well as a red one), a Breakfast Stout plus an American-style pale ale bursting with juicy citrus character. However, as is the case with some of his equally adept contemporaries (Magic Rock's Stuart Ross

immediately springs to mind) it's not just a case of chucking in loads of hops and hoping for the best. Special releases have included a 2.8% QIPA, a Chocolate Milk Stout, an Oatmeal Pale Ale and the luscious Limoncello IPA.

AVOIDING THE BANDWAGON

According to Siren's founder Darron Anley, 'for Siren's approach as a whole we look to ideally find gaps where possible, i.e. an oatmeal pale ale and a breakfast stout, which are part of our year round line up, weren't really being done when we started. We try not to jump on bandwagons: for instance we have wanted to make a sour since we started but everyone started doing it so we held back a while, and then came at it with a different angle, i.e. take a sour beer and heavily dry hop it with a single hop, and then change that dry hop each batch.

"We try not to jump on bandwagons: for instance we have wanted to make a sour since we started but everyone started doing it so we held back a while, and then came at it with a different angle"

'Barrel aging is also great fun and allows us to experiment. We are constantly looking to expand it, but space is an issue, we currently have 120+ barrels with beers varying from Imperial porters, golden barley wines, dry stouts, sour milds and *Brett* [wild yeast] primary-fermented beers. And we are aging in barrels that have formerly held tequila, Banyuls, Grand Marnier, wine, Bourbon and Pedro Ximénez.'

INTERNATIONAL EXPERIENCE

Witter-Merithew is a well-travelled brewer, having worked at Duck-Rabbit in North Carolina in the US, which specialises in full-flavoured beers, and then moved to Denmark where he headed up Fanø Bryghus. He came to Siren after Anley, having been to the Craft Beer Conference in San Diego, told former Thornbridge brewer Kelly Ryan about his hunt for a brewer. Ryan then initiated a Twitter campaign to find him a head brewer and Witter-Merithew was on his way.

'When the concept of the brewery first started I think Darron really wanted to open a brewery making the types of beers he enjoyed, that is American-style beers,' says Witter-Merithew. 'That said I do not think I really have a set-in-stone brewing philosophy other then to enjoy it and brew beers I want to drink. Often little things such as something I taste while enjoying a meal or something I read can get me thinking about

Siren's beer range is broad enough to tempt any drinker: from sour milds to Imperial porters and dry stouts

something we should brew. I often start by just thinking what I want the final beer to taste like. Then if needed I will do some research and reading to work it all out and then just write something up. I am pretty lucky that I have brewed so many different beers by this point that I feel pretty comfortable in just writing a recipe and brewing it.'

Beers to try ...

Soundwave, 5.6%
Vibrant West Coast IPA that hums with resiny hop character that contrasts fantastically with the juicy citrusy character (think oodles of mango, grapefruit and ripe peach); the crisp, dry finish brings the mouth alive.

Broken Dream, 6%
Smoothness is the key to this silky soft so-called Breakfast Stout whose character also brings coffee, chocolate, subtle roast and hints of liquorice to the palate. The finish lingers like an echo.

Westerham is commited to the use of English hops, such as those grown at the Scotney Castle estate and dried in traditional Kentish oast houses

Established: 2004

Founder: Robert Wicks

Beers: Finchcocks Original, Grasshopper, Summer Perle, General Wolfe, God's Wallop, Puddledock Porter, Spirit of Kent, Freedom Ale, British Bulldog, Scotney Green Hop, 1965, Hop Rocket India Pale Ale, Viceroy, Double Stout, Audit Ale

Website: www.westerhambrewery.co.uk

WESTERHAM

Crockham Hill, Kent

The address will soon be out of date as Westerham is on the move, from their current National Trust-owned site to land belonging to the Squerryes Estate. Squerryes is a Georgian stately house and gardens. Grapes are grown on the estate to make sparkling wine and Robert Wicks, founder and owner of Westerham Brewery, plans to restore barley crops there: Maris Otter was grown on the estate until the 1960s.

Wicks is a passionate believer in using local ingredients to reduce carbon emissions. He makes use of just about every variety of hop grown in Kent and says 'There's no point brewing in Kent if you don't use Kent hops. I know every hop farm in the

> *"There's no point brewing in Kent if you don't use Kent hops. I know every hop farm in the county and can trace the plants back to source."*

county and can trace the plants back to source.' He works closely with the local Scotney Castle estate, where hops are grown, as well as with other hop farmers in the area. Among the hops grown at Scotney is the rare Finchcocks Hop X, which Wicks describes as 'full of oil' and celebrates with a beer called Finchcocks Original.

ETHICAL BREWING

Westerham is proof that wearing an ethical heart on your sleeve is not a turn-off for consumers. The brewery is moving home because it needs extra capacity to produce such beers as William Wilberforce Freedom Ale. The beer was launched in 2007 to commemorate the 200th anniversary of Wilberforce's success in winning parliamentary support for the abolition of the slave trade. Robert Wicks is keen to point out that human trafficking continues in the 21st century, and a royalty from sales of the beer is made to the international charity Stop the Traffik. Robert also brews a bottle-conditioned Viceroy India Pale Ale for the National Trust: proceeds go to help pay for the upkeep of

Even the yeast cultures have some history. They came from the Black Eagle brewery in Westerham that delivered beer to British troops in France during World War Two – in special tanks strapped to Spitfires

houses owned by Lord Curzon, which passed to the trust in 1986. Curzon, who restored the Taj Mahal, was a controversial figure in India but he did enjoy good beer. He recalled in his memoirs trekking across Afghanistan, hallucinating about beer and being overjoyed when a servant rode up and gave him a bottle of Bass Ale.

Robert Wicks opened Westerham in 2004. He trained as a biochemist and then worked in investment banking, all the while brewing at home – 'full mash!' His banking background means he has kept a firm grip on finances and has avoided some of the pitfalls of other small breweries that operate on a wing and a prayer, and has been able to invest in new equipment. In order to emphasise the hop character of the brews, he installed a hop rocket, a piece of kit that looks remarkably like the rocket used by the cartoon characters Wallace and Gromit. But this has serious intent. It's packed with hops, as many as 15 kilos per brew, for selected beers that require exceptional hop character. Following the normal copper boil with hops, the hopped wort then rests in the rocket where it picks up additional aroma and flavour.

HERITAGE INGREDIENTS

Even the yeast cultures have some history. They came from the Black Eagle brewery in Westerham that, as well as supplying pubs as far away as London, also delivered beer to British troops in France during World War Two – in special tanks strapped to Spitfires – and by more conventional means to Churchill at nearby Chartwell. The brewery suffered a series of takeovers and was eventually closed in 1968. The last head brewer, sensing the writing was on the mash tun, deposited samples of his yeasts with the National Collection of Yeast Cultures at Norwich, where they were freeze dried. Wicks was able to get samples, re-culture them and use them to get the correct Westerham flavours in his modern beers.

Robert Wicks (foreground centre) with his brewing team

The eight regular beers brewed at Westerham include Finchcocks Original, a 'Kentish hop ale', which is a member of a much-diminished style known as Light Mild. It uses Goldings and Whitbread Goldings as well as the rare Finchcocks' Hop X, and has a punchy 30 units of bitterness, high for the type of beer. Spirit of Kent was first brewed to mark the Queen's Diamond Jubilee and includes a hop grown in every decade of the reign. The brewery's top brand, British Bulldog, launched in 2004 to mark the 60th anniversary of D-day, is brewed with pale malt and a large amount of crystal, and is hopped with Northdown, Progress and Whitbread Goldings.

Robert Wicks, his brewing team, and their kit, will soon be on the way to their new home. They might be tempted to crack open a bottle of the local sparkling wine to mark the move, but they should stick to tradition and reach instead for a strong Audit Ale. Based on a 1938 Black Eagle recipe. it recalls the tradition of breweries supplying colleges and stately homes to celebrate the finalising of the annual accounts. Certainly there's a lot to celebrate.

Beers to try ...

Freedom Ale, 4.8% bottle, 4% cask
Maris Otter and crystal malts, with Goldings and Northdown hops combine to create a deep gold beer with sherbet lemons and biscuit malt on the nose and a big attack of hop resins in the mouth. The finish is lingering and beautifully balanced between juicy malt, tart fruit and bitter hops.

Viceroy, 5%
Brewed for the National Trust, it uses Maris Otter pale malt with Target and Progress hops from Scotney Castle. It has spicy hops, wholemeal biscuits and tangy fruit on the aroma and palate and a hoppy/malty/fruity finish.

Audit Ale, 6.2%
Brewed with Maris Otter and crystal malts and hopped with Goldings and Northdown, it has a maltloaf aroma with rich raisin and sultana fruit, followed by a palate in which hop bitterness grows and a bittersweet finish with burnt fruit, rich malt and peppery hops.

Established: 2010

Founder: Bob and Jim Morrison, Will Calvert and Paddy Johnson

Beers: ParkLife, Knight of the Garter, Canberra, Windsor Knot, ZinZan's Drop, Guardsman, Eton Boatman, Tree Tops, Kohinoor, Mandarin, Republika, Conqueror, Conqueror 1075

Website: www.webrew.co.uk

WINDSOR & ETON

Windsor, Berkshire

The brewery is at the end of a residential street, with trains rumbling over a Brunel railway arch a few yards away and the castle standing sentinel over the Royal Borough in the background. If Windsor and Eton are posh – homes to kings, queens and public school boys – the founders of the brewery are mercifully down-to-earth: 'Four blokes in their mid-50s who wanted to start a brewery,' in the words of Paddy Johnson, the head brewer. He and Will Calvert had worked for Courage at the Reading brewery while Bob and Jim Morrison brought engineering and marketing skills from their previous jobs. They found a site in 2009 and on 23 April 2010 – both St George's Day and Shakespeare's birthday – launched their first brew of Guardsman best bitter.

The four didn't borrow any money. They invested their savings or mortgaged their houses to install a custom-built brewing plant made in the home of brewing, Burton upon Trent. Fittingly, it's a very English piece of kit, based on mash tun and copper but as the fermenters are conical, with yeast cropped from the bottom, they are able to brew proper lager as well as ales. Their lager – conditioned for six weeks and using a yeast culture from the Czech Republic – is called Republika, a brave name to use in Windsor but the people up in the castle don't seem to mind. When the Queen visited the Pope in Rome in 2014, she took him a bottle of Coronation Ale brewed specially for the occasion by Windsor & Eton, and some of the brewery's Maris Otter malting barley is grown on one of the royal farms.

ENGLISH ROOTS

Guardsman, the flagship beer, is English to its fingertips, brewed with Maris Otter, Fuggles and Goldings. Windsor Knot genuflects with a hop called Sovereign and one from the Commonwealth, Nelson Sauvin from New Zealand. Kohinoor recalls

The brewery's founders Bob and Jim Morrison, Will Calvert and Paddy Johnson

the day of Empire with jasmine petals and cardamom seeds added to malt and hops while Knight of the Garter is a fashionable golden ale with big citrus notes from Admiral and Amarillo hops.

A major innovation came in 2014 when, working with the London Amateur Brewers group, Windsor & Eton designed a beer to mark the 800th anniversary of the signing of Magna Carta on 15 June 1215, the document agreed by King John to appease rebellious barons. It was signed at nearby Runnymede, and the brewery wants to be at the heart of the celebrations. A competition to design the best recipe was won by Manmohan Birdi, an osteopath from south-east London and a passionate home brewer. He used some dark malts, as all brewing grains would have been dark in the 13th century, and while he added conventional Fuggles and East Kent Goldings hops, which would not have been available, he also used ground ivy, liquorice and yarrow, which were all used in medieval times as flavourings, and invert sugar to ensure a powerful fermentation. The finished beer, in cask and bottle, will be 7.4%.

A trial brew by Manmohan was dark brown and had a massive aroma of liquorice, herbs and spices with a bittersweet finish. A beer with body or, as they said back in 1215, *habeus corpus*.

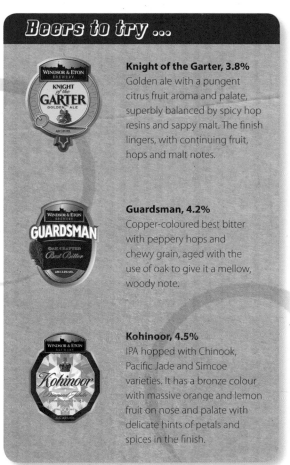

Beers to try ...

Knight of the Garter, 3.8%
Golden ale with a pungent citrus fruit aroma and palate, superbly balanced by spicy hop resins and sappy malt. The finish lingers, with continuing fruit, hops and malt notes.

Guardsman, 4.2%
Copper-coloured best bitter with peppery hops and chewy grain, aged with the use of oak to give it a mellow, woody note.

Kohinoor, 4.5%
IPA hopped with Chinook, Pacific Jade and Simcoe varieties. It has a bronze colour with massive orange and lemon fruit on nose and palate with delicate hints of petals and spices in the finish.

BEER DESTINATIONS

BERKSHIRE, BUCKINGHAMSHIRE, EAST SUSSEX, ESSEX, HAMPSHIRE, HERTFORDSHIRE, ISLE OF WIGHT, KENT, OXFORDSHIRE, WEST SUSSEX

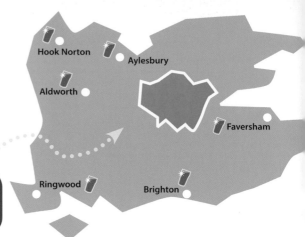

BELL INN
Aldworth, Berkshire
01635 578272

The Bell has been a regular in the *Good Beer Guide* since the 1970s and was a champion of good ale at a time when Courage dominated local pubs. It has been run by the same family for 250 years and has rambling, interconnected rooms with beams, settles and wood panelling, local memorabilia and beer served through a hatch. The local West Berkshire brewery supplies Maggs' Magnificent Mild and a special beer for the pub called Old Tyler. Arkell's of Swindon also features and there are local ciders and perries. The Bell has a vast garden and you can watch cricket on the green, while Mummers perform at Christmas. 'Idyllic' doesn't do it justice.

FARMERS' BAR AT THE KING'S HEAD
Aylesbury, Buckinghamshire
www.farmersbar.co.uk

Chiltern brewery's flagship pub is part of a coaching inn dating to 1455, ranged round a cobbled courtyard with the original stables intact and used today as outlets for small retailers. The inn has given bed and board to many notable figures over the years, including Henry VIII and Oliver Cromwell. The pub, leased from the National Trust, has heavy beams, wooden settles, and a comfortable restaurant area serving food made with local ingredients and suggested beer matches. The bar offers the full range of the brewery's beers, including, occasionally, Bodgers Barley Wine served from an oak cask on the counter that has previously held whisky.

EVENING STAR
Brighton, East Sussex
www.darkstarpubs.co.uk/ eveningstar

The Evening Star is where it all started for Dark Star brewery. Rob Jones, who migrated to Sussex from Pitfield brewery in London, started brewing with a souped-up home-brew kit in the cellar of the pub. Even though the town is awash with good pubs, locals started to congregate here to sample Rob's hop fest beers and soon drinkers were arriving from further afield. The brewery has moved twice and is now big business but it hasn't forgotten its roots and serves the full range of its beer, including seasonal offerings. There's also a selection of world beers on draught and in bottle. It's a small pub and can get crowded but there's seating outside on a patio.

SHEPHERD NEAME
Faversham, Kent
www.shepherdneame.co.uk

Shep's visitor centre is a hive of activity. Groups can tour the brewery, sample the water from the on-site well and view the ancient wooden brewing equipment and Victorian steam engines, along with the modern kit that produces a vast range of succulent beers. There's also a micro plant in the cellars where beers are fashioned using 19th and 20th century recipes, along with new contributions to the range. The centre offers tours that include beer tastings and beer suppers and it can also be booked for weddings and conferences. You will leave better informed about beer, brewing and Kentish hops, and can come away with bottled beers from the shop.

HOOK NORTON
Hook Norton, Oxfordshire
www.hooky.co.uk

Hook Norton is a breath-catching complex of Victorian buildings, with steam billowing from windows and louvres when brewing is underway. The brewery is a now rare example of a 'tower brewery' where the brewing process flows from floor to floor and all the original equipment is still in place. You can marvel at steam engines that provide the power for wood-sided mash tuns and fermenters, while the boiling copper is a burnished vessel made from the genuine metal, not modern stainless steel. In stables alongside you can visit and admire the great shire horses that still pull drays for local deliveries. The visitor centre has a bar where Hooky ales can be enjoyed, with facilities to take them away in draught and bottled form.

INN ON THE FURLONG
Ringwood, Hampshire
01425 475139

An imposing cream-faced Victorian public house that acts as the brewery tap for Ringwood, the first British micro founded by the late Peter Austin, known as the 'godfather of craft brewing'. Ringwood is now part of mighty Marston's but continues to brew succulent ales, with the full range available in the Inn, including Best Bitter, Fortyniner and Old Thumper. You will find other beers from the Marston's range: watch out for Jenning's Cocker Hoop and Marston's Old Empire. The Inn serves breakfasts from 9.30 and holds themed food evenings: tapas are popular. The raised bar serves several interlinked rooms, including one for families plus a conservatory.

Shepherd Neame's visitor centre in Faversham hosts beer and food matching evenings, where diners can enjoy a six-course meal accompanied by specially selected beers

Truman's: Hackney Wick, London

Tap East: Stratford, London

Fuller's: Chiswick, London

Highgate
Hackney Wick
Westbourne Park
Stratford
Clerkenwell
Chiswick
Borough
Blackfriars
Greenwich
Bermondsey

Kernel: Bermondsey, London

Meantime: Greenwich, London

LONDON

GREATER LONDON

London pride: there's a lot of it about in the capital city. First of all there's the ubiquitous beer brewed by Fuller's in Chiswick, amber in colour and malt-forward with a floral hop character courtesy of Northdown, Target and Challenger. Then there's a London pride that is more intangible, which applies to the current spirit of brewing that has made the city one of the hotspots of European beer.

The second sort of London pride can be found in the stainless steel Valhalla of Meantime in London's historic Greenwich, where some of Europe's best lager styles as well as London favourites IPA and Porter have been painstakingly created by brew master Alastair Hook. And in the visionary attitude of Sambrook's in Battersea, started by Duncan Sambrook in 2008, a couple of years after a beery epiphany when he realised that London was deficit in its own brewing culture and he needed to be part of it.

This pride in brewing is echoed by the rock'n'roll attitude of the new kids on the brewing block such as Kernel, Brew By Numbers and London Fields with their railway arches, colourful graphics and beers that are eclectic in their range and incorporative in the way British, American and European influences end up in the mash tun. For these guys, hops, obviously, are a very big part of the scheme, but they are also brewing beers based on 19th century London export stout, India porter and Berliner Weisse.

That's the great thing about London's (and Britain's if it comes to that) brewing revolution, nothing is unachievable when it comes to beer. If you're a former chef like Andy Smith, who started Partizan after a stint learning brewing at Redemption in north London, then making beer is on a par with creating in the kitchen. Want to brew a Belgian Quad or Victorian Mild? Then, as Andy has done, just do it.

BEER DESTINATIONS
> go to page 80

Kernel and Partizan are part of a new wave of breweries based in railway arches springing up across London

BREWING BOOM TOWN

How did this all happen? At the start of the 21st century the London brewing scene seemed bleak. Fuller's, Young's and new guys Meantime, plus a handful of micros, flew the flag for independent brewing (though Guinness and Budweiser were produced in massive plants in the western suburbs). In 2006 Young's closed and merged with Charles Wells in Bedford (ironically where a couple of beers from former London giant Courage are now brewed). A year later, it was estimated that London had 10 breweries and brewpubs; small beer if you consider its 5,000 pubs and the millions living and working within the city limits. How times change. London is now host to well over 50 breweries – such is the constant growth that observers of the scene find it hard to keep track.

This beer revolution seems to have happened so dramatically, over such a short period of time. In a strange case of serendipity, in the same year as Sambrook's started delivering their bittersweet beauty of a session beer Wandle Ale to local pubs, brother and sister James and Lizzie Brodie founded their eponymous brewery in an imposing Victorian pub in Leytonstone, the King William IV. Then as if to smartly underline and dot the i's and cross the t's of this growing London brewing renaissance along came former cheese-monger Evin O'Riordain a year later with the starkly named Kernel, which rapidly caught drinkers' attentions. The floodgates were open; the dam of beer was burst.

TIME FOR A REVOLUTION

And it was about time: London after all was the home of the first beer of the industrial age, porter, which was followed by its younger more vigorous sibling stout. Furthermore, you could also argue that London was the birthplace of what would become known as India Pale Ale (though its spiritual home was Burton upon Trent).

So much history and at one stage so many breweries, but in the decades after World War

This pride is echoed by the rock'n'roll attitude of the new kids on the brewing block such as Kernel, Brew By Numbers and London Fields

Two most gave up the ghost and either deserted the capital or completely removed themselves from brewing (many being swallowed up by larger competitors in the process). Courage's Anchor Brewhouse closed in 1981 when the brewery went to Reading. Meanwhile Whitbread had already left in 1976 – their brewery is now a conference centre. Other names that once made Londoners proud of their beery traditions also joined the rush for the exit: Charrington, Taylor Walker and Truman's (though the latter name has been successfully resurrected with some gorgeous beers).

However, London is not just about the new. Under the tutelage of head brewer John Keeling, Fuller's has not stood still. As well as a range of highly accomplished beers such as London Pride and ESB, Fuller's has also brewed an intriguing selection of bottled beers using recipes from their archives. Called the Past Masters series, the first two were XX Strong Ale and Double Stout, both of late 19th century origin. Another, the third in the series, was Old Burton Extra, based on a 1931 recipe, while the 1966 Strong Ale was based on a recipe from the Swinging Sixties.

We may mourn the death of London's brewing past with its ghosts still lingering on the facades of pubs – the green tiling of Barclay Perkins, the stern stone signs of Truman's – and the city's brewing will never become what it once was, given that the majority of breweries are small outfits. On the other hand, this is a new generation eager to make its mark and more important they are looking backwards and forwards in their efforts to bring great beer back to the capital. London pride indeed.

Insider's view...

Will Hawkes
@CraftBeerLondon

London's beer scene reflects the place itself: energetic, untidy, inspiring, frustrating, original, in thrall to America. There are now over 50 breweries in a city which, a few years ago, had half-a-dozen. When you consider the speed with which pubs are converting to better beer – most notably in East London – it's hard to avoid the conclusion that something really significant is happening in a city whose beery heyday seemed long in the past.

But is the beer any good? Yes (although not all of it) and increasingly so. Many of the most notable names are not cask ale brewers – the likes of Camden Town, Meantime and Kernel – but Fuller's, who have seen it all before, are also thriving. The best of the new breed of pubs – like the Craft Beer Co in Covent Garden, the Euston Tap and the King's Head in Bethnal Green – serve cask and keg and attract punters from all walks of life.

Will Hawkes is a writer and journalist and was British Guild of Beer Writers Beer Writer of the Year 2013

Many of Fuller's beers are available in bottle as well as cask. Some, such as Bengal Lancer and Vintage Age, referment in the bottle; Vintage Ale will improve with age

Established: 1845

Founder: John Bird Fuller, Henry Smith and John Turner

Beers: Mighty Atom, Chiswick Bitter, Seafarers Ale, Front Row, Spring Sprinter, London Pride, Black Cab, Wild River, HSB, Bengal Lancer, London Porter, ESB, 1845, Vintage Ale, Prize Old Ale

Website: www.fullers.co.uk

FULLER'S

Chiswick, London

When you've been brewing for more than 350 years it's easy to get stuck in your ways, but innovation is the mantra at Fuller's. In the past few years the company has invested £5 million to increase capacity to 260,000 barrels annually, of which 150,000 barrels is accounted for by cask beer. Plans are in hand for head brewer John Keeling to launch a series of collaborative brews with breweries including the Camden craft brewery in London and the leading American independent Sierra Nevada in California.

There will be a special brew in 2015 to celebrate Keeling's 40 years in the industry. A voluble Mancunian, he is held in such high regard at the brewery that he can afford to respond cheekily to his directors. 'When they ask me "How can we produce beers with more personality and character", I tell them: "Let people with personality and character make them".'

OLD STYLES AND NEW

Not that the stock beers lack character. London Pride and ESB have picked up so many awards over the years that it takes several trophy cabinets to hold them all: Pride is one of the country's biggest-selling cask ales while ESB is so admired in export markets that it's spawned a style category in beer competitions in the US. But new beers and new styles roll out of the brewery at a breathtaking pace while old styles are revered and maintained. Fuller's was criticised for closing Gale's brewery in Hampshire when it bought the company – with the agreement of the Gales family – in 2005. But it continues to brew several of the Gale's beers, including Prize Old Ale, a 9% strong ale, aged for between six months and a year, and similar in character to a Belgian 'sour red'. The final batch made at Gale's was transferred to Chiswick and a

"When they ask me 'How can we produce beers with more personality and character', I tell them: 'Let people with personality and character make them'."

portion is blended with fresh beer to produce an annual vintage. Fuller's has its own Vintage Ale, 8.5%, bottle conditioned, introduced in 1997 and brewed each year with different varieties of malts and hops. Beer lovers look forward to the latest batch with an anticipation as keen as that of wine drinkers contemplating the release of the new Bordeaux.

Beers with a modern twist include Discovery, one of the brewery's best-selling golden ales, Wild River, an American-style pale ale that uses Cascade, Chinook, Liberty and Willamette hops, and a properly-brewed lager, Frontier, launched in 2013, which is aged for five weeks and is not pasteurised.

"Thirty years ago the instructions were to make beer cheaper and faster, using sugar to speed up production. Now the order is to make beer with more flavour."

John Keeling has joined the headlong rush to produce modern interpretations of India Pale Ale with Bengal Lancer, which is without doubt one of the finest of the new breed.

Fascinated by the added complexities of beers aged in oak, he planned an annual wood-aged beer – and ran into trouble with the excise branch of Her Majesty's Revenue & Customs. When he launched the first Brewer's Reserve, he was accused by the excise officers of the ancient crime of 'grogging' – adding to the strength of beer by the surreptitious addition of spirit locked in the wood. Keeling had to appease the law men by adjusting the strength of the beer, Golden Pride, and producing a final beer at 8.2%. He has since gone on to produce annual vintages aged in Cognac and Armagnac oak barriques and in 2014 was preparing one with the use of Glenmorangie single malt whisky casks.

Keeling has added a Past Masters range to his portfolio, based on Fuller's recipes from the 19th and early 20th centuries. To date the list includes

Fuller's enjoys an idyllic base on the Thames in Chiswick, surrounded by handsome Georgian houses

Bengal Lancer, 5.3 % bottle, 5% cask

It has a deep gold colour and a rich and inviting aroma of hop resins, sherbet lemons and a hint of caramel. Passion fruit and lemon jelly dominate the palate but they are balanced by peppery Goldings. The finish has a bittersweet character but with a massive hop presence – piny, spice and peppery.

ESB, 5.5 %

This massively flavoured beer has an explosion of ripe malt, marmalade fruit and peppery hops on the bouquet, with an attack of juicy malt, orange peel and bitter hop resins in the mouth, followed by a complex finish of malt, hops and tangy fruit, finally becoming dry.

Vintage Ale, 8.5%

Varies from year to year and each vintage will age in bottle and increase in depth and complexity. A young 2013 vintage had a rich bouquet of spicy hops, marzipan, cinnamon, orange marmalade fruit and biscuit malt. Vinous fruit built on the palate with tangy hop resins, spice and ripe grain, followed by a long bittersweet finish dominated by spicy hops, tart fruit and sappy malt.

XX Strong Ale, Old Burton Extra and Double Stout; an Imperial Russian stout is in the pipeline.

A CLOSE CALL

The success of Fuller's, which has an estate of close to 400 pubs, is all the more remarkable when you consider that in the early 1970s a boardroom decision was taken to stop producing cask ale and go over to keg beer. Fortunately, the success of Young's brewery over the river in Wandsworth along with patient pleading by the youthful CAMRA put a stop to such sacrilege. Today the brewery is still run by members of the founding families and enjoys an idyllic location overlooking the Thames and surrounded by stunning Regency houses. The families look to both the past and the future for inspiration. John Keeling sums up the change of attitude. 'Thirty years ago the instructions were to make beer cheaper and faster, using sugar to speed up production. Now the order is to make beer with more flavour.'

And in Chiswick, beer with flavour is reaping a rich reward.

1845 commemorates the founding year of the brewery, which is still run by descendents of the Fuller, Smith and Turner families.

Emma McIntosh stirs hops into one of Kernel's beers. Unlike many other breweries, Kernel's hop recipe changes for each brew

Established: 2009

Founder: Evin O'Riordain

Beers: London Sour, Table Beer, Pale Ale, India Pale Ale, Export India Porter, Export Stout

Website: www.thekernelbrewery.com

KERNEL

Bermondsey, London

The Kernel brewery's branding is a masterpiece of understatement. Its bottles are wrapped with strips of brown paper, with the minimum of information printed on them. There's the name of the brewery, its address in Bermondsey, some information about the fact that the beer is bottle conditioned and the exhortation to 'Please Drink Fresh'.

Oh and there's the name of the beer: it might be an India Pale Ale, with the list of the hop(s) used beneath, something which changes from batch to batch. The hops are added singularly or married together to create a colourful experience on the palate. One thing you can expect from Kernel is the unexpected when it comes to hops.

Within the brewing industry it's an article of faith to maintain the same flavour in every batch of beer brewed. This is not Kernel's way. There might not be massive differences in the variety of IPAs or Pale Ales produced with different hops, but the approach taken by brewery founder Evin O'Riordain

and his brewing team is refreshing, different and erudite (and dare one say, revolutionary).

FREEDOM OF EXPRESSION

'We have certain things we like to taste and feel in our beers,' says O'Riordain, 'a clarity of flavour, a particular intensity (especially aromatic intensity) and an articulate texture. There's also freshness for anything pale and/or hoppy. But the way we brew is not fixed on an ideal goal, or a preconceived notion of what a beer should taste like. When we, say, change the hops on our Pale Ale or IPA, we would like to give the beer space (or give those hops space) to express itself/themselves, rather than conform to what we want it to be. We feel that having a specific image in mind of what the flavours of this beer should be acts as a limit to the potential of that beer. So what we want with our beers is to give them a bit of freedom of expression, within the general parameters above of what we like in a beer.'

"We feel that having a specific image in mind of what the flavours of this beer should be acts as a limit to the potential of that beer"

Almost all of Kernel's beer production is packaged in bottles rather than cask. The bottling, like the rest of the brewing process is done by hand on a micro scale

O'Riordain started his working life with cheese at Neal's Yard Dairy in central London. 'After that I had my own cheese stall in Borough Market for three years,' says the tall and thoughtful O'Riordain, 'but then I experienced an epiphany during a stay in New York. In the evening we would go out and I would be taught about beer. It was amazing to discover that you could treat beer in the same manner that we treated artisanal cheese. One afternoon in the beer garden of a Manhattan bar the thought appeared that I should make beer back home in London.'

This change of direction is no surprise, when you consider that cheese and beer are closely entwined, members of what beer writer Michael Jackson once called 'the family of the fermented'.

BREWING CATALYST

Kernel brewery opened in 2009, beneath a railway arch on the Bermondsey-Southwark border with the beers being an immediate hit with a new generation of beer-loving Londoners (and drinkers further afield) – within two years O'Riordain had been named Brewer of the Year by the British Guild of Beer Writers. In fact, you could argue that Kernel was the trailblazer in the capital city's brewing renaissance that seems to have swept all before it since the end of the past decade. Prior to that the London brewing scene was dominated by Fuller's and – to a lesser extent – Meantime, while a handful of small breweries wandered in their wake. Not long after the founding of Kernel, the numbers started to grow. However, whether Kernel was a brewing catalyst or not, O'Riordain is refreshingly free of pomp and circumstance.

'We brew beers that we enjoy drinking,' he explains, 'and it is our selfish pleasure to do so, without attempting to think how others will respond to them. We feel it is patronising to do so, to give someone what you think they will like (as opposed to giving them something that we feel is good). This is, for example, the reason we have no tasting notes on our labels – you don't need us to tell you how it tastes.'

In 2012, the brewery swapped its railway arch for a bigger one, about half a mile away along the track. This has given them the space to introduce more brewing vessels as well as oak barrels for aging beer (there are several dozen stacked away, filled with beers in a quiet corner of the brewery). It also keeps them within the gastronomic community that inhabits the railway arches that run eastwards from London Bridge.

'The environment of the brewery, the environment in which we work, has a huge effect on the beer (as does being in London),' he says. 'So we make our brewery the best place to be in. Which makes the beer better. We surround ourselves with our community (our friends the cheese makers, ham importers, butchers, coffee roasters) because these things are also essential to our lives. They affect the beer.'

Beers to try...

London Sour, 3.2%
Based on a Berliner Weisse, this is a tangy, tart, juicy and gently sour beer with an aroma reminiscent of fruit chews, and a dry and quenching finish.

India Pale Ale Simcoe, 7%
Ripe peach, melon and grapefruit hover above the glass when poured, while the palate is coated with an essence of tropical fruits in alliance with a brisk and bitter grainy background.

Export Stout, 8.2%
A luxurious dark beer that blends notes of vanilla, rich chocolate liqueur and freshly ground coffee beans with an end-of-palate acidity that adds a delicious contrast.

"We brew beers that we enjoy drinking, and it is our selfish pleasure to do so, without thinking how others will respond to them"

Beer trends...
BREWPUBS

Brewpubs dot the beer scene in London. Some kits are hidden away, such as that used for Howling Hops' beers at the Cock Tavern in Hackney; it's crouched in the cellar, producing small batches for sale mainly at the pub. They're not beers to be coy about though, and include the bristly Smoked Porter and the full-bodied Old London Victorian Stout (though plenty of hop bines are plundered for their IPAs and hoppy pale ales as well).

On the other hand, the slightly larger brewing kit at the Florence in Herne Hill is on full view in the pub, seated in a corner in a glass booth: part of the furniture, its gleaming stainless steel bare to the world. This is a space where brewer Peter Haydon produces beers under two different brand names. Florence beer is for sale in the pub, while beer that goes out into the trade is under the name A Head In A Hat. The latter are beers influenced by Haydon's intense interest in past beer styles using English hops.

There are other brewpubs scattered about the city: London Brewing at the Bull in Highgate; Crate in Hackney, where great beer dovetails with perfect pizza; Tap East (see page 76) in a shopping centre.

Brewpubs have threaded their way through London's beer culture, sometimes thriving, other times spluttering like a dying candle. During the 19th century the capital was crammed with them, until the larger breweries started buying up pubs to sell their running beers in. It wasn't until the 1980s that the brewpub made a noticeable return to the capital through David Bruce's Firkin chain, which offered drinkers what was then a novel glimpse of a brewery at work while they drank.

Come 2000 (incidentally the same year Meantime was founded), the brewpub Zerodegrees opened its first branch at Blackheath; this was in the style of a similar operation called Mash, which had operated in London in the late 1990s and was where Meantime's Alastair Hook was consultant brewer. The Firkin pubs were on the wane and the US model influenced this new brand of brewpub (in style as well as in the type of beer brewed). It was a stylish, ultra-modern fusion of shiny brewing equipment on which highly accomplished versions of beer styles such as Pilsener and pale ale were made, all served with great food. The original branch still thrives and has been joined by ones in Bristol (see page 106), Cardiff and Reading.

Another great pioneer of the London brewpub scene was Brodie's, which is based at the back of a grand old Victorian pub in Leyton called the King William IV. Here brewing began in 2008 under the direction of James Brodie and sister Lizzie (there had been an earlier attempt in the

Top: Zerodegrees in Blackheath
Bottom: Florence, Tap East and the King William IV

same pub a few years ago under the name of Sweet William). James Brodie is often cited as an important influence and inspiration by several brewers: for instance when Evin O'Riordain at Kernel was asked if there was such a thing as a modern London style his reply was succinct: 'If there is, I would like it to be defined by James Brodie.'

Then there's Beavertown which, though it now produces its boldly flavoured beers in an industrial estate in Tottenham Hale, also began life as a brewpub. Founder Logan Plant first set up his kit at an old-school East End boozer that underwent a cool craft bar makeover to become Duke's Brew & Que – Plant brewed next to the kitchen but even such a compact space did not stop him coming up with classics such as Smog Rocket, a 5.4% smoked porter.

This is the great thing about a brewpub, especially during the current climate of beery excitement: there is a freedom of expression that can be often denied to stand-alone breweries – the drinkers are right in front of you and not shy in saying what they think. Or as Plant recalls from his time at Duke's: 'it was great getting instantaneous feedback from the bar.'

Brewpubs: perhaps the most democratic expression of brewing there is.

Meantime's ultra-modern brewing plant cost £7 million and beer production is growing at 60% a year

Established: 2000

Founder: Alastair Hook

Beers: London Pale Ale, London Stout, Pale Ale, Wheat, Raspberry Grand Cru, Chocolate, London Porter, IPA

Website: www.meantimebrewing.com

MEANTIME

Greenwich, London

Meantime is big and getting bigger – 'the fastest-growing brewery in Britain,' according to chief executive Nick Miller. It has a capacity of 200,000 barrels and Miller says the only thing that keeps him awake at night is the prospect of running out of space. Alastair Hook, brewmaster and founder of the South London brewery, has to pinch himself to credit the scale of the success he has achieved since he launched it in 2000.

FROM SMALL BEGINNINGS

Meantime started as a lock-up on an industrial estate opposite Charlton Athletic's ground – a handy base as Hook is a passionate supporter of the football club. The brewery soon outgrew the site and moved to a larger plant a few miles away in Greenwich, where London mayor Boris Johnson ritually pulled the first pint. Johnson was right to promote the business, for Meantime is a draw both domestically and in export markets, attracting 15,000 visitors a year who tour the site and enjoy a glass or two afterwards.

VISITOR MAGNET

The brewery has a second micro plant in Sir Christopher Wren's stupendous Old Naval College, a Unesco World Heritage Site. Here Alastair and his team produce small-run specialist beers, recreating both old and new styles. They include a porter that was brewed for sick sailors who recuperated in the hospital wing of the college in the 18th century. Other beers are aged in whisky and wine casks. The walls are decorated with an illustrated history of brewing in London while the spacious restaurant stages regular monthly beer-and-food evenings.

Back at the main brewery, Alastair Hook leads the way through halls packed with mash kettles, fermenters and conditioning tanks designed by the German manufacturer Moeschle. There are 78 vessels in total. The brewery cost £7 million, raised from a small group of investors who share Hook's passion for good beer. The brewery is growing at the remarkable rate of 60% a year and Hook, adding to Nick Miller's grey hairs, says he will run out of capacity in three years' time.

Beers at Meantime – both lagers and ales – are properly conditioned and aged to deliver powerful malt and hop flavours

Hook and Miller were shell-shocked by the success of their latest venture. They have employed a 'tank beer' system to dispense their beers which they call 'brewery fresh beer'. Unfiltered and unpasteurised, the beer is served from a horizontal tank – visible to drinkers – in pubs and other outlets. Within the tank, beer is contained in a sterile bag and compressed air in the the tank pushes the beer to the bar, enabling easy dispense without the air coming into contact with the beer itself. Hook says 'brewery fresh' was put on the bar of the National Theatre and 1,000 litres went in just 24 hours. 'Imagine,' he said, 'all those luvvies drinking my beer!'

There are 60 varieties of hops in the brewery, sourced from all parts of the world, and they are generously used in the 50 different beers that will be produced in a year

EUROPEAN INFLUENCE

Hook learned the brewing skills at Heriot-Watt University in Edinburgh – a fertile training ground for many new brewers – and the world-renowned Munich Technical University in Germany. What he doesn't know about brewing can be written on the back of a torn beer mat. His lagers are properly aged for up to 120 days while his ales are also made with due reverence: his London Pale Ale, for example, takes a month to brew and condition. He wants fresh beer so hop flavour and character can be fully expressed. There are 60 varieties of hops in the brewery, sourced from all parts of the world, and they are generously used in the 50 different beers that will be produced in a year. The regular beers, which account for 80 per cent of production, are London Lager, Pilsner, London Pale Ale and Yakima Red. Beers in the pipeline include a Jasmine IPA, a Black Russian Imperial Stout and a French-style Bière de Garde. Hook loves German wheat beers and marries the Bavarian tradition with Belgium's by producing a raspberry-flavoured version.

London Pale Ale, 4.3%

The deep bronze beer has a big citrus nose with hop resins and juicy malt, followed by a luscious palate of honeyed malt, hop resins and tart fruit, and a lingering bittersweet finish that ends dry and hoppy.

Wheat, 5%

Bavarian-style bottle-conditioned beer made with 60 per cent wheat and fermented with a Bavarian yeast culture. It has a soft, creamy, spritzy bouquet and palate of banana and bubblegum, with a light underpinning of Perle and Northern Brewer hops and a smooth, quenching finish.

Raspberry Wheat, 5%

The regular wheat beer with the addition of raspberry purée in the conditioning tank. It has a hazy red colour and a tempting aroma of tart fruit and creamy malt. Fruit dominates the palate with a background of smooth malt and gentle hops. The finish is quenching with a lingering note of fresh tangy fruit, rich malt and light hops.

With the exception of a small amount of London Pale Ale, Alastair isn't big on cask beer. His beers come under the heading of 'craft'. He doesn't have an issue with CAMRA and loves cask ale. He is full of praise for the work the Campaign has done to save real ale but he has carved out a different route to market. In spite of his training background, his lodestar is now the United States and he admires the way American brewers have taken beer forward. 'They've invested in beer and looked and learnt from the wine makers. They make brewery-conditioned beers of the highest quality,' he says.

Hook and Miller's events at the Old Brewery include beer and food matching dinners, with dishes cooked by top chefs. In order to keep up with the clamour from visitors, Meantime plans a new visitor centre that will feature a shop along with a bar offering fresh beer and tapas, with regular beer-and-food events. And a hop garden has been laid out on the banks of the Thames, the first such garden in London for a century or more. Meantime proves it has deep roots in London.

The beer range from the new and Old Brewery covers the whole spectrum: from pale to black

Established: 2011

Founder: Richard Dinwoodie and Mike Hill

Beers: Tonic Ale, East End Mild, Jim Wilson Bitter, Poplar Pale Ale, APA, Coffee in the Morning, Smokestack Porter, Tap East IPA

Website: www.tapeast.co.uk

TAP EAST

Stratford, London

Shopping until you drop might be a fun thing to do for some, but the best reason to carve your way through the teeming crowds of Westfield Stratford is to head to Tap East, a funky little brewpub that hides itself away in the 'Great Eastern Market' section of this east London retail mall. Among a bazaar of upmarket food outlets selling tapas, cured meats, coffee and artisanal breads, Tap East is a haven of beery sanity amongst the madness, as well as being a rather revolutionary idea.

Once in the compact space, where recycled wood, painted in a colour scheme reminiscent of a line up of beach huts in Southwold, forms part of the decor, take your time and choose a beer. Look

through to the right of the bar and see burnished copper vessels that look as though they were designed for exploring oceanic deeps: this is where the beer comes from.

How about a smooth, slightly toasted East End Mild, or maybe something a bit more brown? Have a glass of Jim Wilson Bitter, an easy drinking bitter, northern in its character, even old-school, with a highly bitter finish. Or for something more contemporary there's a stout with freshly ground coffee beans and – naturally – an IPA, which gets different hop combos every time it's brewed. Tap East is a serious beery place and you have to admire the foresight of Richard Dinwoodie and Mike Hill who set it up.

BREWING BEER FOR LONDON

'We had wanted for some time to have a brewery,' says Dinwoodie, who along with Hill had founded Borough Market's Utobeer in 1999 and seven years later the groundbreaking speciality beer bar the Rake. 'It just fitted the company's profile and this opportunity came our way. Also we have never been good at doing what everyone else wants so when it was a shopping centre it was different, all the better

The branding is bold and unabashed, with the pump clips giving more than a nod to the US craft beer revolution

and the potential for the area over the next few years is enormous.'

Jim Wilson Bitter is named in honour of Tap East's former brewer who left in the spring of 2014. In his two-year tenure, he is considered to have pushed the brewpub's beers to a higher level, while also organising collaborations with all manner of brewers from around the world. For instance, Smokestack Porter originally started life as a one-off collaboration with Goose Island's former brewmaster Greg Hall. According to Dinwoodie, 'it was so popular that we brewed it

> *"My inspiration for the beers comes from an interest in flavour and the diverse history surrounding brewing. Tap East brews a broad range of styles both traditional and contemporary"*

again and have just decided to make it one of our permanent range. Our thinking behind that is simple; if it's successful, keep doing it'.

Jonny Park stepped into Wilson's big shoes, his interest in brewing developing while working in London pubs. When he started working for Utobeer he managed to put this interest into practice by learning from Jim Wilson. 'My inspiration for the beers comes from an interest in flavour and the diverse history surrounding brewing,' he says. 'Tap East brews a broad range of styles both traditional and contemporary to offer customers something familiar and at times exciting.'

Tap East is not a pub or a bar in the sense of somewhere that has locals but it's still a place to visit even if shopping isn't your god. After all, if coffee and bread can have a craft presence in a place like Westfield, then why not beer?

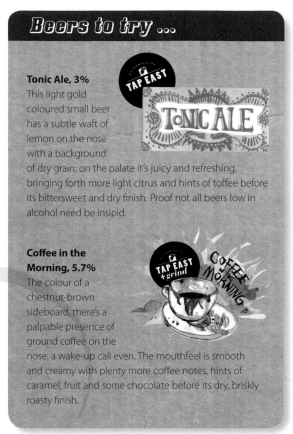

Beers to try ...

Tonic Ale, 3%
This light gold coloured small beer has a subtle waft of lemon on the nose with a background of dry grain; on the palate it's juicy and refreshing, bringing forth more light citrus and hints of toffee before its bittersweet and dry finish. Proof not all beers low in alcohol need be insipid.

Coffee in the Morning, 5.7%
The colour of a chestnut-brown sideboard, there's a palpable presence of ground coffee on the nose, a wake-up call even. The mouthfeel is smooth and creamy with plenty more coffee notes, hints of caramel, fruit and some chocolate before its dry, briskly roasty finish.

Tap East's burnished copper vessels are clearly visible from the bar – a unique sight for a shopping centre

Established: 2013

Founder: James Morgan and Michael-George Hemus

Beers: Swift, Runner, Lazarus, Bold as Brass, Attaboy, Tom Ditto, London Keeper

Website: www.trumansbeer.co.uk

TRUMAN'S

Hackney Wick, London

Truman's has risen from the grave. The brewery founded in 1666 in Whitechapel that grew to become the second-biggest ale maker in Britain after Bass, closed in 1989. It was the victim of a whirlwind takeover that sucked such famous London brewers as Manns, Truman's and Watney's into the leisure group Grand Metropolitan, which was interested solely in the value of their pub estates. East London Cockneys loved the Truman beers, ranging from mild to bitter and stout and promoted with the famous slogan 'There are more hops in Ben Truman', until they were cruelly snatched away from them.

RESURRECTING A LEGEND

The beers were not forgotten: the name and the eagle symbol remain carved into many pubs in the East End and beyond. In 2010 two young entrepreneurs, James Morgan and Michael-George Hemus, planned to restore Truman's beers to the capital and were overwhelmed by the number of East Enders eager to invest money in the scheme. £1 million was raised. Then James and Michael-

George had to find a way through the minefield of who owned the rights to the Truman name, brands and logos. They discovered a trail of destruction that spoke volumes for the cynical way in which once great names in brewing were passed from pillar to post. When GrandMet closed its breweries, the brands passed to Courage, another famous name in London brewing. Courage merged with Scottish & Newcastle, which in turn was taken over by Heineken. Fortunately for Morgan and Hemus, the British arm of the Dutch brewing giant was happy to divest itself of the Truman heritage.

Working with experienced brewer Benedikt Ott, Morgan and Hemus built a brand-new, state-of-the-art brewery in Hackney Wick, just a discus-throw from the Olympic Stadium on the other side of the Hackney Cut canal. Ben Ott was keen to recreate beers with the authentic Truman's character, which meant obtaining the original yeast cultures. Further investigation revealed they were stored at the National Collection of Yeast Cultures in Norwich, a bank that's a vital lifeline for all British breweries: in the event of a catastrophe that destroys the yeast being used, a fresh sample can be obtained from the NCYC, where cultures are stored under liquid nitrogen at minus 196 degrees Celsius.

The owners had a brewery and a yeast culture and were ready to roll. The first beer unveiled was called Runner, a deep copper-coloured beer that took its name from the 'running beers' developed by brewers at the turn of the 20th century. They replaced the porters, stouts and IPAs that were aged for long periods and were the forerunners of today's cask-conditioned beers that need just a few days to settle and 'drop bright' in the pub cellar.

GROWING WINGS

The success of Runner prompted the launch of two more regular and paler beers, Swift and Eyrie: the second took its name from the new brewery and an eagle's place of rest. To celebrate the opening and quick success of the venture, the brewery team added a bottle-conditioned stout called London Keeper with a whopping 8% alcohol. Ott discovered the recipe in old Truman's logs from the 1880s and found it was a double export stout that was kept or aged for months before bottling.

London Keeper is a faithful recreation of a 19th-century stout and it will age in the bottle for 10 years

After just a year in operation, the brewery is growing apace and now has its own tap, the Cygnet, in a former warehouse on the canal. And one of its range of seasonal beers is called Lazarus in honour of the Biblical figure that rose from the grave.

Swift, 3.9%
Brewed with Maris Otter pale malt and a light dash of Munich malt, with Cascade and Saaz hops. It has a juicy malt nose with citrus fruit and grassy hops, a bittersweet palate with honey malt, tart fruit and hop resins, and a quenching finish with juicy malt, citrus fruit and floral hop notes.

Runner, 4%
For a mid-range beer it has a big vinous bouquet and palate with strong hints of chocolate, coffee, caramel and peppery hops. The finish is bittersweet to start but ends dry, hoppy, malty and bitter.

London Keeper, 8%
This bottle-conditioned beer will improve in bottle for 10 years or more. The beer has a big hit of treacle, molasses, bitter coffee and roasted grain on the nose, with bitterness in the mouth coming from both grain and hops, with big hints of chocolate, coffee and liquorice. The finish is long and complex, with burnt fruits, liquorice, espresso coffee, roasted grain and spicy hops.

BEER DESTINATIONS

LONDON

Highgate

Westbourne Park

Clerkenwell
Blackfriars   Bermondsey
Borough

DEAN SWIFT
Bermondsey, London
thedeanswift.com

There's a gorgeous irony about this single-bar, street corner pub: it's a few minutes stroll from the Thames-side site of the onetime brewing giant Barclay Perkins, which is remembered by posters for its London Lager on the wall. Now, the Dean Swift is a modern craft beer and good food place, light and airy with a variety of beer paraphernalia dotted around. Cask beer comes from the likes of Redemption, Tiny Rebel, Ilkley and Moor, while Bristol Beer Factory and Kernel pop up on keg, alongside bottled beers from across the globe.

BLACK FRIAR
Blackfriars, London
www.nicholsonspubs.co.uk

This tall and narrow triangular shaped pub juts out into the joining of two busy city roads with the pugnacious air of a boxer about to start a bout. A pot-bellied friar stands over the entrance as if entreating incomers to join him in his merriment. Inside, it's all art nouveau, marble and mirrors, which makes the Black Friar one of London's most distinctive pubs – when it comes to beer though, it's very much up to date with the likes of Truman's, Adnams and Harbour often propping up the bar.

ROYAL OAK
Borough, London
020 7357 7173

If you stand for a moment outside the Royal Oak and peer through its engraved windows you will see a row of handpumps at the bar standing as straight-backed as Guardsmen. This is one of two London pubs owned by Harveys brewery, and it's a chatty, roomy collection of two bars where the exemplary beers of the Lewes' brewing institution can be studied to your heart's content. You can drink the muscular and bittersweet Sussex Best Bitter, but come winter it's the incredibly complex Porter that demands attention.

RAKE
Borough Market, London
www.utobeer.co.uk/the-rake

What was once a greasy spoon kind of caff, and then became London's first craft beer bar remains a thriving, jiving kind of place to drink great beer. A constantly rotating list of cask and craft keg beers stand proud at the bar top, featuring such magi of the mash tun as Magic Rock, Burning Sky, Beavertown and Oakham, while the glass cabinets behind contain enough bottles of world beer to sustain a gap year's drinking. There's a wall signed by visiting brewers from around the world. The Rake may be Lilliputian in size but it's big in heart and ambition.

CRAFT BEER CO
Clerkenwell, London
thecraftbeerco.com/pubs/clerkenwell

Old school boozer that received a modern craft makeover when it reopened in 2012: the big open bar is light and luminous, with almost the glittery air you would find in an art gallery. Look upwards and you'll see a mirrored ceiling with ornate woodcarvings. However, it's the beer we're here for, with up to 16 handpumps dispensing beers from the likes of Thornbridge, Dark Star and Marble, next to a line of wasp-waisted steel fonts representing rare draft beers from around the world. Beer nirvana indeed.

BULL
Highgate, London
thebullhighgate.co.uk

Historic pub, turned into a restaurant that failed, and rescued by Dan Fox, formerly of the acclaimed White Horse, Parsons Green. Fox has installed a microbrewery with brewer Tom Unwin and their London Brewing Co produces Beer Street pale ale and a changing range of beers that are served both in the bar and in the restaurant. The pub hosts regular talks on beer, and beer-and-food matching.

UNION TAVERN
Westbourne Park, London
union-tavern.co.uk

This was formerly an unremarkable Fuller's pub called the Grand Union until it was redesigned and reopened in 2012 with the brewery's cask beers being served alongside those from other London breweries such as Brew by Numbers, Partizan and, from just beyond the M25, Windsor & Eton. International keg beers are available and Meet the Brewer events are held on the last Tuesday of the month.

The Royal Oak is one of two London pubs belonging to East Sussex-based Harveys brewery, and serves a range of their exemplary beers

Bath Ales: Warmley, Somerset

Bristol Beer Factory: Bristol

Moor: Bristol

Bristol • Bath

Harbour: Bodmin, Cornwall

Dulverton

Exeter • Honiton

Bodmin

St Austell

Otter: Honiton, Somerset

St Austell: St Austell, Cornwall

SOUTH WEST ENGLAND

CORNWALL, DEVON, DORSET, GLOUCESTERSHIRE, SOMERSET, WILTSHIRE

The Southwest may have a reputation for cider, but this is now firmly beer country: a region whose beating heart pulsates to a steady rhythm of vibrant, vivacious beers emerging from all manner of breweries. There are small breweries; medium-sized breweries; family breweries; farm breweries; microbreweries; craft breweries and even the odd cuckoo brewery. From the brooding moors to lively beaches with the crash of the surf, from the tranquil green spaces where sheep do graze to noisy, bustling cities, the Southwest's beer culture thrives.

ALES OF THE CITY

Let's look at Bristol, once more a major beer city with Bristol Beer Factory leading the way and making friends with their judicious use of hops, a lilting lubricious milk stout and various experiments with aging beer in a variety of wooden barrels. This sense of adventure has certainly paid off: in 2011 their 12 Stouts of Christmas won them the best drinks producer category in the BBC's prestigious Food & Farming Awards.

On the other side of the city, Arbor approach brewing in a light, playful manner, producing US-influenced IPAs and deep booming stouts alongside an eclectic range of beers that go under the Freestyle Friday name (India Pale Bock anyone?). Fellow Bristolians Wiper and True are one of the newest on

BEER DESTINATIONS
> go to page 106

Top: The Blue Anchor has been brewing beers on site since the 15th century. **Bottom:** Wadworth still delivers beer by dray horse

the block and don't even have a brewery, relying on renting out space from other concerns. This peripatetic approach to making beer doesn't seem to have harmed them, if their Simcoe-hopped Pale Ale is anything to go by. It's a beautifully balanced beer brimming with fresh citrus and pine notes. And of course there is Bath Ales who, despite their name, brew within the environs of Bristol, while Graze, their onsite restaurant/bar/brewery in Bath, veers towards the wilder shores of craft.

WESTWARD HO!

Further west the sours, saisons and many other intriguing beers of east Somerset experimentalists Wild Beer bowl over beer-drinkers in their droves. Their former neighbour Moor Beer Company (now in Bristol), is headed by American expat Justin Hawke, a devotee of well-hopped beers and a cheerleader for the unfined beer movement.

In Devon and Cornwall breweries such as Sharp's (whose Doom Bar is the best selling cask beer in the UK), Otter, Harbour, Skinner's and Driftwood Spars are also winning awards, making friends and satisfying thirsts. There's even a small brewery on the Scilly Isles, Ales of Scilly, a beery full stop to the region.

BUILDING ON TRADITION

All this beer activity has a precedent: the Southwest has a long and historic tradition of brewing. Porter was made and sent abroad from Bristol at the end of the 18th century; both Exeter and Plymouth were home to thriving regional concerns whose pubs dotted the surrounding countryside. Meanwhile the citizens of smaller towns in the region such as Weymouth, Devizes, Wiveliscombe, Bridgwater and Tiverton were all proud of the breweries in their midst, long gone but still recalled. Then there was barley: that grown in the Vale of Porlock on the northern side of Exmoor was seen as some of the best in the region.

All this ale-accented activity has a precedent: the Southwest has a long and historic tradition of brewing

As well as the youngsters there are plenty of breweries in the Southwest who have survived and thrived: anyone drinking Tribute and Proper Job can give thanks to St Austell, whose grey austere brew house towers over the former clay-mining town of the same name. The centre of the Wiltshire town of Devizes remains home to Wadworth brewery, where the 6X delivery horses still clip-clop by. On the south coast in Dorset the Palmer family remain in charge of making beer as they have done since the 1700s. And let us not forget the venerable Blue Anchor in Helston, a brewpub with its roots in the Middle Ages, and still a lodestone for lovers of their homemade Spingo Ales.

The region had its own specialities in the past: Taunton Ale, Dorchester Ale and the White Ales of Devon, the latter being renowned in the 19th century and made mainly in the South Hams, though some pubs in Plymouth also produced their own versions. Opinions were mixed on this beer that apparently had eggs in the mix, though some whispered that pigeon droppings also made their presence felt: back in the 16th century, the physician and traveller Andrew Boorde tried the Cornish version of White Ale and thought it 'lokinge whyte and thycke, as pygges had wrasteled in it'. It died out during the latter years of Victoria's rule, but more recently Cornish brewery Penpont tried their hand at producing one. It didn't go out into the trade but the very fact that Penpont were interested and intrigued enough by this ancient style to have a go demonstrates the strength of the beer revolution in the Southwest. If by some miracle he came back from the dead, Andrew Boorde would be very happy to drink the beers of the region now.

Insider's view...

Jessica Boak
boakandbailey.com

The West Country is short on really top notch breweries compared to, say, Yorkshire; however, there are some fantastically characterful pubs, particularly in small towns and villages. The Blue Anchor at Helston is one of a handful of surviving traditional pub breweries in the UK and its rich, rather sweet 'Spingo Ales' are truly distinctive.

Cornwall has two other excellent pub breweries, the Star Inn at Crowlas and the Driftwood Spars near St Agnes, both regular haunts of ours. Further afield, in Bristol, there are more and more places to drink every year; however we always make a point of visiting the Grain Barge, a boat overlooking the *SS Great Britain*, which serves Bristol Beer Factory beers in perfect condition.

The Wild Beer Company from Somerset are doing some really interesting things with exotic yeasts, and their champagne-like Ninkasi (made with local apple juice) is a classic in the making, appealing to more than just beer geeks.

Jessica Boak lives in Cornwall and is one half of beer blogging duo Boak and Bailey

Established: 1995

Founder: Roger Jones

Beers: Special Pale Ale, Forest Hare, Summer's Hare, Dark Side, Gem, Golden Hare, Barnsey, Festivity, Rare Hare, Platform 3

Website: www.bathales.com

BATH ALES

Warmley, Somerset

Bath Ales have a comfortable reputation: their pubs have style, a clean, sharp design, a compromise between old school comfort and modernist minimalism. The beers are balanced and drinkable as well, a counterpoint between the sweet, heady bready aromas of malt and the bitter, fruity character of the hop. Gem is the signature beer, 4.1%, the colour of an old sideboard that has been polished slavishly by the family down through the years, yet it still retains a gleam. It looks good in the glass and drinks well: dry, crisp, grainy, with a lasting bitter encore. Boring brown bitter some might say, although this is a robust and roistering best bitter that is always a joy to drink. So that's Bath Ales deciphered, or is it?

If you think you know Bath Ales then you might be surprised by another one of their beers, the 2013 Imperial Stout, 11%, aged in an Islay whisky cask and branded under the Sulis name. This is a big beer that booms away on the palate with the conviction of a foghorn blaring away on a misty night. There's a massive and fantastic counterplay between a high-pitched Islay-style assertiveness and dark chocolate/ coffee sweetness. There have been several different barrelled expressions of this style, as well as a barley wine, which was rich, bittersweet, fruity and smooth.

DUAL FOCUS

The beer is brewed at Graze in Bath, an ambitious restaurant/brewpub that Bath Ales opened next to the railway station in 2012; the brewery is actually called Beerd (Bath Ales also has a bar in Bristol of the same name). Shane O'Beirne is the brewer in charge here.

'To make the Sulis range we sourced a number of whisky barrels from Scotland,' he says. 'These barrels came from a number of the whisky regions, Highland, Speyside and Islay, as we wanted to see the effect that different barrels had on the beer. The stout was made from a blend of pale, brown, crystal and chocolate malt as well as roast barley. After fermentation the beer was racked into the barrels, where it was kept until we were happy with the flavours. We decanted the casks into tanks before bottling. I felt it was important to bottle condition

Top: Gerry Condell, Bath Ales head brewer is an advocate of balanced beers. **Left:** Best bitter Gem is Bath Ales signature beer. **Right:** Darren James, part of Bath Ales' brewery team

this beer so that they could mature and the flavours develop in the bottle over time.'

That's the great joy about British brewing at the moment. We all think we know a brewery, know what direction it's travelling in and then it chooses to go in another way, confounding matters. That's Bath Ales for you.

'Without question this is a great time to be a brewery,' says the brewery's managing director, Robin Couling. 'The marketplace is awash with new brewers and that this brings with it its own commercial challenges and pressures. That said, it is generating a tremendous amount of interest in brewing and beer amongst a new generation of drinkers and this must be applauded, for every challenge there is a new opportunity. It is also a fantastic time to be a beer drinker with myriad choices available from an increasing number of outlets. The modern drinker is perhaps more fickle, aware and agile than ever before, it is therefore critical that we stay relevant with ideas such as our

Beerd craft brewery whilst continuing to appeal to our established Bath Ales audience.'

Gerry Condell has been Bath Ales' head brewer since 2004 and he's an advocate of balanced beers – of which Gem is perhaps one of the best examples. 'It's our flagship beer,' he says. 'It's a wonderfully balanced beer with a bittersweet taste. In my opinion it's one of the finest examples of a best bitter in the country. Balance is very important in a beer. I try to make beers that are well balanced – consistency and quality are also vital.'

He is also enthusiastic about what is happening at Beerd. 'We are very fortunate to have a second brewery under our umbrella called Beerd brewery,' he says. 'This is a five-barrel brewery where Shane is continuously producing new beers in a variety of styles from IPAs to Dunkels and Hefeweizens to Saisons. He uses a variety of different yeast strains depending on the beer being produced and what is most suitable for the particular style. We have recently produced a few whiskey barrel-aged beers

Left: Shane O'Beirne, Bath Ales' experimental brewer. **Right:** The Beerd brewery at Graze in Bath is generating interest with its experimental range of craft-brewed beers

"It is also a fantastic time to be a beer drinker with myriad choices available from an increasing number of outlets. The modern drinker is perhaps more fickle, aware and agile than ever before"

(the Sulis range) and are looking to expand our barrel program this year with additional rum and wine barrels. Beerd brewery allows us to experiment more as brewers and make smaller one-off batches of beer for the UK and abroad.'

Couling is equally excited about the venture. 'When the opportunity came up to secure a premises in central Bath that was large enough to accommodate a small brewery we were delighted. It has added a great point of difference to what is already a pretty dramatic bar and restaurant space. It is wonderful to be able to brew a beer that is unique to the site, and indeed for Bath Ales to be able to now brew beer in the heart of its namesake city. Customers seem to relish the chance to try the house brew and it is particularly popular with our many tourist customers. In time we plan to develop a guest experience centred around the brewing process to further add to the theatre.'

It just goes to show, you should never dismiss a brewery as set in its ways – they might surprise you.

Beers to try ...

Dark Side, 4%
Think roast coffee beans with hints of chocolate on the nose, while the creamy palate also has a bittersweet character edging towards mocha and chocolate.

Barnsey, 4.5%
A stocky, copper-coloured best bitter that is pumped up with chocolate and toffee notes and a dry, roasty character in the background.

Festivity, 5%
Dark chestnut porter that comes out every winter; the nose is a soothing aromatic complex of coffee, vanilla and a hint of rum. On the palate, more of the same along with a subtle wash of liquorice and blackcurrant; the finish is bittersweet.

Bristol Beer Factory operates out of the Tobacco Factory in Bristol – a multi-media centre that also houses a theatre, bar and artisinal bakery

Established: 2004

Founder: Simon Bartlett and George Ferguson

Beers: Nova, Seven, Bristletoe, Sunrise, Bitter Californian, Milk Stout, Independence, Hefe, Bitter Kiwi, Exhibition, West Coast Red, Southern Conspriracy, Saison, Southville Hop, Vintage, Ultimate Stout

Website: www.bristolbeerfactory.co.uk

BRISTOL BEER FACTORY

Bristol

The word factory in the context of beer and brewing usually conjures up a soulless space where machines clank and workers become alienated (Charlie Chaplin in *Modern Times* perhaps); meanwhile the beer that is produced is an equally soulless commodity. So you might be suprised to discover that the beers that Bristol Beer Factory launches into the world can be bright and colourful or brooding and moody according whatever style is in the glass at the time. If you've drunk Independence or the mighty Southville Hop (Southville being the name of the Bristol district the brewery is situated in) then you will know that hops are certainly important but they're not the only piece of ammunition in the brewery's locker as Simon Bartlett, the brewery's co-founder and managing director, explains.

NEW AND WONDERFUL THINGS

'The flavours and aromas that you can get from the American and New Zealand hops are fantastically bold and relatively new so it's great to experiment with these but there are many other flavours that can be obtained from the many varieties of yeast and malts. It's something I am always reminding our brewers.

'All the ideas come from the brewers. They are the ones who are looking at what is new and what is good from beers all over the world. I actively encourage that and get them to experiment on a pilot kit we have. They are the ones with the energy to create new and wonderful things. I do think that the American beer scene massively inspires us but recently we have been looking at Belgium (but not the fruit beers!).'

"All the ideas come from the brewers. They are the ones who are looking at what is new and what is good from beers all over the world"

The result of opening this window onto the world of Belgian beer was seen in the summer of 2014 with the launch of the Unlimited/Limited Edition Range, a result of what Bartlett calls the 'creative brains' of the brewery (brewers, marketing and graphic designers) sitting down with the aim of designing six unique beers that would be produced throughout the following year. The first beer was a scorcher of a double IPA, which was then followed by Belgian Rye. Here the Saaz, Centennial, Amarillo and Cascade hops worked in tandem with speciality and pale rye grain while Belgian Trappist yeast

> *"I want us to be thought of as a brewery that spreads the word of great tasting beer... I want to awaken all of our customers to these wonderful flavours: not just existing beer geeks who buy online but the rest of the community in the pubs"*

added its own fermentation magic. The result was an amber-coloured beer with a warm aroma of a freshly baked rye loaf working alongside hints of grilled banana; on the palate there were subtleties of banana and allspice, alongside the lift of alcohol and a biting bittersweet, rye spice finish.

Other beers in the range included a barrel-aged wheat wine and a 'double' version of the Soriachi Ace-hopped session beer Acer.

REINVIGORATING BRISTOL

The brewery is part of the Tobacco Factory, once home to Wills Tobacco and now a venue hosting a theatre and space for other arts-like things as well as an artisanal bakery. Local architect George Ferguson opened it in 2000 as part of his project to reinvigorate south Bristol. He then wanted beer for the Factory's bar and thought a brewery would fit in well: next on his shopping list was buying what was left of the old Ashton Gate brewery (the fermenting block), which had been swallowed up by Georges in the 1930s (Georges in turn were devoured by Courage). The proposed new brewery was at the

Bristol Beer Factory have added a range of experimental beers to their standard range: producing unique beers with exciting hop and grain combinations

back of the Tobacco Factory and in 2004 Bristol Beer Factory was born. For local man Bartlett, then working for brewery engineers Briggs in Burton, this represented an ideal opportunity. 'I was looking for a way back to Bristol,' he recalls, 'I was already thinking of setting up my own brewery, so this was an ideal excuse to become involved.'

The brewery's modus operandi was initially cautious, with its beer portfolio consisting of best bitter, golden ale and premium bitter, the kind of beers that were consistent and drinkable but hardly likely to set the beer world alight. Things became more interesting with the emergence of the luscious and creamy Milk Stout, which was then followed by the cheese-friendly Bristol Hefe and an earthy Saison. Then there was the 12 Stouts of Christmas, a dozen dark beers that included the aforementioned Milk Stout, Raspberry Stout and a powerful Imperial Stout that was aged in a Glenlivet cask. This range of beers was part of the reason Bristol Beer Factory was awarded Best Drinks Producer in the BBC *Food Programme's* Food & Farming Awards for 2011.

Whether it's a hefty dose of hop character, a groovy riff on Belgian beer or a boisterous bitter this is a brewery that has an ability to appeal right across the drinking board.

'I want us to be thought of as a brewery that spreads the word of great tasting beer of all styles,' says Bartlett. 'I want to awaken all of our customers to these wonderful flavours: not just existing beer geeks who buy online but the rest of the community in the pubs. Even though we produce new beers and ones that may push the boundaries I also want to produce high quality best bitters and traditional English ales.'

This is most definitely a brewery as far away from a factory as can be.

Beers to try ...

Nova, 3.8%
Sunny session beer with bright tangerine notes on the nose and a sherbet-like sweetness; take a swig and enjoy the gentle daub of citrus before the bracing bitter finish.

Milk Stout, 4.5%
From the waft of chocolate buttons on the nose, to the creamy, mocha-like character on the palate to its dry toasty finish, this is a retro-gem

Southville Hop, 6.5%
Ripe peach skin and grapefruit pith dominate the nose, while the palate is a big blast of tropical fruit and citrus followed by a lingering bitter finish.

Established: 2012

Founder: Eddie Lofthouse and Rhys Powell

Beers: Light Ale, Amber, Porter, Pale Ale, India Pale Ale, Pilsner

Website: www.harbourbrewing.com

HARBOUR

Bodmin, Cornwall

The name Harbour, when applied to a brewery, sounds nice and safe, traditional even, evoking a brewery tempted to make beer within its own cloistered perimeters. Base it in Cornwall and you've got the added attraction of cream teas and big beaches. But safe, traditional and twee isn't Harbour's style. Instead if you order a beer brewed by this relatively young set-up you're likely to face American-style pale ale or an IPA bursting with citrus brightness. But then for the co-founders of Harbour it is their mission to produce beers both invigorating and inclusive.

'We strive to strike a balance between bold flavours and drinkability,' says Eddie Lofthouse, who decided to found the brewery with old surfing pal Rhys Powell after the two of them had met in a Padstow pub. 'Beer is at the end of the day something to drink and enjoy, not everything needs to be overly challenging or contemplative.'

INTERNATIONAL APPROACH

There are four main beers, Light Ale, Amber, India Pale Ale and Pale Ale, all of which to one extent or the other seem to be influenced by the American can-do approach to brewing, though as Lofthouse points out, it would be more correct to declare that the whole international beer scene is an influence: a Pilsner is another regular while a saison has been attempted.

'Head brewer Rhys' inspiration for beers basically draws on the vast gamut of styles and techniques used globally,' says Lofthouse, 'and then trying get to grips with a few of them, hopefully producing some good examples, one step at a time. We approach all our beer design with a basic interpretation of a style and tradition. Then we use this as a foundation to build on, but that doesn't always mean straying too far from the original. It's more evolution than revolution. We have a humble approach to what we know, as the more we seem to learn, the more it becomes apparent how little we really know.'

So far there have been imperial stouts made with chocolate and vanilla or aged in bourbon barrels; chillies, mango and lemon peel have found their way into the IPA (not at the same time); and

Spent mash is dug out of the mash tun by hand, filling the brewery with malty aromas and steam

"We strive to strike a balance between bold flavours and drinkability"

different yeasts have been employed, which is the thinking behind the Farmhouse IPA. There have also been several versions of their Double IPA, using different hop varieties, and in one case it has been wood aged. The philosophy behind Harbour's creative restlessness feels as if Lofthouse and Powell (the latter part of the brewing team at Sharp's prior to Harbour) are intrigued and interested to see how certain beer flavours can develop. Maybe that's one of the main aspects of Britain's brewing revolution: brewers approaching their craft with an open mind; everything is possible.

Then there's Cornwall: big skies, the surrounding seas, the slower lifestyle, but definitely no cream teas.

'Cornwall per se isn't really particularly important to our brewing ethos,' says Lofthouse, 'but the lifestyle it offers us as people influences our personalities and therefore our beers. There is a slower more relaxed way of life here where the beautiful rugged coast has in impact on every aspect of your day. There is a honesty to life down here, it's less pretentious and I think that comes through in our beers.'

Beers to try ...

Pale Ale (No 5), 6%
Amber-gold brew with plenty of deep booming orange and ethereal grass notes on the nose, while it's a juicy combination of grapefruit, orange and a grainy caramel malt balance in the mouth. The finish is chewy, dry and bittersweet.

Porter (No 6), 6.8%
The colour of a moonless night in the glass; rich strokes of chocolate and mocha coffee creaminess blended in with the background of roastiness on the nose; smooth mouthfeel, more chocolate and coffee, slightly creamy, berry fruitiness and dry, bitter finish.

Established: 1996

Founder: Arthur Frampton

Beers: Revival, Nor'Hop, So'Hop, Raw, Amoor, Dark Alliance, Illusion, Confidence, Ported Amoor, Radiance, Smokey Horyzon, Hoppiness, Old Freddy Walker, Fusion, Sloe Walker, JJJ IPA

Website: moorbeer.co.uk

MOOR BEER

Bristol

Brewing intensely flavoured beers is the goal of Moor Beer's Justin Hawke, a Californian expat who has made this Bristol brewery one of the craft beer names to drop. There's a ferocity in his devotion to flavour, an evangelical approach even; beers such as the glittering golden ale Nor'Hop – so-called because of its use of Northern Hemisphere US hops (there's also a So'Hop that turns to other side of the world) and the luscious pale ale/barley wine hybrid Hoppiness burst with fresh zingy aromas and flavours.

'Nor'Hop is our best seller and tends to combine a lot of what we're about,' he says. 'It's session strength, intensely flavoured and has a great appearance. I've watched a lot of people try it and stay on it all night. However, if I think of my favourite of our beers it'll probably be Hoppiness. It's not a one-dimensional hop bomb like a lot of them. It's got malt depth to it, enough to have an impact but let the hops out compete it.'

Until the summer of 2014 Moor was located in the middle of the Somerset countryside, not far from Glastonbury, but its relentless growth has meant a move to Bristol. For Hawke the rural location was originally a fine place to hone his brewing technique and develop beers, but this isolation eventually became a barrier to expansion.

'We relocated to the city where we have access to a much broader spectrum of people,' he says, 'and equally important they have access to us. We want to have a direct relationship with our passionate drinkers, which was impossible being where we were. We also wanted a closer camaderie with other like-minded breweries and pub managers.'

CUTTING-EDGE BEERS

Moor Beer began on a farm close to Glastonbury in 1996 but it was bought, moved and revived by Hawke in 2007; there was also a gradual change in the character of the beers being brewed. One of the old brewery's favourites (and award-winners) Old Freddy Walker has managed to survive but Hawke got the brewery to march to a difficult tune.

'We've been at the cutting edge in a lot of areas since 2007,' he says. 'We were barrel ageing years ago, but with a purpose, not just throwing any beer into any barrel just because it will sell to a ticker. We've been at the forefront of hop development, helping launch new hop varieties and getting the public interested in hop forward beers. We've done strong beers and session beers. We've championed new packaging and dispense techniques. And of course we kicked off the unfined beer movement. That's a lot to achieve in seven years.'

Hawke has been single-minded in the way he has championed unfined beer, which was influenced by the naturally hazy *naturtrüb* beers of Germany, which he drank during his time stationed there with the army. All of Moor's beers are now naturally hazy, a move that took great business courage to do given the British drinker's penchant for crystal clear beer, but his persistence has paid off and there's a growing amount of brewers producing unfined hazy beer (though it's not without its detractors).

'After returning from Germany I lived in San Francisco during the craft brewing explosion, which is where I got my love for hops and learned how to brew,' he says. 'But I could never get British pubs and cask beer out of my head so we moved to England with the intention of opening up a brewery here combining flavour forward (usually hoppy) beers with secondary conditioning and a natural haze – a truly global amalgamation that really works.'

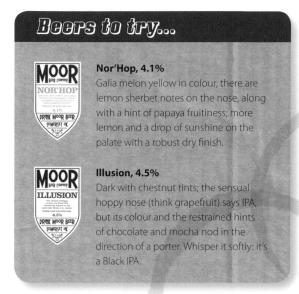

Beers to try...

Nor'Hop, 4.1%
Galia melon yellow in colour, there are lemon sherbet notes on the nose, along with a hint of papaya fruitiness; more lemon and a drop of sunshine on the palate with a robust dry finish.

Illusion, 4.5%
Dark with chestnut tints; the sensual hoppy nose (think grapefruit) says IPA, but its colour and the restrained hints of chocolate and mocha nod in the direction of a porter. Whisper it softly: it's a Black IPA.

Justin Hawke (back) has made collaborative brews with a number of other brewers, including Rypa, a rye pale ale brewed with Beavertown's Logan Plant (centre)

David and Mary Ann McCaig set up Otter brewery on an old farm north of the small market town of Honiton, by the headspring of the river Otter

Established: 1990

Founder: Mary Ann and David McCaig

Beers: Bitter, Amber, Bright, Ale, Witch Otter/Claus/MacOtter/Cupids Otter, Head

Website: www.otterbrewery.com

OTTER

Honiton, Devon

High up in the hills above the small Devon town of Honiton, Otter is at work. They brew exemplary beers – beers that aren't revolutionary in the sense that they use *Brettanomyces* yeast or the latest (probably unnamed or given a code number) American hop – but drinkable and destined to tingle the palates of those in the West Country and far beyond; the brewery is revolutionary however in the way it has embraced the environment.

In a pub somewhere in the area, you might find someone ordering a pint of Otter Bitter, an amber-copper session beer with its earthy nose, robust (especially as it's only 3.6%) mouthfeel and palate and grainy, bitter, dry finish. Further up country, perhaps in the Midlands or on the Welsh borders, it might be Otter Ale with its scales-of-justice balance between biscuit, toffee and pear drop fruity notes; or we could be talking the mighty Otter Head, 5.8%, dark chestnut in colour, with a voluptuous and vinous mouthfeel and big bold dry and bitter finish.

DRINKER APPEAL

'I would describe Otter's beers as well-balanced, never heavy, with loads of drinker appeal and classically English hopped,' says Patrick McCaig, the brewery's sales director, 'and I would say that Otter Bitter is a great representative of what we aim to do and it's our most popular beer because of its full flavour and great condition in what is a comparatively low strength.'

Otter can brew 100 barrels at a time and its brewing kit is a sleek vision of stainless steel, while the fermenting rooms have the sweet hum of light banana and papaya estery notes in the air. This is a traditional brewery. In charge of brewing is Keith Bennett, who was formerly at Hall & Woodhouse; he's also a home brewer. Brewing is in his blood.

BEER IN THE BLOOD

Beer is also in the blood at Otter. The ancestors of Mary Ann McCaig, who founded the brewery with husband David in 1990, once ran the Oak brewery in the Wiltshire town of Westbury, where brewing came to a halt in the 1930s (sadly there's a familiar story in that the building and associated pub were demolished in 2012 to make way for

Otter's new cask-racking shed has a living roof planted with sedum, which insulates the building as well as helping to capture rainwater

There are willow beds, ponds and lagoons at the bottom of the valley, where water is recycled, returning to the ground, clear and clean... the roof is a living sedum roof: this helps to add insulation to the cellar

a supermarket). Husband David learnt his trade at Whitbread back in the 1980s, when he was based at their Liverpool plant. As was the case quite frequently in those days, a closure was on the cards and McCaig was offered a job brewing in Malawi. The alternative was retirement, so he took the latter option and came to Devon and started making furniture. However, his career path diverted from a world of making sideboards and armchairs when he set up Otter on an old farm north of Honiton. As the headspring of the river Otter was very close there really could be only one name for the enterprise. The otter – the animal that is – has become integral to the brewery's branding, though one look at a bottle or beer mat shows that the logo's stylised lines owes more to Picasso

than the classic Henry Williamson novel *Tarka the Otter*. There's an extra dimension to Otter's animal branding: go to most home games of Premiership rugby side Exeter Chiefs and you'll see Derek the Otter on at half-time, offering prizes for the best rugby kicks to selected spectators. The brewery is one of the club's sponsors.

ECO FOCUS

Yet there's a lot more to this well-integrated family brewery than history and snappy graphics. If you take a trip to its bucolic rural location, you will notice how well connected the brewery is with its environment. There are willow beds, ponds and lagoons at the bottom of the valley, where water is recycled, returning to the ground, clear and clean.

Amber, 4%
This bright and cheerful amber-coloured beer has tropical fruit notes on the nose, while the palate is an accomplished balance of more tropical fruit, bitterness and a dry finish.

Bright, 4.5%
Gold-coloured and sparkling in the glass with ripe apricot skin on the nose; on the palate it's softly fruity and refreshing, while the finish has more fruit and a lingering bitterness.

Head, 5.8%
A big and bold strong bitter with toffee, rich malt and resiny hop aromas, while rich malt, citrus fruit, nuttiness and a vinous hint on the palate are balanced by a resiny hoppy finish.

In the cask-racking shed, which was built in 2009, the roof is a living sedum roof: this helps to add insulation to the cellar, and also helps to capture rainwater for barrel and vehicle washing; the walls are clay honeycomb block, have a low carbon rating as well as good insulation properties; finally, over half of the ground floor was built underground helping to keep the cellar cooler and thus doing away with the need for electric chilling systems.

"The building of this was a commitment to the future"

'The building of this was a commitment to the future,' says Patrick McCaig, who also goes on to list the continuing eco-friendliness of the brewery, 'Earlier in 2014 we invested in kit that continues to let us return all our waste water back to its source. This big tank breeds special bugs to feed on the nasties in the waste water, clean it and belch it back out into the willow beds for the final polishing.' Back to the beer. Another recent development at the brewery has been the inclusion of a small pilot brewery that has been used to test the consistency

of regular brews and develop new ones. This has seen the beginning of a seasonal range of beers, which according to McCaig, 'gives head brewer Keith the opportunity to flex his brewing muscles – all the beers are traditionally brewed, using hops and malt to drive flavour and nose and there are plans for a single hop range. Keith has this ability to keep to our character yet explore depths of flavour – for instance the single hopped Admiral Otter.'

Beer and brewing runs through the veins of Otter brewery, like its namesake river on its journey to the sea.

Top: Roger Ryman and his brewing team.
Bottom: St Austell's award-winning beers are produced on a modern brew kit housed in their Victorian brewery

Established: 1851

Founder: Walter Hicks

Beers: Dartmoor Best Bitter, Trelawny, Black Prince, Tribute, Proper Job, Clouded Yellow, Admiral's Ale, HSD, 1913 Cornish Stout, Smugglers Ale, Big Job

Website: www.staustellbrewery.co.uk

ST AUSTELL

St Austell, Cornwall

Prepare to be swept under by a double IPA: bruised gold in the glass, sharp and zestful on the nose, with a blast of tropical fruit and ripe peach. Take a sip from the glass and you'll get a further run of tropical fruit on the tongue, a big boost of bitterness with a juicy malt sweetness holding it together, while its long tail-end finish of bitterness seemingly goes on forever and ever. This is a beast of a beer, seemingly straight from the American west coast. You can almost hear the waves bearing the surfers to shore. Or can you? There are certainly waves and surfers close to the brewery from where this beer emerges, but we're not in southern California but southern Cornwall.

Big Job is crewed ashore at St Austell, the august family brewery that is definitely part of the British brewing revolution. There's a delicious irony at play here – back in the 1990s St Austell (or St Awful as they were known) would have been seen as just another brewery treading water as beer sales fell and pubs closed. Yet the brewery has survived and is rocking the beer world. What happened? One man: Roger Ryman.

A NEW HAND ON THE HELM

Back in 1999, a tall, gig-rowing, rugby-playing Lancastrian took on the top job in brewing, that of a head brewer. He'd come from Maclay's in Scotland, hardly a den of seething innovation but he was iron-like in his resolution to change things at St Austell.

'When I was interviewed for the vacant head brewer's job,' recalls Ryman, 'I made it clear to the MD-in-waiting James Staughton what opportunity I saw for the company. The business had a solid estate of pubs and a strong regional identity, while the brewery itself, although not modern, was housed in a structurally sound granite building, and not threatened with imminent physical collapse. Why would this brewery not be successful? I was clear in my ambition that with the application of good brewing practice, innovation and focus on beer brand development I could see no reason why it could not double its sales in ten years, own a nationally revered cask ale brand and sit proudly at the top table amongst regional and family brewers.'

TRADITIONAL VALUES, MODERN APPROACH

If history, as James Joyce had Stephen Dedalus say in *Ulysses*, 'is a nightmare from which I am trying to awake', then Ryman was the alarm clock for St Austell. Granted they had a heritage going back to 1851, but what Ryman did was merge its traditional values with a modernistic approach that continues to drive the brewery forward to this day.

The beer that made Ryman's name and drew drinkers to the bar was Tribute, a luscious, sparkling ale first brewed in 1999 under the name Daylight Robbery (a reference to that year's eclipse). In his words, 'it was a modern pale ale characterised by significant late hopping with US and continental varieties'. He used Fuggles from England, Styrian Goldings from Slovenia and the American hop Willamette with the result being a zesty, citrus, juicy beer with a boisterous bittersweetness.

However, important and successful as Tribute was (and remains), Ryman, supported by Staughton, has pushed to make St Austell one of the most successful and dynamic English breweries. It is said that some family brewers, when wishing to reinvent themselves, now talk of 'doing a St Austell'. A friendship with Karl Ockert from Bridgeport Brewery in Portland, USA, led to the birth of Proper Job, a sessionable strength (4.5%) American-style IPA. He did nano as well with a small microbrewery that can produce 10 firkins each brew. 'It offers me,' he says, 'as head brewer, the opportunity to get out of the office and back to sleeves-rolled-up-brewing. There is nothing better than a Sunday in the microbrewery concocting a new recipe – no meetings, no e-mail and no phone calls!!'

TRAILBLAZING BEERS

There has been a fleet of beers produced over the years, some of them blazing a trail across the sky never to return, others taking their place in the pantheon of St Austell greats. Dark beer? Then how about a smooth stout based on a 1913 recipe, or a sublime example of that controversial style black IPA, Proper Black. Lager? There have been both Czech and German lagers produced, as well as a Bock complete with a billy goat image on the label,

The St Austell brewery can be toured and visitors can view the complete brewing process

Tribute is one of the brewery's most popular and sucessful beers, but it's since been joined by dozens of others

"St Austell Brewery have been brewing beer for 160 years, and we plan to continue brewing beer for another 160."

while beers from the wilder shores of brewing have included barrel-aging, souring and the addition of all manner of fruits and herbs. Early 2014 saw the emergence of Tamar Creek, which Ryman described as Flemish sour red ale that had been matured in oak barrels with Cornish cherries. The finished beer was polished and pleasing and pulsated with a tart, vinous character on the palate.

These days St Austell's beers take the drinker on an exhilarating voyage around the modern world of brewing, a journey that wouldn't have been possible without Roger Ryman's innovatory approach along with the stellar support he received from James Staughton and, of course, his team on the brewing floor.

'St Austell Brewery have been brewing beer for 160 years,' he says, 'and we plan to continue brewing beer for another 160.'

Beers to try...

Tribute, 4.2%
Pale amber in the glass, this classic session beer pulsates with bags of citrus fruit and hops on the nose while the palate is a zesty zephyr of citrus fruit adroitly balanced against a biscuity malt backbone; the finish is long, dry and gently bitter with more citrus.

Admiral's Ale, 5%
Chestnut/russet in colour this ESB has a toffee-caramel character in the mouth that is balanced by a juicy citrusy hop character.

Proper Job, 5.5%, 4.5% cask
The palest gold in colour; it's an aromatic beer with a well-filled fruit bowl of tropical fruit and resiny hop note ascending from the glass. More tropical fruit appears on the palate but the stern malt base keeps any inclination to over-fruitiness in line; the finish is bittersweet. Magnificent.

BEER DESTINATIONS

CORNWALL, DEVON, DORSET, GLOUCESTERSHIRE, SOMERSET, WILTSHIRE

BRISTOL

Bristol is on the beer trail. City-located breweries such as Bristol Beer Factory, Arbor and Zerodegrees have tempting taps where you can experience their vibrantly flavoured beers (keep an eye out for beers from self-styled cuckoo brewery Wiper and True as well); these have been joined by a clutch of recently opened pubs and bars that actively celebrate the city's ever growing status as an important beer hub. Alongside old favourites such as Butcombe's Colston Yard (the original home of pioneer micro Smiles), the Cornubia and the Seven Stars, we find the Bristol Beer Factory's Barley Mow, Arbor's Three Tuns and Bath Ales' very own craft beer bar Beerd (there's even a BrewDog!). Then on King Street, which leads down to the part of Bristol Harbour that is called Welsh Back, here can be found the city's very own craft beer quarter, with several pubs selling the best of Bristol and other craft breweries. The Small Bar is a high-ceilinged corner bar that hasn't been open for long; the beer menu is chalked up behind the bar, while there's a nano brewery tucked away in the corner ready to produce beers to add to the dozen or more available already. Across the road, we find the Beer Emporium, both an arched cellar bar and a handy bottle shop selling the best in British craft beer as well as classics from around the world. Next door, a bit older but just as craft wise, there is the Royal Navy Volunteer, a pub dating from the 17th century, which nevertheless when it reopened in 2013 went straight for the modern beer jugular with casks, kegs and bottles from some of the brightest brewing stars about. Finally, if you totter down to the harbour,

past a couple more pubs, including the Old Duke and the Llandoger Trow, there is the Spyglass, a barge that is run by Three Brothers Burgers and where beers from Bristol Beer Factor and Tiny Rebel are available. Oh and lest we forget: the city's CAMRA beer festival continues to thrive, while new addition Bristol Beer Week celebrated a successful second year in 2014.

Barley Mow
www.barleymowbristol.com

Beerd
www.beerdbristol.com

Beer Emporium
thebeeremporium.net

Colston Yard
www.colstonyard.butcombe.com

Cornubia
thecornubia.co.uk

Famous Royal Navy Volunteer
www.navyvolunteer.co.uk

Seven Stars
www.7stars.co.uk

Small Bar
www.smallbarbristol.com

Three Brothers Burgers aboard Spyglass
www.threebrothersburgers.co.uk

Three Tuns
0117 907 0689

Zerodegrees
www.zerodegrees.co.uk/bristol

BEER CELLAR
Exeter, Devon
beer-cellar.co.uk/Exeter

The imposing bulk of Exeter Cathedral dwarfs this compact craft beer bar that was set up by Cornish brewery Penpont in 2013 (the brewery also has bars in Launceston and in Truro). Echoing London's Rake, this is also a former café, which perhaps accounts for the laid-back vibe within as drinkers switch between pints from West Country stars such as Harbour, Penpont and Kubla, go continental with the odd Bavarian Weisse or opt for a genteel measure of a mind-blowing hoppy IPA (and even ones of the double persuasion) from the USA.

BRIDGE INN
Dulverton, Somerset
www.thebridgeinndulverton.com

Country pubs are not normally known for their eclectic selection of beers, but the Bridge Inn bucks that trend by bringing in beers that might come from Dark Star, Thornbridge and Bristol Beer Factory, alongside local ales from Exmoor Ales and Exeter brewery. As the River Barle flows gently past the pub, beer lovers inside can be further tempted by Brooklyn Lager on draft and a fridge full of bottles from Orval, Flying Dog, Goose Island, Westmalle and BrewDog.

The Bridge Inn in Dulverton offers draught beers from the likes of Dark Star and Thornbridge alongside bottles from further afield, such as the Belgian Westmalle and Orval

EASTERN ENGLAND

The famous expression 'nature abhors a vacuum' has been borne out in Eastern England. It's a region famous for its barley, thanks to the rich, dark soil, and it was the local grain that gave rise to a powerful tradition of brewing. Today there are breweries in abundance, plucking the best of the golden bounty from the soil to fashion an astonishing variety of beers. Yet just a few decades ago, much of the region was a brewing desert. Mergers, takeovers and closures destroyed breweries and pubs, and forced poor apologies for beer on undeserving drinkers. Slowly, but with growing pace, brewing has been restored with such success that Norwich now has an annual celebration, City of Ale, that's supported by breweries and pubs from both within and beyond the city.

THE RISE OF KEG

How different Norwich is today to the city visited in the early 1970s by the writer Christopher Hutt, author of a seminal book, *The Death of the English Pub*. He found there was just a single pub serving cask beer in a city with a population of more than 200,000. Norwich had been the victim of a giant London brewer called Watneys. It was one of the earliest practitioners of filtered and pasteurised keg beers, and it came to Norfolk to foist these beers on an unsuspecting public. It bought and eventually closed all three of Norwich's breweries, and then – to add insult

Oakham Ales: Peterborough, Cambridgeshire

Batemans: Wainfleet, Lincolshire

Elgood's: Wisbech, Cambridgeshire

Wainfleet

Cromer

Peterborough

Wisbech

Great Yarmouth
Norwich

Cambridge

Southwold
Laxfield

Poppyland: Cromer, Norfolk

Adnams: Southwold, Suffolk

BEER DESTINATIONS
> go to page 130

to injury – developed a new beer for the city's pubs called 'Norwich Bitter' that was brewed in Northampton.

Great Yarmouth on the coast, which combines both an important harbour and a seaside resort, lost its brewery following the arrival of another large London brewer, Whitbread. Lacons dated from the 18th century and sold its beer throughout East Anglia and down into London: its falcon logo can still be found carved into some London pubs. Whitbread, in common, with Watneys, wanted a large pub estate in which to sell its keg beers and its insipid version of Heineken lager. Lacons closed and its historic brewery became a warehouse for Whitbread's products.

LOCAL REVIVAL

Brewing revived in Norfolk in no small measure thanks to the gritty determination of Ray Ashworth. His Woodforde's brewery, named after a famous toping clergyman, Parson Woodforde, has been forced to move twice as a result of fires but has found a strong base at Woodbastwick, close to the Norfolk Broads, where it has its own pub, restaurant and visitor centre. Ashworth was a keen home brewer who moved into commercial production

with such award-winning beers as Wherry Best Bitter and Norfolk Nip. The 8.5% Nip recalls a barley wine from the 1920s brewed by Norwich brewery Steward & Patteson. Woodforde's has grown production to around 18,000 barrels a year and is now a fully-fledged regional brewery.

Two other key players in the restoration of brewing in Norfolk are Wolf Witham and David Winter. Witham brewed at the Reindeer pub in Norwich before moving to a bigger site at Attleborough while Winter, who brewed with both Ray Ashworth and Wolf Witham, went on to make beer at Chalk Hill brewery before opening his own Winter's brewery. Witham has built a deserved reputation for not only good quality beer but also a strong sense of humour with such beers as Granny Wouldn't Like It, playing on the Red Riding Hood story, and – celebrating the irrepressible local dialect – a strong mild ale called Woild Moild.

Another key player in Eastern England's beer revival is Colin Keatley who opened the Fat Cat pub in Norwich in 1991 and drew beer lovers like a magnet with his wide choice of cask ales and Belgian specialities. Spurred on by this success, he followed with the Fat Cat Brewery Tap with its own brewing plant – designed by Ray Ashworth – and then the Fat Cat & Canary, a pub handy for Norwich City football ground, home of the Canaries. In Great Yarmouth, young entrepreneurs have opened a new Lacons brewery dedicated to both modern beer styles and the recreation of old Lacons brands, including stout and an Audit Ale once brewed for Cambridge University.

NATIONAL SUCCESS

It took the collapse of Suffolk's major brewery to open the floodgates in the county. Tolly Cobbold

The unassuming street-corner Fat Cat is a Mecca for beer-lovers and cements the new brewing pedigree of Norwich

in Ipswich dominated brewing and pub retailing to such an extent that even Greene King looked like a minnow by comparison. A combination of poor management and abysmal beers led to the slow death of Tolly. As a result, Adnams and Greene King blossomed. Adnams, with an uncompromising devotion to characterful, hoppy beers, is now represented nationally. Greene King followed a less-than-popular course of mergers and takeovers that saw it become a national giant courtesy of such brands as Ruddles and Old Speckled Hen. In 2013 it responded to criticism of its beer range by installing a new specialist plant at Bury St Edmunds that can produce small-run beers with more profound flavours. Green Jack in Lowestoft has grown from brew-pub status to a 25-barrel plant that recalls the town's long fishing history with such beers as Trawlerboys, Red Herring and a 10.5% export stout called Baltic Trader. St Peter's has achieved international success from its base in an old medieval hall with its flagon-shaped bottles and a range that includes organic and fruit beers.

In Cambridgeshire and Lincolnshire, Batemans and Elgood's continue to fly the flag for family breweries. Both have developed new brands to appeal to a modern audience while maintaining a commitment to such traditional styles as dark mild and bitter. Elgood's proved how a younger generation of the family can bring new concepts to beer-making when in 2013 it brought back into use two redundant open cooling vessels to make Belgian-style lambic beer, using wild yeasts in the atmosphere. Milton at Waterbeach is one of several artisan breweries in Cambridgeshire that has deepened choice for drinkers with imaginative beer ranges that include both dark ales and fruity golden ones. Milton's Marcus Aurelius, called an Imperial Roman Stout, inspires the thought that beer in Eastern England can rightly proclaim: *Veni, Vidi, Vici*.

Insider's view...

Dawn Leeder
cityofale.org.uk

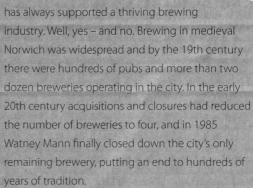

The fields of East Anglia are blessed with fertile soils which produce, arguably, the finest malting barley in the world. So, naturally, one might assume that the region has always supported a thriving brewing industry. Well, yes – and no. Brewing in medieval Norwich was widespread and by the 19th century there were hundreds of pubs and more than two dozen breweries operating in the city. In the early 20th century acquisitions and closures had reduced the number of breweries to four, and in 1985 Watney Mann finally closed down the city's only remaining brewery, putting an end to hundreds of years of tradition.

Thankfully those days are gone and the region has undergone an extraordinary brewing renaissance; currently there are 60 breweries in Norfolk and Suffolk with a further 26 in Cambridgeshire. East Anglia's picturesque, historic towns and cities enjoy a thriving pub trade and are home to some of the largest regional beer festivals, at Cambridge, Peterborough and, especially, Norwich which holds two major festivals each year.

These great annual festivals give shape to the year, attracting visitors to the region to celebrate its rich brewing heritage, sample the huge variety of ales available and, most importantly, secure a vibrant future for this most vital industry.

Dawn Leeder is the co-chair of Norwich City of Ale, an annual celebration of beer and pubs in Norwich and Norfolk

Established: 1872

Founder: Ernest and George Adnams

Beers: Sole Star, Lighthouse, Southwold Bitter, Gunhill, Explorer, Ghost Ship, Broadside, Old Ale, Tally Ho

Website: www.adnams.co.uk

ADNAMS

Southwold, Suffolk

For a brewery founded in 1872, Adnams is a thoroughly modern company not only producing a wide range of challenging beers but also thinking carefully about its impact on the environment. A new brewhouse, installed in 2008, is low carbon: it uses 58% less gas than the equipment it replaced and all the steam created during mashing and boiling – and that's a lot of steam – is recycled. Spent grain and hops are also recycled in the nicest possible way as food for local cattle and pigs.

A new warehouse in Reydon, just outside Southwold, is based in an old gravel pit and is partially submerged. The walls are built of compressed hemp rather than concrete and they maintain an even temperature inside without the need for refrigeration or heat. Solar panels also help heat the building and the roof is made of sedum,

The new beers are complex. Fitzgerald is not content to make fashionable golden ales with pale malt alone

a succulent plant that acts as insulation. Rain water is collected on the roof and is used to wash equipment and delivery vehicles. The company has twice been given the Queen's Award for Enterprise and the second award in 2012 was specifically for its contribution to sustainable development.

21ST CENTURY BREWERY

All this has been going on in a genteel seaside town best known for its inshore lighthouse, antique shops and multi-coloured beach huts. But Southwold was once an important stop on the stage coach route to Ipswich, Essex and London, and brewing has been going on behind the stately Swan Hotel since the 14th century. Ernest and George Adnams bought the brewery in the 1870s and were joined in 1902 by the Anglo-Irish Loftus family: both families control the company to this day, though George Adnams had only a brief career with the brewery. Tiring of urban life, he went to Africa where he was promptly eaten by a crocodile. The driving force at the brewery today is chairman Jonathan Adnams, who has worked at the brewery since he was 19. In common with his predecessor

Master brewer Fergus Fitzgerald has rolled out a wave of new beers that has cemented the brewery's reputation

Simon Loftus, he was determined to make the brewery and its beer fit for the 21st century as well as making an important contribution to the environment.

Today beer is only part of the mix: to one side of the impressive pale brown-stone Victorian facade overlooking East Green is the new Copper House that includes stills making gin, vodka and whisky. As all three products are grain-based, it's a simple step to take the mash from the brewhouse and distil it, ageing the whisky in wooden casks and adding 'botanicals' to the gin and vodka. It's from the distillery that visitors can catch one of the finest views of the town, with the Sole Bay Inn fronting the lighthouse and red-tiled cottages lining the streets down to the beach and the sea.

COMMITMENT TO FULL-TASTING BEERS

Change has been fast and spectacular. At the time of the 'real ale revolution' of the early 1970s, beer lovers made the long trek to Suffolk to sample the uncompromisingly hoppy beers brewed in Southwold. There was mild ale in those days and a winter barley wine, Tally Ho, but the main brand was Bitter, packed with peppery and spicy Fuggles and Goldings hop character. If anyone was brave enough to suggest the beer was a tad too bitter, Simon Loftus would respond: 'Drink someone else's beer then – we're not changing'. The commitment to full-tasting beers remains but the technology has altered out of all recognition. Adnams sprang on to the national stage with a premium bitter, Broadside, introduced in the late 1980s. Only 6 to 7% of the brewery's production goes to its 70 pubs and its beers are on sale in free trade outlets along with pub companies large and small nationwide.

Demand put a terrible strain on the creaking Victorian mash tun, copper and wooden fermenters. In 2008, the new brewhouse was installed, German-built and based on the continental system of mash mixer and lauter vessel that allows more brews a day to pass through. Master brewer Fergus Fitzgerald, who arrived at Adnams in 2004 via Murphy's in Cork and Fuller's in London, seized the opportunity to use the flexible new kit and rolled out a wave of regular and seasonal beers. Traditional Fuggles and

Adnam's traditional brewery now houses a modern brew kit as well as a newly-installed distillery.

The main brand was Bitter, packed with peppery and spicy Fuggles and Goldings hop character. If anyone was brave enough to suggest the beer was a tad too bitter, Simon Loftus would respond: 'Drink someone else's beer then – we're not changing'

Goldings have had to make room in the hop store for such American varieties as Cascade, Chinook, Citra and Mosaic. The last named, first grown in 2012, is also the name of one of the beers: hops are added four times during the boil in the copper and they add powerful notes of melon and peach.

The new beers are complex. Fitzgerald is not content to make fashionable golden ales with pale malt alone. Fat Sprat, with a portion of sales going to support the Maritime Conservation Trust, is brewed with Munich, black and cara malts alongside pale, and is hopped with Cascade, Chinook, Columbus and Goldings varieties. Explorer was the result of the brewing team exploring the Yakima Valley in Washington State, one of the major hop-growing regions of the US, and rushing home to make a citrus-rich pale beer with Chinook and Columbus varieties. Ghost Ship takes its name from the many ships wrecked off the coast, and uses caramalt, rye, crystal and pale malts. The hops are American Citra and Chinook with Motueka from New Zealand. The whisky casks in the cellar are also put to good use, with a new stout aged in them to pick up oak and vanilla notes.

Fittingly, Fergus Fitzgerald has switched to a new variety of East Anglian malting barley called Concerto that's perfectly in tune with the harmonious beers he brews.

Beers to try ...

Southwold Bitter, 3.7%
The brewery's workhorse, a pale copper colour, brewed with pale and crystal malts and hopped with First Gold, Fuggles and Goldings. There's pronounced orange fruit on the aroma and palate, with peppery hops and juicy malt. The finish is finely balanced between biscuit malt, tart fruit and bitter and peppery hops.

Ghost Ship, 4.5%
A pale ale with a complex grain recipe made up of pale malt, rye crystal malt and caramel. The main hop is American Citra, with a helping hand from Chinook and New Zealand Motueka. The beer has an aroma and palate of violets, citrus fruit, hop resins and malt biscuits, followed by a dry and bitter finish that interweaves between biscuit malt, hop resins and tart citrus fruit.

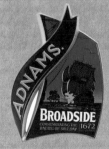

Broadside, 4.7%
The beer that gave Adnams a national presence is a deep bronze colour and is brewed with just pale malt and a touch of caramel. The hop make-up is identical to Bitter's and the beer has tangy fruit, biscuit malt, and spicy hops on nose and palate, with a long and quenching finish balanced between rich malt, orange fruit and an uncompromising hop bitterness.

Top: Jaclyn and Stuart Bateman have led their family brewery to success.
Bottom: Batemans windmill houses the brewery and visitor centre

BATEMANS BREWERY

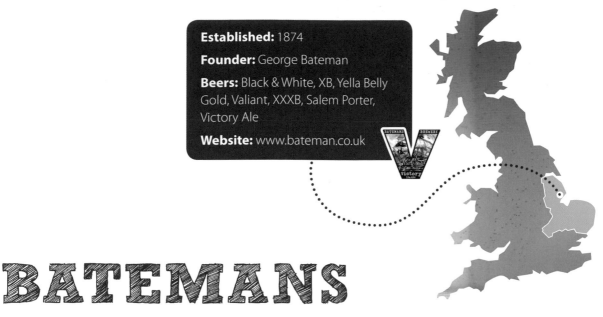

Established: 1874

Founder: George Bateman

Beers: Black & White, XB, Yella Belly Gold, Valiant, XXXB, Salem Porter, Victory Ale

Website: www.bateman.co.uk

BATEMANS

Wainfleet, Lincolnshire

Stuart Bateman is a cheerful man with a warm smile and a sharp sense of humour. But he's also proud and protective of his family's brewing heritage and he doesn't take prisoners.

In the spring of 2014, he threw a hand grenade in to the rumbling debate in the brewing industry when, along with his sister Jaclyn, and the brewers and staff at the Wainfleet brewery, he launched a major rebranding of his beers with the theme: 'Batemans – craft brewers since 1874'.

'I'm fed up with being told I can't call myself a craft brewer because I've been making beer for more than two years,' he declared. 'People who say that are denigrating the industry. I may not have a pony tail, ear-rings or tattoos, but I'm producing craft beer.' Warming to the theme, he added: 'Heritage is a good thing – it's not old fashioned. If you Google

the word "craft" up comes "artistry" and "attention to detail" but you will also get "skills passed on from generation to generation". When you're in a brewery on the edge of a river with a windmill, that makes you even more passionate.'

FAMILY BREWERS

Jaclyn and Stuart are the fourth generation of the Bateman family to run the brewery, founded 140 years ago. They run an estate of 62 pubs but they also supply a free trade that's buckling under the weight of the vast range of beers now available as a result of the boom in new breweries. Drinkers want distinctive beers with exciting malt and hop character and the Bateman siblings knew they had to adapt to demand while remaining true to their core cask ales.

"I'm fed up with being told I can't call myself a craft brewer because I've been making beer for more than two years. I may not have a ponytail, ear-rings or tattoos, but I'm producing craft beer"

Visitors to the brewery are invited to explore the museum of brewing before sampling some of Batemans award-winning ales in the beer garden

They are used to a challenge. A split in the family in the 1980s almost led to the closure of the company. But George and Pat Bateman, then in charge and with the full support of daughter and son Jaclyn and Stuart, managed to raise the cash to buy out the relatives who wanted to quit brewing.

In 1986, as if a divine hand had written the script, Batemans won CAMRA's Champion Beer of Britain competition with their strong XXXB bitter and they became one of the best-known breweries in the country. With Jaclyn and Stuart now in charge, they knew they had to adapt to a changing industry. They introduced both dark and golden ales in the shape of Salem Porter and Yella Belly Gold.

Yella Belly Gold has proved an enormous success for the brewery, standing out from the crowded field of golden ales. Brewed with lager malt as well as pale malt, it uses American Cascade and Chinook hops. The finished beer has a booming citrus hop note balanced by rich creamy and juicy malt. The name comes from the yellow waistcoats once worn by members of the Lincolnshire Regiment.

REBRANDING SUCCESS

Buoyed by the sales of the beer, the Batemans went full bore for a total rebranding exercise in 2014. The old-fashioned windmill logo was given a sharp makeover and the cask ales in pubs – Dark Mild, XB and XXXB – have new clover-shaped pump clips with distinctive colours. To prove their commitment to traditional styles, Dark Mild was uprated from 3% to 3.6% and renamed Black & White. It's brewed with Challenger hops and roasted malts and has a rich coffee-and-chocolate character underpinned by peppery hops. It's been received with something akin to adulation by drinkers and publicans, proving that there's still room in the pub trade for distinctive dark beers.

Yella Belly Gold has proved an enormous success for the brewery, standing out from the crowded field of golden ales

There's a new range of seasonal Biscuit Barrel Beers that includes Oatmeal, Barley, Bourbon and Chocolate biscuits. The aim is to show that barley malt and its many biscuit-like characteristics make just as important a contribution to beer as hops. Award-winning bottled beers include Mocha brewed with coffee, along with fruit beers.

The Batemans theme is that beer is more than pleasure – it's fun. The brewery has a spacious bar inside the ivy-covered windmill that used to grind the grain for the brew house. A new brew house, installed early this century, is called the Theatre of Dreams, emphasising Stuart's love of football, though he's a supporter of Nottingham Forest, not Manchester United. Families are welcome and there's a fascinating museum that traces the history of not just Batemans but brewing in general. Dioramas in the museum feature mannequins sporting Luciano Pavarotti and former President Bill Clinton masks. To stress the fact that the brewery is fighting fit for the modern age, there's an annual rock concert on the river bank overlooking the brewery, with lots of well-crafted beer available.

Beers to try ...

Black & White, 3.6%
Bateman's revamped Dark Mild, brewed with pale, crystal and roasted malts and hopped with Challenger. It has a luscious aroma of chocolate and coffee, with hints of liquorice. Spicy hops appear in the mouth, countering the richness of the grain. The finish is bittersweet, spicy hops countering the burnt grain and chocolate and coffee notes.

Yella Belly Gold, 3.9%
Named to commemorate the yellow waistcoats of the Lincolnshire Regiment, Bateman's entry into the golden ales category is brewed with lager malt and American hops. It has a bittersweet aroma of citrus fruit, toasted malt and tart hop resins. Tart fruit builds in the mouth with biscuit malt and bitter hops while the finish has a grapefruit note from the hops with biscuit malt; it finally ends dry and bitter.

XXXB, 4.5%
A classic strong bitter that bursts with rich, vinous fruit, honeyed and creamy malt, and tangy hop resins. The malts are pale, crystal and wheat, and the hops are Challenger and Goldings. There's ripe fruit and malt in the mouth, balanced by peppery hops. The luscious finish has a hint of banana with biscuit malt and a powerful peppery and earthy hop note.

Beer trends...
PUTTING SOMETHING BACK

To make good beer, brewers turn to the bounteous land to source grain, hops and water. Now a growing number of brewers are committed to 'putting something back', aiding the environment by returning used grain and hops to farms, and recycling water. In some cases, power is supplied in part or in total by solar panels and wind turbines.

Hobsons was one of the earliest artisan breweries to aid the environment. It's based at Cleobury Mortimer in Shropshire on a former farm where Nick Davis and his family were keen to use every available source to reduce carbon footprints and use local ingredients. They have the advantage of being close to the major hop fields of Herefordshire and Worcestershire – famous for the Fuggles variety – and they also buy barley for malting from a neighbouring farm. Davis installed a rainwater harvesting system that's used for washing vessels and floors, while power to drive machinery and move ingredients is supplied by a wind turbine. Spent malt and hops are supplied to farmers as cattle feed and fertiliser. Allotments have been created on brewery land where local people can grow flowers, fruit and vegetables with the aid of compost created by used malt and hops.

In nearby Ludlow, the Ludlow brewery, founded in 2006, follows in Hobsons' minimal carbon footprints with a system that reclaims heat generated by the brewing process to warm floors while rainwater is captured and recycled for washing. Solar panels have been installed to supply power and all lighting is low-energy. In 2011 the brewery was given the Ludlow Heritage Award for its contribution to both the history of the ancient market town and its support for the environment.

Two major contributors to the environmental cause are Otter in Devon (see page 98), and Adnams in Suffolk (see page 112). Otter, near Honiton, has developed willow beds, ponds and lagoons where water from the brewery is cleaned by nature and returns to the plant. The roof of the partially-submerged brewery is made of sedum that captures rainwater used for cleaning vessels and vehicles.

Other environmentally-friendly breweries include Digfield, Enville, Heart of Wales, Hop Fuzz, Little Valley, Malt, Mill Green, Rother Valley, Rowton, Saffron, Shottle Farm, Stamps, Stringers, Yates (Cumbria).

Purity brewery, Great Alne

Paul Halsey, managing director of Purity Brewing at Great Alne in Warwickshire, not only ensures the brewery is eco-friendly but also advises pubs he supplies on how to conserve energy by using correct cellar and serving temperatures for his beers. At Great Alne he has developed a wetland system where waste water from the brewery is recycled and cleaned. Spent grain is supplied as animal feed to local farmers.

Adnams brewery, Southwold

Adnams has invested heavily in modern equipment that uses far less energy than its original brewhouse. Its warehouse is based in an old gravel pit and has walls made of hemp rather than concrete and a sedum roof captures and recycles rainwater. Solar panels have been installed to supply additional energy.

Buntingford brewery, Royston

Buntingford brewery, founded in 2001 by Steve Banfield, is based on a farm near Royston in Hertfordshire and both brewery and farm are involved in encouraging wildlife. The Maris Otter barley used in the brewery has the lowest possible carbon footprint as it's grown on the farm while water comes from a borehole on site. Used water runs into a pond that attracts wildlife and since the scheme started the endangered corn bunting has settled on the site.

Purity brewery uses a reed bed system to filter their waste water before it's discharged into the water course

Established: 1795

Founder: Thomas Fawsett

Beers: Black Dog, Cambridge Bitter, Golden Newt, EP, Black Eagle Imperial Stout, North Brink Porter, Coolship

Website: www.elgoods-brewery.co.uk

ELGOOD'S

Wisbech, Cambridgeshire

In spite of the title, there are no sons at Elgood & Sons – but there are three sisters. It's the only brewery in the country run by a sisterhood.

The attractive brown stone buildings stand alongside the River Nene in a small market town on the edge of the brooding Fens, land hauled from the encroaching sea over many centuries. The buildings that form the present brewery started life in 1682, became a grain store and made the logical move to brewing in 1795. The Elgoods arrived in 1877 and haven't budged since then. Today Belinda Sutton is managing director, Jennifer Everall is the company secretary and Claire Simpson looks after sales and exports: those are their married names but they are Elgoods to the core.

EUROPEAN INFLUENCE

When head brewer Alan Pateman arrived in the 1990s, his first act was to stop using copper cooling trays known as coolships. 'I haven't come here to make Belgian lambic,' he joked, proving the old saying that many a true word is spoken in jest. In 2014 he launched a beer known by the house name

of Cambic: a Fenland version of the famous 'wild' lambic beers of Belgium.

The launch of the beer, now officially known as Coolship, proves the Elgoods are not living off past glories. They own some 40 pubs but, facing stiff competition from both bigger regional breweries as well as newer artisan ones, they know they have to diversify. As well as staple beers Black Dog Mild and Cambridge Bitter – both award winners in CAMRA's Champion Beer of Britain competition – Elgood's has a range of monthly seasonal beers and has attacked the export market with a full-flavoured, roasty Black Eagle Imperial Stout that has attracted attention from American beer lovers.

And then came Coolship. Bob Leggett, the American importer of Black Eagle, was visiting the brewery, noticed the decommissioned cool ships and urged Pateman and the sisters to consider making Belgian-style lambic for the US, where sour beers are all the rage. Coolships, from the Flemish word *koelschip*, are a key vessel in the making of lambic. A mash that's a mix of malted barley and unmalted wheat is boiled in the copper with a large amount of aged hops that have lost most of their bitterness but add tannins for flavour and prevent oxidation. Following the boil, the hopped wort is pumped to the coolship: it's a dramatic moment when Pateman calls 'Open the taps!' and boiling wort floods into the coolships, filling the brew house with steam.

The wort stays overnight in the trays while windows are left open to encourage air-borne yeasts to float in and attack the malt sugars in the liquid. Alan Pateman uses a 60-40 blend of English Maris Otter malting barley and wheat, with 'a massive amount' of old Styrian Goldings hops. Once fermentation is underway in the coolships, he pumps the liquid to fermentation tanks with a bed of oak and chestnut chips, which create a home for the wild yeasts. Some six to nine months later, the beer is moved again, this time for a further few months ageing in barrels bought from Bordeaux wine makers.

The finished beer has all the hallmarks of a true lambic: acidic with oak and vanilla aromas and flavours, creamy malt, vanilla from the wood and a musty note that brewers call 'horse blanket'. The first batch delighted Bob Leggett who has sold most of it to eager Americans.

Head brewer Alan Pateman has brought back into use Elgood's decommissioned coolships to brew an acclaimed Belgian-inspired lambic beer

Beers to try ...

Black Dog, 3.6%
A classic Fenland dark mild that has won a fistful of awards. It's brewed with Maris Otter pale malt, crystal malt and roasted barley, with Fuggles hops. The roasted grain gives the beer a pleasing chewy character with roasted notes and earthy Fuggles resins on the nose. Dark malt, vinous fruit and light hops dominate the palate followed by a dry finish well balanced between dark grain, rich fruit and spicy hops.

Cambridge Bitter, 3.8%
A firmly traditional English bitter, it's brewed with locally-grown Maris Otter pale malt, with a touch of wheat malt and roasted barley. The two English hops are Challenger and Fuggles. The copper-coloured beer has a creamy malt aroma with spicy and fruity hops with a plum-like fruit note. Biscuit malt, tangy hop resins and tart fruit fill the mouth with a dry and hoppy finish with a good balance of vinous fruit and biscuit malt.

Coolship, 6.7%
Elgood's version of Belgian Lambic, brewed with pale malt, unmalted wheat and aged Styrian Goldings: the hops used in the spring 2014 brew were picked in 2011. Aged in oak casks, the beer has an acidic aroma with oak, vanilla and a musty note known as 'horse blanket' to brewers. The palate is tart and tangy with creamy malt, vanilla and an acid sourness. The finish is uncompromisingly acidic and musty with strong notes of oak and vanilla.

Production director John Bryan brews experimental beers on the compact kit which can be viewed at Oakham's Brewery Tap in Peterborough

Established: 1993

Founder: John Woods

Beers: JHB, Inferno, Citra, Scarlet Macaw, Bishops Farewell, Hawse Buckler, Green Devil IPA

Website: www.oakhamales.com

OAKHAM ALES

Peterborough, Cambridgeshire

Oakham's beers are bold and vivid in the glass, bursting with flavour, crisp and zesty on the palate, complex in their palette of flavours and yet friendly and approachable. American hops lead the charge and the beers' drinkability has landed them with plenty of awards and accolades down through the years. The branding is equally dramatic with splashes of primary colours and highly stylised characters on the labels and pumpclips, such as a humanoid hop cone and a brilliantly plumaged parrot.

HOP FORWARD BEERS

If you think of Oakham's beers, chances are it will be Citra (the one with the humanoid hop) that first springs to mind, though JHB's victory as Champion Beer of Britain in 2001 still reverberates through the beery universe; the latter's triumph also set off several years of golden ales winning this prestigious award. Citra is a favourite of hopheads everywhere, with its riotous assembly of lychee, grapefruit and ripe gooseberry aromas and a

dazzling array of tropical fruit notes kept in line by a stern bittersweet and dry finish. The beer is a noble expression of the Citra hop variety, and production director John Bryan can still recall when he first encountered the hop.

He's been going on an annual hop research trip to the Yakima Valley in Washington State ever since 2002, usually in the company of other brewers and Paul Corbett from hop merchants Charles Farham. 'In 2009 we went to see John I Haas of major hop suppliers the Barth-Haas Group,' he recalls, 'and we were told that there were some spare Citra and I rubbed it in my hands and it was the most exciting thing I have ever enjoyed in brewing. I knew then I wanted to brew with it and I wanted to be the first as well, so I had my hops flown back, while supplies for other breweries were being shipped over.'

When the shipment of Citra hops eventually arrived at the brewery, Bryan recalls that it smelt even better than it had in the US; you could say that his response to the arrival was a sign of his passion and love for making boldly flavoured beers: 'I was

"we were told that there were some spare Citra and I rubbed it in my hands and it was the most exciting thing I have ever enjoyed in brewing. I knew then I wanted to brew with it and I wanted to be the first"

rubbing my face in the hops and taking bits of hop sack off to wear.'

Therefore it comes as no surprise to learn that Oakham is one of the biggest buyers of this fragrant hop, though Bryan and head brewer Alex Kean also maintain a watch on what else is happening in the hop world. 'We keep an eye on hop trends,' he says, 'in both the US as well as the UK, where there is some interesting new hop breeding coming through.'

MOVING AROUND

Oakham first saw the light of day in 1993 in its namesake town in the tiny county of Rutland – it was very much a one-man band with founder John

Wood doing the brewing. There were two beers, the ever-present JHB and the charmingly named Old Tosspot (which is no longer brewed). Bryan, who comes from a farming family in the Fens and had only home-brewed up until then, joined as a brewer a couple of years later, when Wood had sold the business on. 'After an interview with the then owner Paul Hook,' he recalls, 'I got the job, went on a course and began brewing. It was a bit scary at first.'

When Bryan first started, the brewery was producing 10 barrels a week; it soon went up to 30 and now 75 can be brewed in one go. The brewery has also moved around. It left its original home and moved to the Brewery Tap in 1998, a

Oakham's award-winning beers are brewed at their purpose-built site just outside Peterborough

former unemployment office in Peterborough, which doubled up as lively bar and restaurant (it spent several years at risk of being demolished due to the local council's plans for redeveloping the North Westgate area but that risk has now diminished as the development of the area is on hold). It got the removal vans in once more in 2006 to travel to its current home on a purpose-built site in Peterborough's northern suburb of Woodston, though the Tap still has a compact kit on which experimental beers are occasionally brewed.

INTERNATIONAL SUCCESS

There are five regular beers with Citra and JHB being joined by Inferno, Scarlet Macaw and Bishop's Farewell. Alongside the various seasonals and the one-offs for members of the Oakademy of Excellence, there is a quartet of intriguing beers that are barrel-aged. These include the heady (7.5%) and fruity Attila and the bright and breezy Green Devil IPA, which was described as the big brother of Citra. 'I like to age these beers in barrels,' says Bryan, 'for secondary conditioning and a different flavour profile. I'm always open to experimentation and innovation.'

Bryan was delighted when Green Devil IPA was named Champion Cask Ale at the International Brewing Awards in 2013, held at the National Brewing Centre in Burton upon Trent. He was joined in his delight by Oakham's managing director Adrian Posnett who remembers 'to win a gold and silver medal when competing with over 1,000 beers from over 45 countries was a fantastic honour, particularly as we were being judged by our peers. This is Green Devil's fifth gold medal at a brewing competition, and it was only launched in 2011.'

Another accolade for Oakham came their way in the summer of 2014 when Citra was awarded Champion Golden Ale at CAMRA's Great British Beer Festival. The beer then went in to become runner-up in the overall competition.

Beers to try ...

JHB, 3.8%
Bright gold in colour, this inviting session beer blossoms onto the nose with lime-citrus notes, while its light bubblegum-like juicy fruitiness and a pronounced bitter finish invites further exploration.

Hawse Buckler, 5.6%
A dark soothing beer with a triumvirate of aromas: chocolate, raisin and roasted malt. On the palate, toffee, mocha and chocolate collide with an earthy, slightly spicy and bittersweet character.

Green Devil IPA, 6%
A robustly hopped beer whose aromas veer between a green earthiness, grapefruit, hints of lemon tart and a Riesling-like sprightliness; ripe peach skin and ripe mango pulp start the tango on the tongue followed by a mid-palate sweetness and an assertive bitter finish.

This clutch of awards are testament to the quality and of the beers, and to John Bryan's brewing skill. Think what beer and brewing would have lost if he had chosen to follow in his father's footsteps and become a farmer.

"I like to age these beers in barrels for secondary conditioning and a different flavour profile. I'm always open to experimentation and innovation."

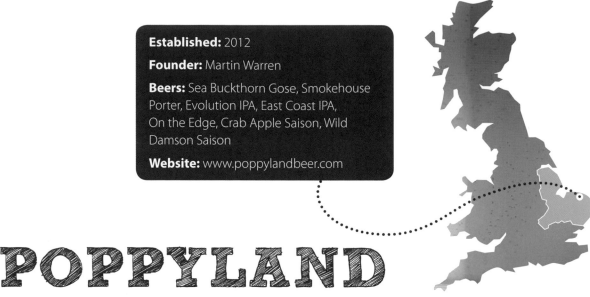

Established: 2012

Founder: Martin Warren

Beers: Sea Buckthorn Gose, Smokehouse Porter, Evolution IPA, East Coast IPA, On the Edge, Crab Apple Saison, Wild Damson Saison

Website: www.poppylandbeer.com

POPPYLAND

Cromer, Norfolk

Martin Warren won't mind if you call him a scavenger, though forager is the preferred term. He scours the highways, byways, hedgerows and beaches of North Norfolk in search of ingredients for his beers.

Damsons, crab apples, petals, wild hops and even crab have found their way in to his brews. 'Why not crab?' he asks. 'That's what Cromer is famous for.'

Poppyland opened in 2012 in a former car repair workshop. Martin had brewed at home intermittently since he was 17 or 18 but only thought of making it a full-time profession when he was made redundant by Norfolk County Council in 2008. He'd been a museum curator for some 25 years and had developed a database of both the history of the Cromer area and its wildlife. He sank some of his pension in a 2½-barrel brewery that was designed and built for him by Brendan Moore of Iceni brewery in Thetford. Moore's advice was succinct: to make extraordinary beers and sell them at prices that would make Martin some money. That meant making bottle-conditioned beer in attractive and distinctive packaging and pricing it at around £6 a bottle.

EUROPEAN INFLUENCE

Martin Warren has followed this sage advice. 'There are no rules where beer is concerned any more,' he says. 'You don't have to be identikit.' He has a passion for recreating the traditional Belgian farmhouse style known as Saison. They are strong beers, ranging in colour from gold to copper, and generously hopped, sometimes with the addition of herbs and spices. His Saisons include Wild Damson, Crab – the label says 'good with sea food' – and Evolution, an 'IPA Saison' brewed with American and New Zealand hops.

He discovered a rare German beer style called Gose, originally from the town of Goslar in the Leipzig area. It's made with 50% wheat as well as malt, lightly hopped, with salt added. It's a 'sour mash' beer, which means a portion of the grain is removed from the mash tun and allowed to turn sour by the action of *Lactobacillus*. The bacillus can be injected but Warren allows it to happen naturally

Above: Martin Warren sank his pension into his 2½-barrel brewery. **Right:** The beers are all bottle-conditioned

from bacteria in the atmosphere. The sour grain is then returned to the rest of the mash. Warren adds salt from the Cromer marshes and also a touch of coriander. His Sea Buckthorn Gose has a further addition of thorns from the Cromer cliffs.

Smokehouse Porter is brewed with Norfolk Maris Otter malt and New World hops: the ingredients are placed on shelves in a local fish smokery and smoked.

One of Warren's first beers was Days of Empire, a strong Victorian-style pale ale. It used wild 'landrace' hops and a historic barley variety called Chevallier, popular in the 19th century, that has been revived and grown by the John Innes Centre in Norwich.

LOCAL FOCUS

These intriguing beers are available from the brewery, one local pub, the Red Lion, local markets and the occasional specialist beer shop. Martin doesn't sell online but the beers can be bought on- and offline from the Real Ale Shop near Wells-Next-the-Sea – a great supporter of Norfolk breweries. If the brewery is closed, the phone number is shown in the window and if you call Warren, who lives over the road, he will come and open up. This is localism of a special kind.

Beers to try ...

Smokehouse Porter, 5.7%
The beer is made with Maris Otter malted barley from Branthill Farm near King's Lynn and New World hops, both smoked in a fish curing house in Cromer. The deep russet-going-on-black beer has a herbal and spicy nose with smoked grain and hints of liquorice. Oak and smoke blend in the mouth with vinous fruit, liquorice and bitter hops. There's some balancing sweetness in the finish that leads to a dry, smoky and hoppy end.

Wild Damson Saison, 7.4%
A hazy brown beer with acidic fruit on the nose, sweet biscuit malt, herbal hints and floral hops. Sweet-and-sour in the mouth, it has tart fruit, rich biscuit malt and spicy hops. Hops are more present in the finish, with continuing acidity from the fruit, smoky grain and gentle, herbal hops.

BEER DESTINATIONS

BEDFORDSHIRE, CAMBRIDGESHIRE, LINCOLNSHIRE, NORFOLK, SUFFOLK

Wainfleet

Great Yarmouth
Norwich
Cambridge
Laxfield

CAMBRIDGE BLUE
Cambridge
www.the-cambridgeblue.co.uk

The Blue wears its heart on its sleeve and a cask on its pub sign: a large wooden barrel hangs on the exterior. The term 'permanent beer festival' may be over-used but it fits here as the publicans have turned this Victorian pub into a shrine for beer lovers. There are as many as 14 cask beers on offer, mainly from East of England breweries, and a vast range of world beers, both draught and bottled. There are more than 100 Belgian beers and around a dozen each from Germany and the US, with Australia and other countries also featured. The pub was built to refresh railway workers and is now a true community local, welcoming students, university lecturers, commuters and beer lovers from far and near. The Blue was also listed in the *Observer* newspaper's food awards, as the tucker here has a good reputation.

LACONS BREWERY AND VISITOR CENTRE
Great Yarmouth, Norfolk
www.lacons.co.uk/visitor-centre

It's more than a brewery, it's a celebration of a major force in Norfolk brewing: cruelly snuffed out in 1968 and brought back to life in 2013. Lacons dates from 1760 and built a vast estate of pubs as far south as London, all adorned with a falcon logo. It was bought and closed by national brewer Whitbread, which wanted to stuff the pubs with its insipid version of Heineken. Lacons came back to life in 2013, on a different site in the town, and its brewery is augmented by a visitor centre and museum. There are tours of the brewery and an illustrated history of the company, including old recipe books, pub signs, and brewing and pub equipment. And there's the opportunity to taste the new Lacon's beers in a tap room.

KING'S HEAD
Laxfield, Suffolk
www.laxfieldkingshead.co.uk

It's known as the Low House to distinguish it from another pub on higher ground beyond the village church: the name is not a comment on the quality of the customers. The Low House is one of the few pubs left in the country without a bar. This wonderful old thatched inn has beams, high-back settles, uneven tiled floors that show the passage of time and a large room at the back where casks of beer are set up. You wander into the room and ask for a glass of whatever takes your fancy. Bob and Linda Wilson have the full range of Adnams beers, with guest ales and local cider. The food is simple but nourishing pub grub: sausage and mash or lasagne, for example. There's a large garden and B&B accommodation can be arranged. The freestanding pub sign is unusual, showing Henry VIII on one side and Charles I on the other but it does mean both Stuarts and Tudors are welcome.

FAT CAT BREWERY TAP
Norwich, Norfolk
fatcattap.co.uk

Colin Keatley is a beer superstar in Norwich: a London publican who came east and opened the first Fat Cat pub in 1991 when the city and the county were still suffering from the hammer blows of Watneys, which had bought and closed all three Norwich breweries. Keatley brought variety and choice back to the Fair City and such was his success that he opened a second Fat Cat, complete with a small in-house brewery. The kit was built and installed by Ray Ashworth, founder of Woodforde's brewery at Woodbastwick, which also played a major role in bringing back choice to the parched county. The large open-plan Tap is decorated with memorabilia of Norwich's lost breweries while the brewing plant knocks out Fat Cat Bitter, Marmalade Cat, Cougar and Wild Cat. Keatley has added a third pub, the Fat Cat & Canary, near the football ground, and you can visit all three courtesy of a special bus.

BATEMANS BREWERY VISITOR CENTRE
Wainfleet, Lincolnshire
www.bateman.co.uk/visitors+centre

There are two cottages for hire at the brewery, which is a few minutes' stroll from the train station. And you'll need time to take in all the pleasures of the centre, which includes a tour of the brewery, with ancient and modern vessels, and a museum. Mr George's Bar, inside an old windmill, invites you to sample the full range of beers and enjoy a good lunch: the mill used to grind the grain for the brewery in the 19th century. The museum traces the history of brewing in Wainfleet and further afield and is done with Batemans rare humour: there are lookalike models of Bill Clinton and Luciano Pavarotti performing such vital tasks as cask washing. You can play traditional pub games and, when the weather's kind, take your pint and sit by the River Steeping.

The Cambridge Blue serves as many as 14 cask beers, mainly from the East of England, as well as world beers both on draught and bottled

THE MIDLANDS

DERBYSHIRE, HEREFORDSHIRE, LEICESTERSHIRE, NORTHAMPTONSHIRE, NOTTINGHAMSHIRE, RUTLAND, SHROPSHIRE, STAFFORDSHIRE, WARWICKSHIRE, WORCESTERSHIRE, WEST MIDLANDS

Brewing in central England has historically been dominated by both a small town and England's second city. Today Burton upon Trent and Birmingham have lost their precedence as brewing centres but the region is now awash with thriving new breweries. Derbyshire, once in the shadow of Burton, has an astonishing array of beer makers. Nottingham, too, has lost substantial breweries but the gap has been filled to overflowing with new practitioners of the art in both the capital city and the county: Nottingham itself has eight breweries, with Castle Rock at the forefront.

All regions have factors that influence their beer styles, and in the Midlands it's water that plays a defining role. The waters of the Trent Valley enabled Burton to emerge in the late 19th century as the most important brewing centre on the globe, an astonishing achievement for a small Midlands town. But, as the driving force of India Pale Ale and pale ale, it not only exported to all parts of the British Empire and beyond but also attracted brewers from other countries. They came to study Burton's brewing practice and, in particular, the technologies of the Industrial Revolution that made the production of pale malt possible on a vast commercial scale. The first golden lager beer, Pilsner from Bohemia,

Salopian: Hadnall, Shropshire

BEER DESTINATIONS
> go to page 156

Buxton: Buxton, Derbyshire

Thornbridge: Bakewell, Derbyshire

Buxton • Bakewell

Nottingham

Derby • West Bridgford

Burton upon Trent

Castle Rock: Nottingham

Birmingham

Shrewsbury • **Dudley**

Northampton

Marston's: Burton upon Trent, Staffordshire

Bathams: Brierley Hill, West Midlands

owes its existence to brewers from Central Europe visiting Burton and even importing a British-made malt kiln. English pale ale the godfather of golden lager? You'd better believe it.

THE HOME OF IPA

Today one of the great revivalist beer styles is IPA. It had largely disappeared by the end of the 19th century but now brewers in Britain, the United States, Belgium and Australasia have fallen in love with a beer that's synonymous with Burton and which offers a complex blend of sappy malt and tart hop bitterness.

Burton had been an important brewing centre since the monks of Burton Abbey produced ale for their abbot, his guests and visiting pilgrims. Centuries later, nut-brown Burton ale became a cult drink in London and was exported as far as the Baltic. The Burton brewers lost much of their export trade during the Napoleonic Wars but by sheer good fortune were offered a lifeline and new overseas sales by the mighty East India Company.

A brewer in East London called Hodgson had cornered the market in beer for India in the late 18th and early 19th centuries but he'd fallen out with the East India Company, which encouraged the Burton brewers to make a pale and bitter beer for 'the Raj'. The brewers found that the spring waters of the Trent Valley, rich in such sulphates as gypsum and magnesium, were ideally suited to making pale ale: sulphates are flavour-enhancers and draw out the full piquancy of malt and hops. Within a few years, the great Burton brewers, Allsopp, Bass, Ind Coope and Worthington, had built a highly profitable trade with India and other parts of the British Empire.

BLACK COUNTRY BEERS

Birmingham, Wolverhampton and the 'Black Country' had to meet different demands from drinkers. The brewers there were less involved in export and had to quench the insatiable thirsts of an army of industrial workers labouring in mines, foundries and factories. The water in the area is radically different from Burton's: low in gypsum, high in chloride and best suited to the production of dark beer. Dark mild became the signature beer of the area: not overly hopped and with some brewing sugars left in the beer to produce a full-tasting, sweetish brew. Such mighty brewers as Ansells and Mitchells & Butlers produced enormous volumes of dark mild.

The Midlands is home to established breweries such as Marston (left) and a new wave of craft brewers like Thornbridge (right)

Marverine Cole
www.beerbeauty.co.uk

Britain's second city, Birmingham, is packed to the rafters with an impressive selection of city-centre pubs for the tourist to drop into. These include the very old, such as Fuller's Old Joint Stock pub and theatre, a former bank from the late 19th century and which has probably the tallest ceilings in the city; here you can drink guest ales from Midlands breweries, as well as supporting small burgeoning theatre companies. On the other hand, the Wellington pub is probably known as the city's finest among the CAMRA crowd with 16 handpulls! It's even more of a destination since its recent revamp, adding another bar, function room and a rooftop garden. City-centre breweries aren't in abundance, yet the four-year-old Two Towers brewery holds its own and is expanding, as news spreads of its locally-inspired offerings – Jewellery Porter and Livery Street Mild – to name a couple.

The new breed continues – and spans both Birmingham and Warwickshire when you look at Purity Ales. Based on a farm near Stratford-upon-Avon, the brewery has aimed at and won fans amongst the younger craft beer drinker with Lawless, Longhorn IPA and many more. Sponsoring local music and comedy festivals has broadened appeal and they've recently fused that with food, opening Pure Craft Bar and Kitchen in Birmingham's business district. All backed by one of the region's best chefs.

Head out into the area known as the Black Country and you move into beers and breweries which often garner rockstar legendary status: Batham's brewery in Dudley, with the deliciously smooth Best Bitter; while in Sedgley, tucked away behind the Beacon pub, is Sarah Hughes brewery (a teeny-weeny Victorian Tower brewery) which dishes out the dangerous and fruity Dark Ruby Mild. As I said, the Midlands is a vast and beautiful beast.

Marverine Cole is a journalist, broadcaster and unashamed beer lover

The big Birmingham brewers are long gone but dark mild has made a spirited recovery in the hands of new and older family producers. Bathams and Holden's in the Black Country have never departed from the style while Beowulf in Brownhills shows with Dark Raven (4.5%) that mild doesn't need to lack strength. In Sedgley, the Sarah Hughes brewery in the Beacon Hotel brews a remarkable Dark Ruby mild at 6%, based on a recipe from the 1920s. In Wolverhampton, Banks's, a member of the Marston's group, continues to produce Mild as a major member of its portfolio.

Burton has also lost its world-famous names though Marston's continues to fly the flag for pale ale and still uses the idiosyncratic 'Burton Union' system of fermentation. Burton Bridge is one of the oldest new-wave breweries in Britain and produces a wide range of beers that include interpretations of Burton ale, pale ale, porter and stout. In Stoke, the Titanic brewery, another long-standing artisan brewery, remains true to mild and also offers bitters, porters and an award-winning stout. Derbyshire's staggering number of new breweries includes the acclaimed Thornbridge in Bakewell – one of the vanguard of the British brewing revolution – which brews pale, gold and black ales and stouts. Its award-winning Jaipur IPA proves that a truly great beer style will never go out of favour.

Established: 1877

Founder: Daniel Batham

Beers: Mild Ale, Best Bitter, XXX

Website: www.bathams.com

BATHAM'S

Brierley Hill, West Midlands

People sigh with pleasure when they arrive at the Vine pub, the brewery tap next door to Batham's brewery. It receives visitors from all round the world, as well as locals from the British Isles. Many Americans make the long trek to this suburb of Dudley in the Black Country to go all misty-eyed over 'a real pub'. The brightly-painted exterior tells you that Bathams brews 'genuine home brewed Mild & Bitter Beers' while a fascia board carries a quote from Shakespeare's *Two Gentlemen of Verona*: 'Blessings of your heart: you brew good ale'.

Inside, it's all tradition, with a public bar to the right and a carpeted lounge to the left. Locals sup pints and talk in the sing-song burr of the Black Country, a region that gets its name from the smoke and soot generated by thousands of factory chimneys when Britain still had heavy industry. And to many drinkers supping a pint and munching a cheese cob, the pub is not the Vine but the Bull & Bladder – a name that pays reference to the former slaughterhouse next door.

PLAYING TO THEIR STRENGTHS

With the myriad range of beer styles that many breweries are rushing to experiment with, it may not be considered innovative to concentrate on mild and bitter, but as Batham's sends its bitter out to pubs in 54-gallon hogsheads – a size of cask scarcely used by brewers these days – it's clearly meeting the demands of modern drinkers. Tim and Matthew Batham are the fifth generation of the family to run the company and are sufficiently young to know what their customers want.

Change tends to be slow in this part of the world and the brewery had been going for 70 years before it brewed a bitter. Dark mild was the drink of choice – not only personifying the landscape of the Black Country, but the ideal brew to slake the thirsts of workers toiling in coal mines and iron foundries.

The brewery was founded by Daniel Batham after he lost his mining job in 1881. In 1912 the family took over the Vine and centred brewing and pub-running there. Today Batham's owns 11 pubs and supplies beer to many other outlets in the region: Tim Batham has had to add two additional fermenting vessels to keep up with demand. Bitter was an also-ran until it was named the Best Bitter in Britain in a competition staged by the *Daily Mirror*

The Vine – better known as the Bull & Bladder – is an iconic Black Country pub and Batham's brewery tap

in the 1970s. Sales soared and overtook Mild, though the dark beer holds up well and doesn't have an 'old boys' image in this part of the world.

Tim Batham describes his Mild Ale as 'dark pale ale'. He is refreshingly open about his brewing methods and describes the two beers as 'parti-gyle'. When he has made a batch of Best Bitter, using a traditional mash tun, copper and fermenters – some of the fermenters are built of wood and are more

than 100 years old – he adds brewing water to a portion of the Bitter to reduce its strength from 4.3% to 3.5%. Caramel is added for colour and flavour, and casks are heavily primed with sugar to ensure a powerful second fermentation. Both Mild Ale and Best Bitter are dry hopped in cask with Goldings, giving the dark beer a powerful hop note not often found in milds. But that's the way they like it in the Black Country.

Beers to try ...

Mild Ale, 3.5%
A superb example of the style, with a vinous fruitiness reminiscent of blackcurrant on aroma and palate. The finish is bittersweet and ends dry with Goldings hop notes.

Best Bitter, 4.3%
A deceptively easy-drinking beer, straw coloured with biscuit malt and rich hop resins from Goldings and Northdown on the nose. It's bittersweet on the palate and finish but ends dry with peppery Goldings.

XXX, 6.3%
A beer brewed for the Christmas period. Amber malt is blended with Westminster pale malt and the beer is hopped with Fuggles, Goldings and Northdown. In true Christmas tradition, it has a Dundee cake/marzipan character with succulent grain and spicy hops.

Head brewer Colin Stronge leads a brewing team which concentrates on crafting experimental new beers with bold flavours

Established: 2009

Founder: Geoff Quinn

Beers: Jacob's Ladder, Moor Top, Rednik Stout, Special Pale Ale, Far Skyline, Red Raspberry Rye, Jaw Gate, Wild Boar, New World Saison, Imperial Black, Tsar, Double Axe

Website: www.buxtonbrewery.co.uk

BUXTON

Buxton, Derbyshire

Lovely old Buxton, the cultural centre of the Peak District as well as a place where those who fancy it can take the waters. Nowadays there's another reason to visit this beautiful spa town. It's the home of Buxton brewery, which opened its doors back in 2009, part of the wave of breweries that emerged around the start (or just a year or so on each side) of the current decade (think Kernel, RedWillow and Magic Rock for starters). These are all breweries who are keen exponents of assertively flavoured beers, whether brimming with hops or sleeping the sleep of the just within wood.

So if you're looking to take the waters, then why not do so in the form of a glass of Axe Edge, their robust IPA, a phantasm of flavour and hop character; or for something lighter but equally full of character perhaps you should plump for a pint of Moor Top, the brewery's sensual session beer with its powerful punch of Chinook hops.

SHARED VISION

Colin Stronge is the man in charge of the mash tun, a head brewer who started his career in the now defunct Liverpool Brewing Company and moved onto Manchester's Marble brewery – another key player in Britain's brewing revolution – where he spent nine years. Here, as second brewer, he developed his appreciation for hops: 'I had previously viewed them as more for their preserving quality than flavouring,' he recalls. After Marble it was a move up to Scotland with Black Isle before family commitments brought him south to Buxton. 'When I heard that the then head brewer had given his notice I got in contact with owner Geoff Quinn and it was apparent very quickly that we shared a similar vision of what we wanted for the brewery.'

The beer vision of Buxton, as expressed through the work of Stronge and his brewing team, is a mixture of bold flavours and ever increasing ripples

"For me it is about pushing beer flavour forward beyond what can be achieved just by malt, hops and yeast"

Solomon's Temple, just outside Buxton, is a fortified Victorian tower that appears on the brewery's logo

of experimentation. 'I try to treat each brew like the most important beer I will ever make,' Stronge says. 'Attention to detail, whether it is about selecting the malts and hops, choosing the combinations of flavours or the weighing out of salts, each piece of the puzzle must be meticulously handled. Influences come from everywhere: a new hop strain, a beer you've tried, a flavour you'd like to recreate or just seeing something on your travels. We made a sour raspberry beer last year after seeing how many were growing in the area near to the

"Our outlook is to never be afraid to try new things. We have experimented with fruit beers, Brett fermentation, Lacto fermentation and combinations of these"

brewery and thinking on how those flavours would work in a beer.

'Our outlook is to never be afraid to try new things. We have experimented this year with fruit beers, *Brett* [wild yeast] fermentation, *Lacto* fermentation and combinations of these. I guess we are still best known for our stronger, hoppier brews but we like to have a wide roster of styles available.'

As you might expect with such an open-minded brewing stance, barrel aging is also high on Buxton's agenda. This process has included the rich and virtuous Imperial Russian Stout Tsar Bomba, which was Buxton's normal Imperial Stout put into a barrel and inoculated with a yeast strain taken from a 1978 bottle of wood-aged Courage Imperial Russian Stout.

'For me it is about pushing beer flavour forward beyond what can be achieved just by malt, hops and yeast,' says Stronge, 'and combining the flavours of wood, spirit, wine and beer to create interesting new flavours which we couldn't otherwise achieve.'

Spoken like a true brewing revolutionary.

Beers to try...

Moor Top, 3.6%
This brilliant gold session beer has a bright aromatic nose of citrus (think lime and grapefruit), while the palate tingles and rings away with plenty of lemon and lime all kept in line with a crisp, biscuity character.

Imperial Black, 7.5%
Dark chestnut brown in colour, with a fragrant hop-forward nose suggesting melon and passion fruit plus a hint of liquorice. It's juicy and creamy on the mouth with plenty of citrus and tropical fruit. The finish is long, dry and bitter.

Buxton have had success with barrel-aged beers. Their Imperial stout Tsar was aged in a barrel innoculated with a Courage yeast from 1978 to create Tsar Bomba

Established: 1998

Founder: Chris Holmes

Beers: Sheriff's Tipple, Nottingham Gold, Black Gold, Harvest Pale, Hemlock Bitter, Snowhite, Preservation Fine Ale, Elsie Mo, Midnight Owl, Screech Owl

Website: www.castlerockbrewery.co.uk

CASTLE ROCK

Nottingham

They must have engraved the word 'innovation' into the walls of the brewery, built over the road from Nottingham's central train station and within a longbow shot of Nottingham Castle. There's a restless determination to develop new beers in this brewing city, home to many other breweries. In 2014, Castle Rock launched a series of beers to commemorate World War One. They will include beers called Tommy Atkins (the generic name for a British soldier at the time) and Christmas Truce: a donation from sales will go to relevant charities, including Amnesty International. An old fermenter from the original brewing plant has been brought back into commission to produce short-run beers called Traffic Street Specials, named after the road that runs alongside the brewery. The beers are strong, 6% or more, and will include an unfiltered, highly hopped IPA; a beer made with the addition of lemongrass and tarragon; and a dandelion and burdock ale.

AWARD-WINNING BEER

Castle Rock grew out of a pub group called Tynemill, founded in the late 1970s by Chris Holmes, a former national chairman of CAMRA. In an area dominated by such big brewers as Hardys & Hansons and John Smith's, Tynemill found a ready audience among people in need of distinctive beer and good pub food. The brewery was added in 1997 and at first produced just 30 barrels a week. But regular updates, including a brand-new, custom-built plant in 2010 costing £600,000, has increased production to 300 barrels a week. The group owns 22 pubs and the demand from those pubs and the free trade means further expansion at some point in the future can't be ruled out.

The new plant came under immediate strain in 2010 when Harvest Pale Ale won CAMRA's Champion Beer of Britain competition and sales went through the roof: the beer now accounts for half of Castle Rock's production.

Castle Rock's brewing team create award-winning beers that demonstrate a dry sense of humour from their plant in Nottingham

Chris Holmes has retired but his legacy lives on. He believed in putting something back into the community and a monthly series of special beers helps support Nottingham Wildife Trust. A 'Nottinghamian' celebration beer is brewed quarterly and some of the special brews, such as Sheriff's Tipple and Screech Owl, have become regulars on the bar. There's also a good, dry Nottingham sense of humour connected to Castle Rock: its brewery tap is called the VAT & Fiddle as it's adjacent to the local offices of HM Customs & Excise. Let's hope the brewery is never late with its tax return...

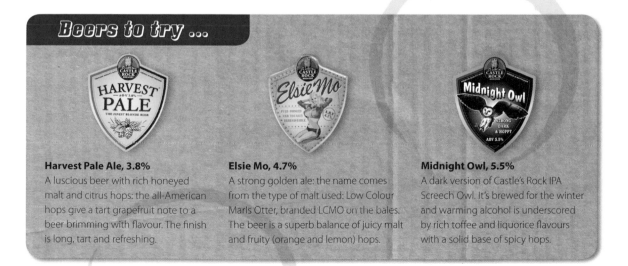

Beers to try ...

Harvest Pale Ale, 3.8%
A luscious beer with rich honeyed malt and citrus hops: the all-American hops give a tart grapefruit note to a beer brimming with flavour. The finish is long, tart and refreshing.

Elsie Mo, 4.7%
A strong golden ale: the name comes from the type of malt used: Low Colour Marls Otter, branded LCMO on the bales. The beer is a superb balance of juicy malt and fruity (orange and lemon) hops.

Midnight Owl, 5.5%
A dark version of Castle's Rock IPA Screech Owl. It's brewed for the winter and warming alcohol is underscored by rich toffee and liquorice flavours with a solid base of spicy hops.

Beer trends...
LOCALISM

Farmers' markets are an increasingly popular destination to buy locally-produced food; the shelves and stands at farm shops groan beneath the weight of foodstuffs, a lot of it often grown in the surrounding fields.

Shoppers like local food, and if there's local food then there should be local beer, which is why CAMRA's LocAle scheme was launched in 2007 after being developed by Nottingham CAMRA's Steve Westby. At the time, Westby was quoted as saying that he was motivated by Greene King's takeover of one of his local breweries – Hardys & Hansons – the year before.

'I dreamt up what became LocAle over a pint one evening,' he said in 2008, after been awarded the prestigious title of CAMRA's Real Ale Campaigner of the Year for his innovation. 'I had been mulling over the impact of the takeover and cynical closure of Nottingham's last major brewer and it is pleasing that such a simple idea has become so successful.'

He was right – it is a simple idea. All pubs need to do to sign up to the scheme is have at least one cask beer from a local brewery permanently on offer. Local means a brewery within 20-30 miles radius of the pub (different distances apply in different areas, and are decided by the scheme's local administrators) – the beer doesn't always have to be the same, which helps with rotation, and pubs can

CAMRA's LocAle scheme – pioneered in Nottingham – provides accreditation for pubs selling beers brewed in their local area

Guy Shepherd, SIBA chairman

Nottingham CAMRA's Steve Westby

choose to support a number of breweries, as long as they are within the correct distance.

Guy Shepherd is the owner and brewer at Exe Valley just outside Exeter; he is also chairman of the Society of Independent Brewers (SIBA). As can be expected, whichever hat he wears, the idea of localism and supporting local brewers has his approval.

'From a brewer's perspective,' he says, 'LocAle makes complete sense. With no disrespect to the product we make and love, beer is about 95% water and it makes no sense to transport large quantities of it around the country. I am delighted to supply beer within a tight radius of the brewery. It keeps transport costs well down and ticks the boxes that many consumers are now looking for to search out and support local producers. The "buy local" ethos of the likes of farmers' markets is also very evident in many consumers' buying patterns today; being a brewer in an area dependent on the tourist industry it is very noticeable how they also want to search out and try local beers when down in the Southwest.

'From SIBA's point of view, we have used the term 'Local Beer' as part of our strapline for some years now. The Direct Delivery service that SIBA provides for brewers is largely driven by the need for pub groupings to have access to locally-produced beers, with many now insisting that beer supplied through the scheme must be brewed within a certain mileage of each pub (often around 30 or 40 miles). Successful pubs are very often the ones that have the best selection of local beers on their bars.'

From a publican's point of view getting involved in the LocAle scheme also makes perfect business sense. As Shepherd points out, when tourists visit pubs in holiday areas, one of the first things they do at the bar is ask what the local beer is. Pub regulars are also keen on celebrating local beers: after all, pride in a local brewery is a long established aspect of pubgoing. So next time you visit a LocAle pub and order a pint of the local ale, don't forget to raise a silent toast to the local brewers who have provided your refreshment.

> *"I am delighted to supply beer within a tight radius of the brewery. It keeps transport costs well down and ticks the boxes that many consumers are now looking for"*

Brewmaster Genevieve Upton has helped to develop Marston's new range of Revisionist beers

Established: 1834

Founder: John Marston

Beers: Burton Bitter, Pedigree New World Pale Ale, Pedigree, Revisionist California Common Steam Beer, Old Empire, Owd Roger

Website: www.marstons.co.uk

MARSTON'S

Burton upon Trent, Staffordshire

Marston's is a powerhouse of beer, the only surviving Burton brewery from the 19th century where the miraculous waters and a bizarrely fascinating method of fermentation made pale ale an international style and its place of birth the most famous brewing town in the world. If you take the short walk from Marston's to the National Brewery Centre, now part of the Canadian-American Molson Coors group, you will find, weather-beaten and forlorn, a row of large wooden casks in the car park. They are the old Bass Union fermenters, unloved and unwanted, a memento mori of Victorian brewing. But back at Marston's, the brewery has not only retained its Unions but has added to them and dubbed them 'the Cathedral of Brewing'. Visitors to the fermenting halls are occasionally regaled by the sight of a member of staff dressed in a bishop's mitre and full clerical dress saying benediction over the wooden vessels.

Marston's dates from 1834 and in 1898, as a result of mergers in the town, Marston, Thompson & Evershed moved to the impressive red-brick plant that had been operated by the London brewer Mann, Crossman & Paulin. It was another 'outsider', the Liverpool brewer Peter Walker, who introduced the Union Set method of fermentation when he, too, opened a second plant in the town. The Unions coincided with commercial glass production. Beer drinkers switched from pewter to glass and expected star-bright, sparkling beer, not murky darker ones. The Unions were designed to cleanse pale ale of yeast but yeast is sensitive to its surroundings and the cultures used in Burton adapted themselves to Walker's system. Marston's believes, with quiet passion, that the yeast culture created in its Union Sets has a fundamental impact on the beer, Pedigree Bitter in particular. Its flagship brand was originally called Pedigree Pale Ale and it's a classic example of the Burton style.

CATHEDRAL OF BREWING

The great oak casks that stand at the heart of the system each contain 144 gallons of fermenting beer. The casks are linked by pipes and troughs or, to use the quaint Victorian expression, 'held in union'. Beer is driven by the force of fermentation up swan-

Marston's rolling programme of Single Hop beers uses the same pale malt base but employs a different hop for each new brew

neck pipes placed in the bung holes of the casks where the beer drips into trays above: the trays are placed at an angle and as a result the beer runs back through pipes into the casks below, leaving most of the yeast behind. Sufficient yeast remains in the casks to ensure a continuing fermentation. The end result is a clear, sparkling ale with a superb balance of malt and hop flavours and a sulphur note from the brewing water known as 'the Burton snatch'.

Unions rapidly fell out of favour in the 20th century: they are labour-intensive and need full-time coopers to repair them. But Marston's devotion to the system can be measured by the fact that in the 1990s it invested more than £1million in a second hall of Unions, with the finest oak imported from Germany. But the company is not rooted in past glories and vigorously develops new beers to meet the demands of modern drinkers. It has a large internal market to supply as Marston's is

now a national group that owns Banks's, Brakspear, Jennings, Ringwood and Wychwood breweries, with more than 2,000 pubs and 3,000 free trade accounts. Curiously, considering Marston's home base, it never produced an IPA in the 19th century but it filled that gap in the 21st with the introduction of Old Empire. It has taken a keen interest in hops and its rolling programme of Single Hop beers uses the same pale malt base but employs a different hop for each new brew. Drinkers have been able to taste the differences – pine, cedar, citrus, pepper and spice – between English, American, New Zealand and even Polish varieties. Marston's has also worked with the British Hop Association to develop a new variety called Endeavour that's a cross between an American Cascade and an English variety to give British brewers a more restrained version of a citrus/ fruity hop: the variety is named in honour of Chief

Pedigree, 4.5%
Classic Burton pale ale brewed with pale malt only and Fuggles and Goldings hops. There's juicy malt, hop resins and sulphur on the nose. Biscuit malt and spicy hops build in the mouth and lead into a long, dry finish with a gentle hint of apple fruit.

Old Empire, 5.7%
A modern IPA, brewed with pale malt and Fuggles, Goldings and American Cascade. Sulphur on the nose gives way to floral hops, succulent malt, vanilla and light citrus notes, with a tangy lemon character dominating the finish.

Owd Rodger, 7.4%
A strong ale occasionally available in cask for beer festivals. Thanks to a new bottling line at Burton, Marston's may turn the packaged version from filtered to bottle conditioned. Rich, vinous, with coffee and sultana and raisin fruit.

Inspector Endeavour Morse, a keen imbiber of malt and hop beverages.

The most recent development is a Revisionist range of beers, available in cask, keg and bottle, that has given brewers at all the Marston's plants free rein to introduce their own ales. They include a Pacific Hop Red Ale with three hops from New Zealand, a Belgian-style Saison and a German-inspired wheat beer. Among the most popular is California Steam Beer, brewed by Genevieve Upton at Burton. Genevieve is not the only woman 'brewster' with a big say in the group. The former head brewer at Burton, Emma Gilleland, is now in overall control of beer quality at all the group's breweries. Women running breweries – what would the Victorians think!

Brewery cooper Mark Newton

Established: 1995

Founder: Martin Barry

Beers: Shropshire Gold, Divine Comedy, Oracle, Darwin's Origin, Hop Twister, Lemon Dream, Entire Butt, Golden Thread, Kashmir, Automaton, Black Ops

Website: www.salopianbrewery.co.uk

SALOPIAN

Hadnall, Shropshire

If we're talking about dark horses in the British brewing revolution then Salopian is definitely one. Their beers have always been well regarded, popular with the local audience around Shrewsbury as well as in the wider free trade, but in the words of managing director Wilf Nelson, 'until 2008 we were making fairly typical, lightly hopped Midlands style ales'. And so what you might say. Business was good, as was the brewery's reputation. However, the arrival of a new sales manager Jake Douglas, once of Oakham brewery, shook things up.

'Jake isn't a brewer,' laughs Nelson, 'but he loves beer and understands flavours, he is also cleverly persuasive, and boy does he love hops! He lured me to pubs selling hoppy beers in the modern style, and having opened my eyes we decided a change was in order – it was plain that there was a fast growing market for that style of beer, and that no one was making it in our area. So a fourth category of required traits in our beers is now a pronounced hop character – aroma and flavour.'

This means that alongside the likes of Shropshire Gold, Golden Thread and the elegant pale ale Oracle,

which Nelson regards as representing Salopian ('it has a massive hop aroma and flavour, a perfect balance between the bitterness and the hint of body, and an effervescence that makes it dangerously drinkable'), Salopian's head brewer Kev Harris makes forays into the wilder side of craft brewing with small batches of IPAs (using different hops), black IPAs and Imperial stouts.

"it has a massive hop aroma and flavour, a perfect balance between the bitterness and the hint of body, and an effervescence that makes it dangerously drinkable"

KEEPING UP WITH THE COMPETITION

'Most Fridays, at the end of the day, we'll sit down and taste a variety of bottled beers,' says Nelson, 'mainly American, Danish cuckoo, British new wave, traditional Belgian and the like. It makes me proud that our first attempts stand up to the best of them.'

Salopian's managing director Wilf Nelson has seen the brewery shake up its range and add new beers

Until the autumn of 2014 the brewery was based in an old dairy on the outskirts of Shrewsbury, but it moved a few miles to the north to a new site in the village of Hadnall, installing a larger, better brewery. Nelson says 'it is our intention to diversify our production and produce bigger quantities of our "specialist" bottled beers. What styles we intend to produce though is another matter!'

So far, 'specialist' Salopian beers that Nelson is proud of have included Black Ops, a rich and smooth Imperial stout, the boisterously bitter American-style pale ale Kashmir and Automaton, a sensuous IPA.

The late Martin Barry founded Salopian in 1995; he was a former chef who brewed a variety of strikingly flavoured beers. These included a ginger wheat beer, an Altbier and Kriek. Nelson came on board in 1998 when the business got into difficulties. Barry left in 2004 and was replaced by Harris, who apparently was keen to become a town planner, though as Nelson says: 'I persuaded him that brewing was better.'

Beers to try...

Divine Comedy, 3.9%
New wave mild with hints of blackcurrant jam on the nose. In the mouth berry fruits tumble about in the company of a crisp, grainy chaperone followed by a dry finish.

Lemon Dream, 4.5%
Tangy golden Shropshire ale with peppery, herbal, elderflower-like, notes on the palate before a long dry finish.

Kashmir, 5.5%
Passion fruit and ripe orange peel on the nose; tropical fruit rules the roost in the mouth with a hint of caramel in the background. The finish is bitter and lasting.

Thornbridge opened their new brew plant just outside Bakewell in 2010, creating exemplary beers that are exported around the world

Established: 2005

Founder: Jim Harrison

Beers: Wild Swan, Brother Rabbit, Lord Marples, Ashford, Sequoia, Kipling, Jaipur IPA, Saint Petersburg Imperial Russian Stout, Bracia

Website: www.thornbridgebrewery.co.uk

THORNBRIDGE

Bakewell, Derbyshire

Thornbridge's Jaipur is the benchmark for modern British IPAs, a zap of grapefruit freshness combined with malt sweetness stitched onto a frame of bracing bitterness. It can't help but win awards and make friends. Despite this, there has always been more to Thornbridge than a hefty dose of hops (though the brewery isn't averse to that). Their other beers are just as exciting. St Petersburg is an impenetrably dark imperial stout with a seductive smoothness; Bracia is a creamy, rustically roasty, tenderly burnt and burnished beer with chestnut honey in the mix; Kipling is luscious and luminescent in the glass with a great blast of tropical fruit. More recently, the brewing team took on the complex style of West Flemish brown ale with Sour Brown, and produced a remarkable grand old master of a beer that could easily stand up to the best of the region. Then there is Otto, a rich Weizenbock; Twin Peaks, which was brewed in collaboration with Sierra Nevada; Reverend and the Makers, a bittersweet beauty of an American Brown Ale. There is a palpable sense of exploration with Thornbridge.

QUALITY, CONSISTENCY AND INNOVATION

Rob Lovatt is the head brewer. For him, getting the beer right requires a triumverate of conditions: quality and consistency are paramount and once that is achieved innovation can follow.

'I am very style driven and feel that classic styles have evolved as they are because they are a proven formula that inherently works,' he says. 'There is nothing more satisfying than nailing a classic style. That's not to say I am adverse to experimentation and brewing beers which are a bit more left field; however, a lot of thought needs to go into making beers like these to make sure the final beer is balanced and any novel ingredients complement the other components within.

Jaipur is Thornbridge's flagship beer – a multi-award winning India pale ale which combines hop bitterness and malt sweetness

"We've always said that as a 'new' brewery we didn't have a heritage to follow like many other British breweries so we felt no constraints"

'I think that the Parma Violet Porter and Peanut Butter Brown that we brewed in 2014 are two good examples of this, though the beers that I believe best represent Thornbridge are Chiron, which is packed full of fresh flavour but so damn drinkable as well. Then the Sour Brown because of the complexity and depth but again its drinkablility.'

BREWING TALENT

Looking back, there seems an inevitability about Thornbridge's rise to brewing prominence. In 2005 a small brewkit of 10 barrels was set up in an outhouse at Thornbridge House on the edge of the Peak District. The House was a 19th century stately home that had been bought by local business folk Jim and Emma Harrison. The late David Wickett of Kelham Island brewery in Sheffield was a friend and suggested to Harrison that he might like to install a brewery. Two of the first brewers were young Scotsman Martin Dickie, who went on to co-found BrewDog, and Stefano Cossi, an Italian science graduate who had come to England to deepen his knowledge of the brewing process. Dickie and

Cossi have long moved on, along with ebullient New Zealander Kelly Ryan, who was also on the team until 2010. Lovatt joined in the same year from pioneering London craft brewery Meantime. 2010 was a significant year for Thornbridge as they opened a spanking new palace of stainless steel outside Bakewell, while the old brewery back at the Hall became a play pit and a place of experimentation, whose beers, such as Sour Brown, are released under the Thornbridge Hall name.

'We've always said that as a "new" brewery we didn't have a heritage to follow like many other British breweries so we felt no constraints,' says Jim Harrison, the brewery's CEO, 'so we could brew what we liked and we think our range of beers reflects this. So our ethos has always been about experimentation and ambition for quality and we have supported this with investment in people – recruiting the right ones that fitted the culture and making sure we continued to develop them. But it is also about investing in the best equipment to allow the brewing team to do their job to the best standard possible.'

Wild Swan, 3.5%
A swoon of a session beer with a subtle citrus nose, a refreshing, crisp mouthfeel, hints of bitter lemon on the palate and a dry refreshing finish.

Sequoia, 4.5%
Fragrant hop-forward interpretation of an American amber ale with soothing toffee and caramel notes harmonising alongside a rich orange character. The finish is crisp and dry.

Wild Raven, 6.6%
Black IPA with a hefty aromatic hit of tangy orange and mocha; the creamy mouthfeel works alongside orange citrus and cappuccino notes before a bitter, peppery finish.

THE FIRST BRITISH CRAFT BREWERY

Thornbridge are an integral part of the British beer revolution, arguably the first British craft brewery, as they have bolted together a creative sense of brewing along with consistency and steady business principles (they also run 12 pubs). As for the future, one of the most exciting developments, according to Lovatt, will be barrel aging on a larger scale than before as well as developing more new beers. However, amid this sense of giddy excitement he is keeping a clear head.

'The passion and experience of our brewers is what makes us special,' he says. 'We only select brewers who really buy into what we are trying to achieve. There is no room for anybody to kick against the pricks. Our key objective is to produce the best beer possible for our customers.'

Thornbridge brewery: superstar craft beer pioneers or restless souls keen to discover how far they can take the beer experience? Take your pick. Or maybe it's easier to say that Thornbridge is a remarkable brewery whose brewers have always produced remarkable beers. And why not toast that with some Jaipur.

Thornbridge's chief executive Jim Harrison and chief operating officer Simon Webster

"The passion and experience of our brewers is what makes us special"

BEER DESTINATIONS

DERBYSHIRE, HEREFORDSHIRE, LEICESTERSHIRE, NORTHAMPTONSHIRE, NOTTINGHAMSHIRE, RUTLAND, SHROPSHIRE, STAFFORDSHIRE, WARWICKSHIRE, WORCESTERSHIRE, WEST MIDLANDS

OLD CONTEMPTIBLES
Birmingham, West Midlands
www.nicholsonspubs.co.uk

This striking red-brick Victorian corner building is part of the specialist Nicholson chain of historic pubs. It serves Nicholson's Pale Ale, a house beer brewed for the chain by St Austell, along with beers from Purity and Thornbridge, all of which can be enjoyed in sumptuous surroundings. The pub is a shrine to the Victorian age with chandeliers and deep leather settees. It's named in honour of soldiers who formed the British Expeditionary Force in World War One.

WELLINGTON
Birmingham, West Midlands
www.thewellingtonrealale.co.uk

'The Wellie' has rapidly become a Birmingham institution, a permanent mini-beer festival, with 16 beers on offer. Rather like a Chinese restaurant, you order beers by the numbers listed on screens. The pub is owned by Black Country brewery and you'll find Black Country's Bradley's Finest Golden and Pig on the Wall as regulars, alongside Oakham Citra and Wye Valley HPA and many, many other brews. No food is served but customers can bring their own, and plates and cutlery are supplied.

NATIONAL BREWERY CENTRE
Burton upon Trent, Staffordshire
www.nationalbrewerycentre.co.uk

The centre started life as the Bass Museum and is now run by an independent company within the grounds of the giant Molson Coors Brewery,

successor to Bass. The museum traces the history of brewing in Burton and further afield and has a collection old brewery vehicles. Old locomotives stress the importance of trains to the town in the 19th century and there are models of Burton breweries in its Victorian heyday. Tableaux trace the rise of Burton Ale and India Pale Ale. The museum includes the William Worthington brewery that brews for the on-site Brewery Tap and recreates famous beers from the past, including Worthington E, an infamous keg beer in the 1970s but now in delicious cask form. The centre stages regular conferences and events, including live jazz.

BRUNSWICK INN
Derby
www.brunswickbrewingcompany.co.uk

An arrow-shaped, end-of-terrace pub, it was built in 1842 by the local railway company as part of a model estate for their workers. It fell into disrepair and was rescued by the local conservation society with the support of CAMRA. When it re-opened, landlord Trevor Harris added a small brewery that can be viewed at the end of a long corridor from the bar. There are several comfortable rooms leading off the main bar. The pub is now owned by Everards of Leicester and the brewery is independently run: its big range of beers, including Triple Hop, Porter and Father Mike's Dark Rich Ruby, adorn the bar along with Everard's ales. The food is excellent and the inn is a good stopping off point from nearby Derby Station. The Brunswick is worth missing a few trains for.

MALT SHOVEL TAVERN
Northampton
maltshoveltavern.com

The Malt Shovel has long been an institution in the town. It attracts customers from far and near and is especially popular with workers at the Carlsberg brewery over the road. The spacious tavern with plenty of seating is now owned by the Great Oakley brewery and its Wot's Occurring, Harper's and Gobble are regulars on a bar that groans under the weight of 14 handpumps. There are regular guest beers, including the ever-popular Oakham Ales from Peterborough. There are regular beer festivals and live blues is played on Wednesday nights.

TRENT BRIDGE INN
West Bridgford, Nottinghamshire
www.jdwetherspoon.co.uk

A vast red-brick building, thought to be the biggest pub in the Wetherspoon estate, it's a pub that spawned one of the principle cricket grounds in England, Trent Bridge. The pub predates the cricket ground: William Clarke staged the first match in a field behind the inn in 1838 and married Mary Chapman, the inn's landlady. It remained in the hands of the Chapman family until it was sold to the cricket club. It passed to JD Wetherspoon who spent £3 million on a major overhaul before re-opening it in 2011. There's a vast array of cricketing memorabilia and beers from Batemans, Nottingham Rock, Theakstons and many others.

The Brunswick Inn in Derby is owned by Everards, but it is also home to its own microbrewery which brews a wide range of excellent ales

Purple Moose: Porthmadog, Gwynedd

Conway

Porthmadog

Waen: Llanidloes, Powys

HELLISH GOOD BEER
PAMPLEMOUSSE
ABV **4.2%** *Hand crafted in Wales*
The WAEN BREWERY

Llanidloes

Otley: Pontypridd, Mid Glamorgan

Pontypridd   Newport

Llantrisant

Cardiff

Tiny Rebel: Newport, Gwent

Brains: Cardiff

BEER DESTINATIONS
> go to page 182

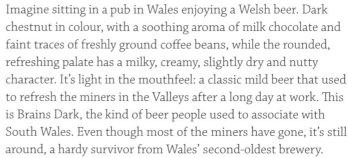

WALES

Imagine sitting in a pub in Wales enjoying a Welsh beer. Dark chestnut in colour, with a soothing aroma of milk chocolate and faint traces of freshly ground coffee beans, while the rounded, refreshing palate has a milky, creamy, slightly dry and nutty character. It's light in the mouthfeel: a classic mild beer that used to refresh the miners in the Valleys after a long day at work. This is Brains Dark, the kind of beer people used to associate with South Wales. Even though most of the miners have gone, it's still around, a hardy survivor from Wales' second-oldest brewery.

Order another Welsh beer. This one has a golden gleam, an upward thrust of ripe apricot and malt sweetness on the nose, while in the mouth it has a juicy apricot sweetness that is kept from going completely over to the saccharine side by liberal doses of Centennial hops in the kettle. It is dry, quenching and bittersweet in the finish. It's called California: a pale ale from Conwy brewery, who have only been around since 2003.

There are other Welsh beers: highly-hopped double IPAs, roistering best bitters with Sahara-dry finishes, beers made with different yeast strains that throw all manner of shapes in the glass, fruit-infused porters, Bible-black saisons and, as if to show kinship with another small country, a Belgian Tripel with dried orange peel in the mix (the latter being a collaboration between the Celt Experience and London's Tap East).

So what is a Welsh beer? The whole brewing scene seems to have changed in the last 15 years or so. Old certainties have weakened but not vanished – as the survival of Brains Dark shows – but new and unorthodox approaches to brewing beer have emerged, giving rise to the variety of beers being now brewed across the country.

ENGLISH INFLUENCE

It wasn't always like this. At one stage, mirroring the regionally split popularity of football and rugby, Welsh beer was also roughly

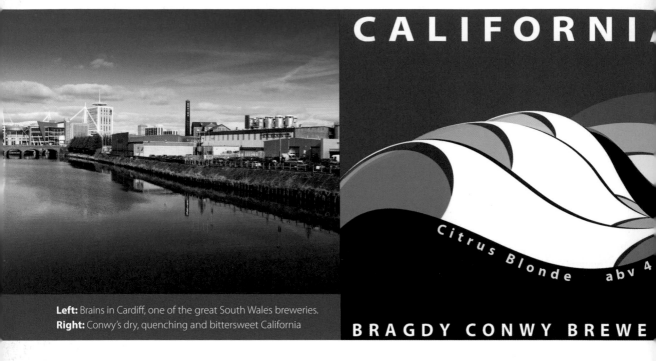

Left: Brains in Cardiff, one of the great South Wales breweries.
Right: Conwy's dry, quenching and bittersweet California

divided between north and south. In the north, the main breweries servicing the pubs and clubs were English, firms like Robinsons, JW Lees and Greenall Whitley, whose beers followed tourists to the holiday towns. Legend has it that the brewery directors even bought pubs in Wales so they could sample their own beers whilst on holiday; there could be a grain of truth in it as Robinsons and JW Lees have a strong presence on the coast all the way to Anglesey, while there is a Bathams house high up on the A5 below the Berwyn mountains (Vaux once kept a pub in a nearby village).

In the near past you couldn't really say that North Wales had its own beer style as these malty bitters and soft milds from over the border dominated the pubs; mellow tasting beers that were not overly hopped. They also influenced the handful of local breweries such as Border, though Wrexham, which was often known as the Burton of North Wales, was famous for its lager brewery, which first opened in the late 19th century

(it closed in 2000, though a microbrewery now produces the beer).

However, in the 1990s matters started changing with a handful of micros opening (and most just as promptly closing). In the early part of the 21st century the likes of Conwy, Purple Moose, Facers and Great Orme appeared and managed to tap into the growing interest in local cask beer. Since then they have been joined by the likes of Bragdy Nant in Llanrwst and Heavy Industry in the small market town of Denbigh (briefly home to the much lauded Four Thumbs in the 1990s).

VALLEYS BEERS

Down south, where the major cities of Newport, Cardiff and Swansea remain tied to the Valleys as if by umbilical cord, there's been an even more frenetic pace of change, possibly influenced by the higher concentration of people in the area. Brains still dominates, the last of the great South Wales breweries that once included Rhymney (there's a micro of that name now), Hancock's, Ely and Crown Buckley (Simon Buckley, a member of the family, still brews under the name of Evan Evans). And let's not forget Felinfoel, which is still brewing in Llanelli and claims the crown of oldest brewery in Wales, as well as being the first brewery in Europe to put their beer in cans.

These veterans have now been joined by the coruscating presence of Tiny Rebel in Newport, while in Caerphilly Tom Newman's Celt Experience manages to blend an eclectic sense of branding with some seriously intriguing beers. The beer scene in Wales has never been so healthy.

Here's another Welsh beer. 'The ale was indeed admirable, equal to the best I had ever before drunk – rich and mellow...and though so pale and delicate to the eye nearly as strong as brandy. I commended it highly.'

The latest craft/artisanal beer? No, George Burrow writing in 1854's *Wild Wales* about a glass of beer he had in a pub in Bala. Wales is back in its rightful place as a great beer nation.

Tiny Rebel have embraced bold and modern branding and an urban art aesthetic to appeal to younger generations

Insider's view...

Stuart Chapman-Edwards
albionalehouse.weebly.com

Wales used to seemingly be a real ale semi-desert: barren and dry apart from the occasional giant cactus of brewing. But in the late 90s and early 00s small shoots began to emerge – to the relief of the thirsty traveller and Cymro alike.

We are blessed with beautiful and useful geology in North Wales: the limestone pavements filter our water and add some delicious ale-friendly elements. In the south it was historically safer to drink the local ale than the water – happily for the legions of weary coal miners. Looking back, I remember the excitement I felt drinking a pint from Felinfoel or Tomos Watkins, knowing it was crafted from the land I live in.

Latterly we are spoiled with the likes of Tiny Rebel, Purple Moose, Great Orme and Nant. We are inundated with the experimental, small-batch brews from Conwy brewery (lamb-infused ale anyone?).

Welsh folk are immensely proud of their land and what it produces, just ask the regulars at the Red Cow, Aberdare or at the Snowdonia Park, Waenfawr: two brewpubs that are bucking the trend of pub closures.

I truly believe that this is a golden age of brewing and real ale-led pubs in Wales, and I feel privileged to be a part of it.

Stuart Chapman-Edwards is the landlord of the Albion Ale House in Conwy, a multi-award winning pub run jointly by Bragdy Nant, Conwy, Great Orme and Purple Moose breweries

Brains' acclaimed beers, brewed in Cardiff are sent out to their estate of 270 pubs throughout Wales, and further afield

Established: 1882

Founder: Samuel Arthur Brain and Joseph Benjamin Brain

Beers: Dark, Bitter, SA, SA Gold, Rev James, Bragging Rights, Barry Island, Boilermaker

Website: www.sabrain.com

BRAINS

Cardiff

'It's Brains you want' the advert for Cardiff's long established family brewery used to go, but these days, with so many offerings to choose from you might have a job working out which Brains' beer you want. Will it be Dark with its creamy chocolate character, a historic mild that would have poured like a biblical flood down the throats of miners in the Valleys? This was a beer that the thirsty men could lubricate their parched throats with in great volume and still get up smiling for the next shift? Or will it be SA, a clean and refreshing best bitter, with grainy biscuity notes on the palate and a bittersweet finish. Back in the 1970s when there were not so many strong beers around as there are today, this was infamously nicknamed Skull Attack even though 4.2% is pretty small beer now.

Or is the Brains beer that you want Dissolution, a rich, full-bodied Belgian Dubbel draped in an aromatic cloak of many flavours? Or perhaps A-Pork-Alypse, a so-called double chocolate and bacon porter, with grilled bacon added to the boil? That's the thing about Brains these days – the brewing team, led by Bill Dobson, has a Janus-like face with which to bedevil the drinker. On the one hand, there are the bread-and-butter beers such as Dark, SA and SA Gold, but then there are also the beers that pour out of the Brains Craft Brewery. In common with several other family breweries such as St Austell, Greene King and Thwaites, Brains are riding the craft beer revolution, happy to show the geeks that they're not just brewers of 'brown beer'.

THE CRAFT BEER REVOLUTION

When asked about the motivation behind the establishment of the 10-barrel brewing kit that was installed in 2012, Dobson cites a desire to develop new brands to appeal to younger consumers as well 'as experiment on the fringes of the beer category without having an impact on our core brands. With the craft brewery we wanted to have the link back to the heritage and quality of our main brand but also appeal to a new set of consumers'.

A magnificent range of beers has been brewed on the micro-kit, some of them in collaboration with publicans and beer writers, but most have been the work of Dobson and the team, demonstrating that family brewers can be just as creative and esoteric as any hopster/hipster start-up.

SA Brain (to give it its proper name) has been brewing in the Welsh capital since 1882, and is the second oldest Welsh brewery (Felinfoel in Llanelli is the grandaddy). The brewery's beers have long been associated with South Wales and the Valleys but it is only in the last few years that they have been creeping both northwards and across the border into the rest of the UK. The brewery has also been associated with the Welsh rugby team in various ways; at one stage the name appeared on the team's tops, which caused some problems when they played France in 2005. The advertising of alcoholic drinks is banned across the Channel, but the resourceful brewery got round this by substituting the word Brawn for Brains. In 2007, the words Brawn Again appeared on the shirts.

CARDIFF ROOTS

The brewery itself was originally in the city centre, where brew days would drape the streets with the warm fug of the boil. In 1999 the plant was decommissioned and Brains moved half a mile over the river to the former Hancock's brewery. This site was first used for brewing in 1868 and was the home of another great South Wales beer, Hancock's HB (which is now contract brewed by Brains). It's a traditional brewery, though uniquely its coppers are outside; and the building is busy and bustling. On brew days steam swirls and twirls from the roof, while inside the brewers check temperatures, write out brew sheets or glide along to the hop store and take their pick. And at some stage during the day brewers will be dipping in and out of the sampling cellar, aiming to check out the quality of the beers brewed. 'Beer tasting should be by committee,' says Dobson, 'we all know each other's strengths. When we start we always start with beer that has the lowest flavour impact. This is a working cellar, it's not something for the pensioners of the company or for entertaining.'

Left: The Yard Bar & Kitchen stands on the site of the original Old Brewery. **Right:** Brains' coppers are on the outside of the brewery

Beers to try...

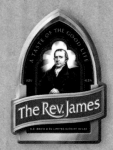

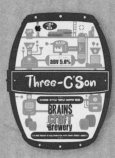

SA Gold, 4.3%

Orange fruit gums on the nose, while there's more orange fruitiness on the palate, contrasting well with the firm but friendly bitterness that lingers around in the finish.

Rev James, 4.5%

Formerly brewed by Buckley's, this has caramel hints on the nose, along with a whisper of toffee; the mouthfeel is spritzy and creamy while the finish is dry and bittersweet.

Three-C'son, 5%

Pale and hazy saison, with a sweet-sour nose; on the palate a green apple snappiness, medium sweetness, a hint of white pepper and a mousse-like carbonation. *This limited-run special from the craft brewery was brewed with Brains by Adrian Tierney-Jones.*

Walk round the city and you'll see a variety of Brains' pubs (the company has over 270 throughout Wales). The Goat Major is a venerable three-storied gem with dark wood and brass railings, while the Yard Bar & Kitchen is a brilliant re-imagining of the former Old Brewery into a slick and comfortable place; the modern world of design making use of yesteryear. Then there is the City Arms, within a dropkick of the Millennium Stadium; for want of a better word this is Brains' craft pub where their beers and others are proffered to eager drinkers.

The great thing about Brains is that not only have they survived the rollercoaster ride that British brewing and beer has been on since the late 19th century, but that they have learnt and earned their accolades and place in the British (and Welsh) sun. Meanwhile their craft brewery shows that the trend for regional brewing experimentation can only add to the excitement that surrounds beer at the moment. Boring brown beer? I think not.

The City Arms is one of several Brains pubs in the centre of Cardiff, serving a good selection of their beers, including examples from the craft brewery

MOTLEY BREW
ABV 7.5%
500ML

Motley Brew is Otley's American-style double IPA. Like all of Otley's beers, the beer name pays reference to the name of the brewery

Established: 2005

Founder: Nick, Charlie and Matthew Otley

Beers: O1, O4 Colombo, O2 Croeso, O3 Boss, O9 Blonde, O5 Gold, Oxymoron, O6 Porter, Motley Brew, O8

Website: www.otleybrewing.co.uk

OTLEY

Pontypridd, Mid Glamorgan

It's lunchtime at the Otley brewery, on an industrial estate just outside Pontypridd in Mid Glamorgan, and a scene similar to that being played out at hundreds of breweries up and down the land can be seen and heard.

In the stainless steel kettle the boil is rolling and roiling to its natural end, while a fermenting vessel is being made ready to welcome the new brew. Around the brewery the clanging of metal casks competes with the radio, while the swish of water intrudes from outside as a high-powered hose is used to dowse and wash casks. There's a sugary and tea-like aroma in the air, warm and slightly heady, the familiar scent of a brewery on brewing day.

This is the hour when the labour of the day starts surging to its climax; the result of the 8.30am session, when the brewers stood around, mugs of tea in hand, looking at brewing sheets, and deciding what to make; this is the time when that beginning comes to its glorious fruition. And as soon as the fermenting vessel is full of the cooled hopped wort, up the stepladder goes head brewer Matthew Otley with a bucket of beige-coloured sludgy yeast ready to pitch it in and start fermentation.

Today the beer being kick-started into life is O1, the brewery's debut beer when they started in 2005. Within four weeks this bittersweet barnstormer of a session beer, which is the colour of a sun-dried bale of summer hay, will be in countless glasses up and down Wales and beyond. Otley has come a long way since it took up the brewing game.

CRAFT BEER PIONEERS

Nick Otley is the brewery's co-founder and managing director, a cordial soul who has been quoted as describing the secret to good brewing as 'consistency, innovation, cleanliness and a dose of insanity'. He's hardly your typical beer industry type, having spent 10 years as a fashion photographer around the world before returning to Pontypridd to set up the brewery with his cousin Charlie and nephew Matthew; the family already had their roots in the pub trade with Nick's father

the secret to good brewing is "consistency, innovation, cleanliness and a dose of insanity"

Otley's O9 wheat beer was previously called O-Garden – a tongue-in-cheek reference to the iconic Belgian beer

O-GARDEN
ABV 4.8%
500ML

buying his first pub in Pontypridd in 1975. This was the Otley Arms and there are now two other family-owned pubs in the district: the Bunch of Grapes and the King's Arms in Pentyrch.

As well as looking after the brewery, Nick is the landlord of the Bunch of Grapes, where great food and superlative beer, wine and cider are dispensed in a modern and comfortable ambience. The Bunch of Grapes also hosts a Beer Academy: a focal point and social club for beer enthusiasts.

'We started because we couldn't find anyone brewing the type of beer we wanted to drink and sell,' he says, 'we wanted a bigger punch of hops and a cleaner lighter beer than what was being produced,

which was mostly mass-produced bland and malt-led. We knew from running pubs already it was the type of beer our customers would want to drink also. It was really hard to get out there at that time, it was before craft beer had become fashionable and there were only a handful of microbrewers producing beers. We were the eighth brewery in Wales, I think now there are nearly 100.'

STYLISED AND SMART

Otley's route into the beer world was a slightly different one to the one that a lot of breweries were taking at the time. For a start the branding of the bottles and pump clips was stylised and smarter,

"We started because we couldn't find anyone brewing the type of beer we wanted to drink and sell. We wanted a bigger punch of hops and a cleaner lighter beer than what was being produced"

"We aren't though prepared to rest on our laurels, we are continually re-inventing and we want to push our boundaries and still surprise people with innovative and inspiring beers."

while the beers were named O1, O2 and so on – this was a modern and artful way of making and selling beer. The beers were also pale and golden in colour, which was very much in keeping with the zeitgeist of the time. The brewery celebrated hop character (or 'punch' as Nick Otley would have it) with plenty of aromatic and citrusy notes on the nose and the palate (US hops were somewhere in the mix, though not exclusively).

Since then darkness has wormed its way into the Otley canon, best represented by the ironically named Oxymoron, which is that most divisive of beer styles, a Black IPA. There's also O6 Porter, a deep flavoured and rich porter with plenty of chocolate and coffee notes.

'When we started BrewDog wasn't around,' recalls Otley, 'and it was rare to see Sierra Nevada in any form other than the odd bottle. Wye Valley's HPA was the beer we modelled our first beer on, other than that we made a decision not to be influenced by others and to just make beers that we wanted to make.'

However ask Nick Otley what beer most represents the spirit of the brewery you get a definite answer. 'O8 our 8% golden ale,' he says, 'sadly it's not made as often now as it once was, thanks to beer duty, but it delivers flavour and complexity you don't expect but never forget.

'We are still a fairly new brewery but now one of the established micros. We aren't the type of brewery that wants to "rebel or revolt", against what

Beers to try...

O5, 5%
A luscious golden ale that has the chiming, ringing notes of a Riesling and is light and fruity on the palate; imagine a duet between local Ponty boy Tom Jones and Cardiff girl Charlotte Church.

Oxymoron, 5.5%
Midnight black in colour with a massive aroma of pine, earthy hops and some subtle roastiness. On the palate, it's spicy, citrusy, piny and has an assertive bitterness in the finish; one of the best of this much-maligned style.

O8, 8%
Bruised gold in the glass, with a rich, pungent fruity nose, think citrus and ripe apricot skin. It's rich and indulgent in the mouth, with plenty of fruit and easy to drink for its strength. Very cheese friendly.

I don't know? We are quietly confident and go about our business. We aren't though prepared to rest on our laurels, we are continually re-inventing and we want to push our boundaries and still surprise people with innovative and inspiring beers.'

Managing director Lawrence Washington

Established: 2005

Founder: Lawrence Washington

Beers: Cwrw Eryri/Snowdonia Ale, Cwrw Madog/Madog's Ale, Calon Lân, Cwrw Ysgawen/Elderflower Ale, Myrica Gale/Bog Myrtle Ale, Cwrw Glaslyn/Glaslyn Ale, Ochr Tywyll y Mws/Dark Side of the Moose, Merry X-Moose

Website: www.purplemoose.co.uk

PURPLE MOOSE

Porthmadog, Gwynedd

Brewery founder Lawrence Washington is a Pink Floyd fan, which is why one of his most popular and award-winning beers is called Dark Side of the Moose. A bit of a painful pun perhaps, but there's no doubting the exemplary nature of this rich dark beer with its complex grid of grain, roast barley and citrus fruit on the nose, followed by a blast of coffee beans, smoke, caramel, rich citrus fruitiness on the palate and finally ending its sojourn in the sun with a dry finish in which the flavour of fruit gums briefly appear. The beer drinker's need for taxonomy when it comes to the liquid in our glass could be flummoxed when trying to put this beautiful beer in a style category – is it a stout, a strong mild, a porter or even an old ale?

Such thoughts of style classification do not trouble Washington, for whom Dark Side of the Moose is one of two beers (the other is the elderflower-flavoured Ysgawen) that best exemplify what Purple Moose is about.

'It does not really fit into any of the traditionally established British beer styles,' he says, 'it came about through my own preference for dark beers and earlier experiments with beer recipes. We simply refer to it as a dark bitter. Anyway, whether or not you can pigeon-hole this beer, I think it has done rather well for itself, creating quite a following among beer enthusiasts and regular pub-goers.'

The brewery was originally a 10-barrel plant operating out of a former furniture warehouse, but new equipment was installed in 2013, significantly increasing production

"What we did set out to do though, right from the outset, was to make our beers to the highest possible standard we could achieve"

CREATING A RANGE

Purple Moose can be found down a backstreet in the small town of Porthmadog, which sits between Snowdonia and the Lleyn Peninsula – it's a beautiful part of the world and hot-spot for tourists. The brewery is diagonally opposite a chapel, an ironic comment, perhaps, on the twin attractions of pub and pulpit that often used to get the Welsh in such a lather. Washington opened the brewery in 2005, having spent the previous years visiting the area to work on the Welsh Highland Railway and walk in the hills. He was also a consummate home brewer, with plenty of experience, so his beers started winning awards early on.

'When we started out in 2005 I didn't see any point in re-inventing the wheel,' he says. 'It was more a case of creating a range of beers of well-established British styles to suit different tastes. What we did set out to do though, right from the outset, was to make our beers to the highest possible standard we could achieve and maintain that standard without fluctuations in consistency.'

Lawrence Washington brews his award-winning beers on a 40-barrel plant in the coastal town of Porthmadog

You could say that he has succeeded as nearly a decade after it opened, Purple Moose has seen a steady stream of awards for its beers; these triumphs have helped to establish them in an area that in the past was not noted for its artisanal brewing. The brewery was also was one of the first of a new wave of North Wales breweries that now include Conwy, Great Orme and Bragdy Nant (the four of them share the lease and running of the Albion Ale House in Conwy, which showcases their beers alongside guest ales and Welsh ciders).

LOOKING FOWARD

As for the future, Washington says that the aim is 'to carry on doing what we do best – creating really popular beers for all tastes. I have no great desire to be too experimental. I take the view that while it is working, and working really well, why change anything? That's not to say that we don't have a little spare capacity to try something a little different now and then.

'It will be our tenth anniversary in June 2015. I feel this should be suitably marked with a special beer of some form or other, but I'm keeping a tight secret on my plans for this just now!'

Beers to try ...

Cwrw Eryri/Snowdonia Ale, 3.6%
Sparkling golden in colour, this crisp and bittersweet session beer has a hint of citrus on the nose, with more citrus on the palate, alongside some pine notes; the finish is dry and bitter.

Cwrw Ysgawen/ Elderflower Ale, 4%
Refreshing summer beer that sees Cascade hops added alongside elderflowers; the result is a fragrant fruity nose while on the palate it's bittersweet and honeyed with a crisp finish.

Ingredients...

SAVING BRITISH HOPS AND BARLEY

The French word *terroir*, widely used in the wine industry to indicate that the character of grapes is influenced by geography, soil and climate, is equally applicable to barley and hops, and brewers are becoming increasingly conscious of the *terroir* of their ingredients. Hops need sandy and loamy soil that retains the water needed for them to grow and flourish. East Kent is ideal for growing, which is why the East Kent Golding is a much prized hop.

Unfortunately English hops have been in crisis as a result of another growing trend among artisan brewers in Britain – importing hops from the US to brew American-style aggressively hopped ales. The problem has been compounded by global brewers based in Britain who import hops developed for lager production from Europe and the Far East. But a spirited campaign has been launched to save and revive the fortunes of the plant. Dr Peter Darby, a world expert on hop development, has set up Wye Hops. Based in Kent, Dr Darby has developed new hop varieties such as Boadicea and Sovereign by taking pollen from selected plants and cross-breeding them. His work has been boosted by the arrival of Ali Capper, who has transformed the sleepy British Hop Association as a result of a whirlwind of activity. With her husband Richard, she grows hops at Stocks Farm in Worcestershire on 100 acres of land, and also tirelessly tours the country delivering talks to brewers on the wonders of English hops and the need to use and preserve them.

As a result of this campaign, English hops are beginning to enjoy a small revival as drinkers' tastes change. Ali Capper says, 'English hops are more delicate yet complex and give great drinkability to beer'.

But Capper and Darby are not oblivious to the popularity of more pronounced citrus flavours. They crossed an English hop with American Cascade to launch Endeavour in 2013, grown at Stocks Farm. The result is a hop with a more restrained grapefruit/peach/melon character than American varieties but one that nevertheless should appeal to those entranced by 'hop forward' beers.

Brewers are also responding to the challenge. Both Hogs Back Brewery in Surrey and Meantime in London are developing their own hop gardens and the plant is also being grown in East Yorkshire. Home brewer Matt Hall and farmer Chris Bradley have joined forces to grow hops on 2½ acres at Ellerker Farm near Hull and the first crop was used in 2014 by small brewers in the region.

Barley

Britain has the good fortune to be an island where it's possible to grow the finest 'maritime barley' – varieties that grow in dark, alluvial soil, much of it reclaimed from the sea, and warmed by both sun and sea breezes. While hop farmers are forward-looking and develop new varieties, it's a case of 'back to the future' for barley. There is great demand from craft brewers for Maris Otter, a variety of barley phased out years ago by big farmers and malting companies on the grounds that it is 'low yielding' compared to newer varieties.

Teddy Maufe grows Maris Otter on 220 acres at Branthill Farm near King's Lynn in Norfolk. He says the coastal climate and loamy soil are ideal for growing the barley. Maufe has introduced a system of traceability and can tell brewers precisely where their supply of grain is grown. 'One brewer even puts the grid reference of the field on his bottle label,' he says.

Many brewers make perfectly tasty beer without Maris Otter. The Concerto variety plays harmonious tunes in the brewery while the aptly-named Tipple has quickly become popular. But, overwhelmingly, Maris Otter remains the barley of choice for artisan brewers.

Ali Capper is a hop grower based in Worcestershire, as well as a tireless advocate of the use of English hops

Established: 2012

Founder: Gareth Williams, Bradley Cummings

Beers: Doc Brown, Hank, Flux, Fubar, Beat Box, Goldie Lookin' Ale, Loki, Billabong, Cwtch, The Full Nelson, Zool, Dirty Stopout, Urban IPA, The Vader Shuffle, Oldstock, Chocoholic, Hadouken

Website: www.tinyrebel.co.uk

TINY REBEL

Newport, Gwent

There's a brashness and boldness about Tiny Rebel's branding that is explosively mirrored in the beers they brew. They use graffiti-style fonts and the central character of their branding is a slumped, slightly dishevelled teddy bear in a hoodie, who looks like he's just slunk back from a good night out. The beers are equally rock'n'roll: plenty of hops; experimentation with various yeast strains and the occasional dabble in barrel-ageing.

Tiny Rebel have come a long way since bursting onto the Welsh beer scene in 2012. A year later they swept the board at CAMRA's Champion Beer of Wales competition, winning gold, silver and bronze; 2013 also saw the opening of their dedicated craft beer bar in Cardiff, the Urban Tap House.

'Our inspiration for beers are quite simple, we brew styles that we like to drink ourselves,' says brewer Gareth 'Gazz' Williams, who co-founded the brewery with brother-in-law Bradley Cummings. 'We would describe ourselves as a brewery that not only makes diverse beer but one that tries to connect with people through our branding and marketing. What we like to call a new-age brewery trying to change the perception of ale being old-fashioned and for the older generation.'

FILLING A VOID

Williams is another home brewer who has made a passion and hobby into his day job. He started brewing in his early twenties, inspired by his grandfather who made his own ginger beer. In 2010 he and Bradley decided that they would have to go pro, but it took another two years for Tiny Rebel to open for business.

"As over-enthusiastic home brewers we felt there was a big void in the brewing industry with very little connection to the younger generations of beer drinkers, hence the reason for our bold and modern branding."

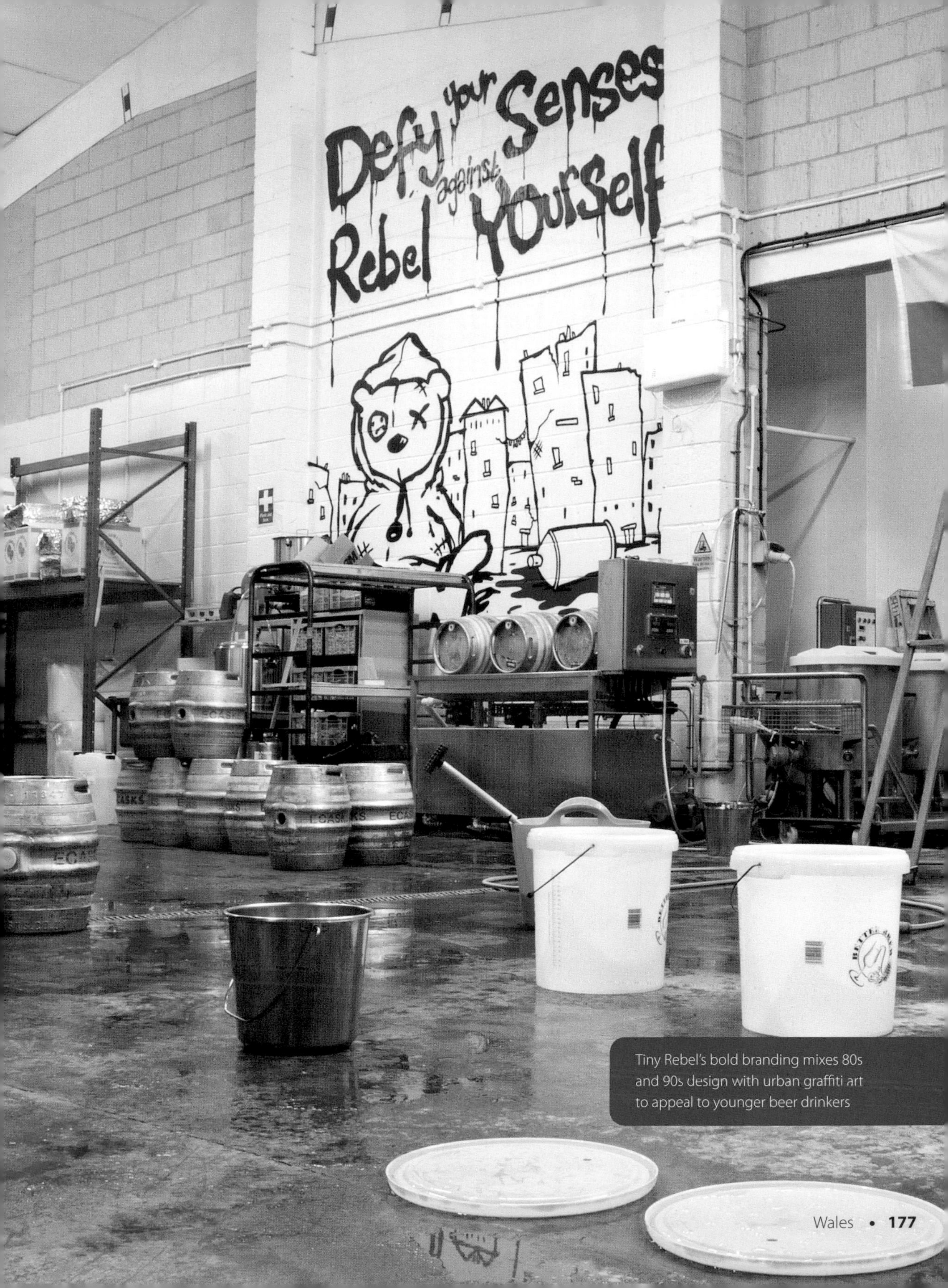

Defy your Senses
against
Rebel Yourself

Tiny Rebel's bold branding mixes 80s and 90s design with urban graffiti art to appeal to younger beer drinkers

"Our head brewer is a bit of a yeast addict"

'As over-enthusiastic home brewers we felt there was a big void in the brewing industry with very little connection to the younger generations of beer drinkers,' says Williams, 'hence the reason for our bold and modern branding. A lot of our branding ideas are reminiscent of 80s and 90s style genres with a good mix of urban style graffiti art. Coming from Wales we didn't grow up being blessed with the option of variety because of the dominance of our regional brewery. This almost subconsciously pushed us to be more progressive in what we're doing.'

BEERS WITH ATTITUDE

For Williams and Cummins, this attitude translates into beers such as Fubar, which is described as a classic American Pale Ale, and the 'amplified IPA' Hadouken, muscular in the glass and hopped with three US varieties. On the other hand, Oldstock is a nod to English brewing traditions and has black treacle and six different malts in the mix. Beers are also barrel-aged with up to eight oak barrels used a year. 2013 saw Ardbeg, Jim Beam, Jack Daniels, Kentucky Rye, Morgan Spiced Rum and Canadian

Bourbon-aged beers, while 2014's beers slept the sleep of the just in Chardonnay, Ardbeg, Woodford Reserve and Heaven Hills oak casks; Tiny Rebel is a brewery that believes in exploration.

However, ask Williams which beers best express what Tiny Rebel is all about, then he points to the 'Tiny Batch' editions that use specialist yeast strains from around the world.

'Our head brewer is a bit of a yeast addict,' he says. 'We have brewed beers with authentic style Belgian strains, Belgian blended strains, saison strains, *Brett* strains, lactic style strains, Bohemian lager style strains, English strains, American strains, German Weisse strains and American strains. We have banned dry yeast in the brewery!'

Tiny Rebel's growth has been phenomenal and as well as Fubar being pronounced Champion Beer of Wales in 2014, it has also opened the Urban Tap House in Cardiff. 'People used to ask us what our goal was,' says Williams, "ultimately it was to operate a comfortable size brewery and own our own bar in South Wales, serving the best beers from around the world. What makes it special? 120+ beers, 30+ ciders, enough spirits to keep you busy and Cardiff's best burgers.'

Not bad for a dishevelled teddy bear in a hoodie.

Beers to try ...

Dirty Stopout, 5.2%
Creamy smoked-oat stout brimming with mocha, liquorice and smoke aromatics, while chocolate, coffee and cola claim the palate before the dry, lightly smoked finish.

Urban IPA, 5.5%
Lemon pie initially makes the running on the nose, followed by a whiff of green, earthy hoppiness; the mouthfeel is juicy, citrusy and bittersweet with a growing bitterness in the finish.

Hadouken, 7.4%
Powerful aromas of Cointreau, grain, resin and pine; the palate has an orange and tangerine surge followed by a dry graininess and long ranging bitter finish.

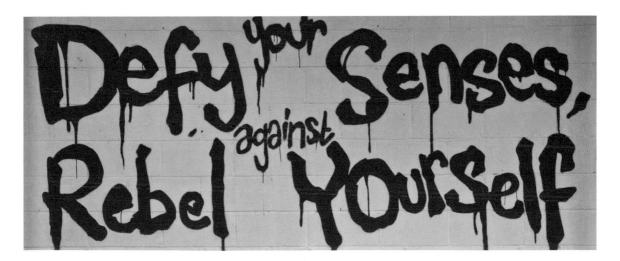

Established: 2009

Founder: Sue Hayward and John Martin

Beers: TWA, Blackberry Stout, Pamplemousse, Janner's Pride, Festival Gold, Landmark, Chilli Plum Porter, Snowball

Website: www.thewaenbrewery.co.uk

WAEN

Llanidloes, Powys

We brew what we like to drink. It's a sentiment shared amongst many of Britain's brewing revolutionaries and something that Waen Brewery's co-founder and brewer Sue Hayward passionately believes in. 'I have a personal dislike of mediocrity,' she says, 'I loathe "safe beers" that are there to please the masses. Anyone can brew those... and plenty do.'

These are not safe beers. Chilli Plum Porter which, as the name suggests, is a dark chocolaty porter with chilli and plums added to the mix. Or maybe it's the Blackberry Stout, an equally brooding beer where the mocha coffee notes smoothly blend in with an undertone of subtle tart fruitiness.

'I want to experiment, and push the boundaries a little whilst still making excellent quality beer,' she says. 'I have a liking for things a little out of the ordinary, so it is natural that this comes through in

"I loathe 'safe beers' that are there to please the masses. Anyone can brew those... and plenty do."

the beers we make. Having said that, I have tasted some awful "speciality beers" that are just flavours thrown in for effect. The beer still has to be a good one and the flavours subtle. We sell as much of Chilli Plum Porter as we do any other beer, and that's because it is drinkable and moreish, as well as being unusual.'

LIGHT BULB MOMENT

One-time home brewer Hayward and her husband John Martin started Waen in Penstrowed in 2009. Looking back at the early beers you could argue that they were a mixture of outliers such as the Blackberry Stout and more restrained beers, very much on a par for the micro-brewing course. However, after a conversation with fellow brewer and hophead extraordinaire Gazza Prescott from Hopcraft brewery, a light bulb flashed on above Hayward's head.

'I immediately wiped most of our "regular" beers off the brewing schedule and decided that from now on we would be brewing what we want, when we want, and would be constantly going to be producing something different.'

Brewing is a family endeavour for John Martin and Sue Hayward

'and this seems to transpose into taste and aromas to me in beer recipes. We've not had a beer that doesn't work yet!

'I really can't characterise us as we change constantly. We are innovative, and don't bow to the mass brown beer drinker but we are neither bonkers nor mediocre, hopefully we sit somewhere in the middle!'

Part of this constant restlessness has seen the opening of the Gravity Station in Cardiff, Waen's hybrid bottle shop and bar. All the cask beers are gravity dispensed, while the bottles on sale are from lesser-known UK brewers as well as ones from around the world. Even here, Hayward tried to demonstrate her single-minded approach, but this time she met her match.

'We are lucky we have a good manager because for instance I'd have no Belgian beers at all, fantastic though they are. Everyone has them, so to my way of thinking that's a reason for us not to! However, Jim [Swidenbank] persuaded me otherwise and we have a good selection now including Boon, Orval and Rodenbach!'

For her brewing inspiration, Hayward is equally quixotic, looking beyond the world of beer, to that of food and, more obliquely, art and design. 'Colours and textures go or don't go together,' says Hayward,

Beers to try ...

Pamplemousse, 4.2%
Bruised gold in colour, and packed full of fresh US hop goodness, this is a juicy, sun-blessed pale ale with a zingy bitterness and an appetising dryness in the finish.

Chilli Plum Porter, 6.1%
Creamy, chocolaty, rich and warm-hearted, with a mild invigorating chilli hit at the back of the throat. A stunning example of how to use chilli in beer.

Snowball, 7%
Luscious chocolate-coconut-vanilla stout with a smooth, creamy mouthfeel, sensuous vanilla and coconut notes and a deep rugged chocolate character. Bittersweet with a dry finish.

BEER DESTINATIONS

Conwy

Pontypridd
Llantrisant
Cardiff

CITY ARMS
Cardiff
www.thecityarmscardiff.com

Peer through the mullioned windows at the front of the City Arms and you'll see the Millennium Stadium looming at the end of the street. Take a stroll through the pub and note the walls dotted with sepia-toned prints of yesteryear, including old rugby teams and star players, plus plenty of beery memorabilia. Rugby and beer have always scrummed down together but in the City Arms their comradeship is celebrated with try-scoring gusto. So it's just as well that there's plenty of beer to drink. The bar sits in the middle of the pub, an engine room of beer offering four cask beers from owners Brains, as well as a brace of their specialist craft beers and four others from all over the country, plus a couple more served straight from the barrel. Breweries making their appearance include Thornbridge, Oakham, Driftwood Spars, Brentwood and RCH, while the bottled speciality beers range from Schlenkerla's Rauchbier to a variety of imported American hop bombs.

URBAN TAP HOUSE
Cardiff
www.urbantaphouse.co.uk

Tiny Rebel opened this energetic beer temple in the autumn of 2013 and it fast became a destination go-to place in an area that has become known as Cardiff's 'craft beer quarter'. Here drinkers sample the Newport brewery's boldly flavoured beers, whether it's regulars such as Dirty Stop Out or their quirky (often well-hopped) specials. As for other beers, expect pints from equally crafty breweries such as Magic Rock, Alechemy and Arbor,

alongside a great selection of foreign bottled beers. The Tap dispenses this great beer-flavoured fun across five different rooms on two floors, with music and video games adding an extra frisson.

ALBION ALE HOUSE
Conwy, North Wales
01492 582484

The Albion Ale House is an architectural time capsule, which has been basically left alone since the 1920s when its then brewery owners remodelled it in the style of the times. Think Art Nouveau tiling in the lobby, Art Deco flourishes here and there and plenty of timber and red brick throughout its three drinking spaces. It was shut in 2011 but a local businessman organised four local breweries (Conwy, Bragdy Nant, Purple Moose and Great Orme) to come together and run it. This is unashamedly a place to celebrate the pub and beer, with eight cask beers normally available (made up of beers from the four local breweries and guests from far and wide). In 2013 it was awarded CAMRA Wales' Pub of the Year.

WHEATSHEAF ROOMS
Llantrisant, Mid Glamorgan
www.wheatsheafllantrisant.com

Old-school town hotel that was home to a microbrewery under the previous landlord. When he left locals and lovers of beer feared the worse but Caerphilly-based Celt Experience rode to the rescue and they have turned it into a stunningly celebratory palace of beer. As well as the brewery's own beers, punchy and pulsating with hop character, there are selections of boldly flavoured beers from across the country. The interior

is minimalist stone and wood and each room has a name such as the Porter Room, where there's a stylised map of the route Imperial porters took to Russia, as well as an open fire for when the weather turns Baltic as well. The Tap Room features a tantalising wall-mounted display of cask and keg taps, the numbers on them referring to the beer list of constantly rotating guests chalked up on the wall.

BUNCH OF GRAPES
Pontypridd, Mid Glamorgan
www.bunchofgrapes.org.uk

When Otley brewery took over this 19th century former alehouse in 2001 they stripped it back to its basics, uncovered an old fireplace and set about making it a beer paradise in the heart of Pontypridd. The brewery was successful. Now the interior is comfortable and modern where regulars enjoy their beers at the front bar or settle in various nooks and crannies. The food is excellent (food and beer nights are a regular occurance), while the beer choice includes nine hand pulls, dispensing some of Otley's boldly flavoured beers as well as beers from craft breweries up and down the land (there are also beer festivals). The fridges are also rammed by beery delights, including bottles from London stars such as Kernel and Brew By Numbers, plus the international likes of Founders, Flying Dog and Norge.

The Wheatsheaf Rooms in Lantrisant has been turned into a stunning celebration of beer by Caerphilly-based brewery Celt Experience

NORTH WEST ENGLAND

CHESHIRE, CUMBRIA, GREATER MANCHESTER, LANCASHIRE, MERSEYSIDE

Is Manchester bitter? It could be if you went into a pub run by JW Lees, where the drink of choice would be their robust bitter: a classic Mancunian pint, smooth and luscious in its mouthfeel, a twang of dryness mid-palate and brisk and bittersweet on the finish, the kind of beer usually associated with this part of the Northwest. If you're doing a pub-crawl in the city you can also discover bitters from Hydes, Holts and Robinsons, though they also have mild and golden ale in their portfolios, alongside seasonal choices. Meanwhile, Robinsons' Old Tom (which is also available in forgettable ginger and chocolate versions) is a peerless old ale/barley wine crossover that has few equals. There's more in Manchester: once a year JW Lees adds to this celebration of muscle-flexing, Samson-like beers when they brew their magical Harvest Ale and some of it is put to slumber in a variety of wooden barrels, including those that once hosted calvados, port and sherry.

Yet let's not cast aspersions on the bitter culture of Greater Manchester and the breweries in the rest of the Northwest. There is a groundswell of support for the traditional bitters that several generations have

BEER DESTINATIONS
> go to page 208

Cumbrian Legendary Ales: Hawkshead, Cumbria

Hawkshead: Staveley, Cumbria

Dunham Massey: Altrincham, Cheshire

Marble: Manchester

RedWillow: Macclesfield, Cheshire

Liverpool Organic: Liverpool, Merseyside

Hawkshead

Staveley

Liverpool

Manchester

Altrincham

Macclesfield

been brought up on. Burnley-based Moorhouse's continues to thrive, producing beers brushed with a distinctive bitterness such as the creamy Premier Bitter and the full-bodied and fruity Pendle Witches Brew. Even though it's classed by the brewery as a speciality ale rather than a mild these days, the brewery's Black Cat is both smooth and chewy, an exemplary beer. Let's also think of Allgates, who returned brewing back to Wigan for the first time in over 30 years; the brewing team mixes and matches bitter and mild, alongside US pale ale and their rich and intense imperial stout Mad Monk. At 7.1% and

The Baltic Fleet pub in Liverpool brews a range of beers in its cellar brewery

only available during the first month of the year this makes a delicious nonsense of 'dry January'.

Thwaites is another giant of the Northwest, whose bread-and-butter beers are also a best bitter and a mild, with seasonal beers thrown in (they also contract brew Kaltenberg Hell). However, they added to the complexity of beer in the Northwest in 2007 with the launch of the golden ale Wainwright to celebrate their 200th anniversary. This seemed to be a catalyst for the brewery to delve deeper into a totally different beer universe. The result was the 'Crafty Dan' range of beers, brewed on a micro kit, including the American-style IPA 13 Guns, a black IPA, a chocolate stout, a fruit beer with loganberries and a cherry mild. It might not seem revolutionary compared to many US craft breweries, but this is the Northwest and for a regional brewery like Thwaites this is revolutionary.

South of Manchester, Liverpool and its surrounding area continues to thrive as breweries spring up: Liverpool Organic mixes up bold flavours with an ecological approach, while old-school dockside pub the Baltic Fleet uses its cellar brewing kit to bring out beers as diverse as a sprightly golden ale and a brooding smoked porter. For anyone au fait with the London beer scene there's a familiar style about Liverpool Craft Beer Co: they brew in a railway arch and beers include a Cascadian Dark (another name for black IPA) and a 'wheat ale'.

Finally, let's take ourselves further north, past Manchester and up to Cumbria. Is Cumbria bitter? It might be, but not if you order a bottle of Hardknott's Vitesse Noir, a self-styled Triple Imperial Vanilla Mocha Stout, which is midnight in the glass, the darkness softened by a gentle breeze of mellow mocha and vanilla on the nose while chocolate and mocha notes all wrap themselves up in a vanilla elegance before a long bittersweet finish. Or you might like to head eastwards from Hardknott to the Lake District to the village of Staveley, where Hawkshead have their brewery

Liverpool Organic mixes up bold flavours with an ecological approach, while old-school dockside pub the Baltic Fleet uses its cellar brewing kit to bring out beers as diverse as a sprightly golden ale and a brooding smoked porter

(and adjoining Beer Hall, bar, visitor centre, beer shop and beer kitchen all rolled into one). Here, you can enjoy such stunning beers as New Zealand Pale Ale with its fawn-like leap of grapefruit and grassy aromatics on the nose, a palate upon which sparks of bitterness, ripe orange peel and banana sweetness shimmy before a dry finish in which citrus notes linger. There are plenty of other highly accomplished breweries in the county: Stringer's Beer in Ulverston and Coniston brewery to name just two, whose beers include traditional session-style ales, potent award-winning barley wines, roasty stouts and smooth oatmeal stouts.

As is common with most other regions of the UK, the Northwest's beer profile is a fractured and complex one. Gone are the days of just mild and bitter (as clichéd an image as whippets, pigeons and clogs). The contemporary beer scene of the region is vital, explorative and gladiatorial: meeting the challenges of modern beer drinking head on. You could even argue that the whole idea of regional beer is vanishing as brewers look to the US and Europe for their inspiration, though there will always be beer drinkers who define their tastes by their location. That doesn't mean that their favourite brewery won't be afraid to experiment, and that is the all-embracing joy of the British brewing revolution: every brewery in every region now has a beer that speaks for it.

Insider's view...

Peter Alexander
tandlemanbeerblog.blogspot.co.uk

Manchester – all swagger and confidence – excites with its vibrant independent brewing scene and eclectic bars and pubs. Try the Northern Quarter's Soup Kitchen for great grub and beers from near and far. Or the Marble Arch with its tiled grandeur, own-brewed ales and a sloping floor to reckon with. Liverpool has the ornate Philarmonic or the grand Vines, stunning Victorian gin palaces and a certain something about the place.

But the Northwest is more than its powerhouse cities. In Cumbria, Hawkshead brew fantastic stuff in their Stavely Beer Hall and brewery. Lancaster has fine canal-side pubs and history. Or how about Ramsbottom? Travel on the preserved railway from Bury and drink Ramsbottom Craft Ales, or a hoppy pint from First Chop Brewing Arm in the tiny First Chop pub.

From leafy Cheshire to the Scottish border there are brilliant beers and pubs everywhere you look.

Peter Alexander blogs under the name Tandleman. He lives in Northwest England and is a beer author and beer reviewer

On the shores of Esthwaite Water, the brewing team at Cumbrian Legendary make their award-winning beers

Established: 2003

Founder: Roger Humphreys

Beers: Old Hall Dark Fruit Mild, Loweswater Pale Ale, Esthwaite Bitter, Langdale, Rannerdale Robin, Grasmoor Dark Ale, Loweswater Gold, Rothay Red, American Invasion

Website: www.cumbrianlegendaryales.com

CUMBRIAN LEGENDARY ALES

Hawkshead, Cumbria

If there's an award for the most idyllic brewery location in Britain, Cumbrian Legendary Ales would win hands down. The brewing plant is situated in converted barns: one barn dates from the 16th century and is of ancient cruck design with curved wooden timbers. The barns stand on the shores of Esthwaite Water. It's beautiful in summer, but in winter – with mist rising from the lake, hoar frost dusting the trees and snow-crusted Helvellyn mountain glowering in the background – it has a magical quality.

But you can't drink the view, so owner Roger Humphreys and his staff of eight have to turn their attention from the lake to their mash tun and copper and get on with the serious business of making beer.

They make it with considerable success. In 2011 their Loweswater Gold, a strong golden ale, won its class in the Champion Beer of Britain competition. The success not only put the brewery on the national map but it boosted sales, requiring additional fermenters to keep pace with demand. It's now Cumbrian Legendary's main brand and accounts for 70% of production, which runs at 60 barrels a week.

GOING FOR GOLD

The brewery started in a small way in 2003 in a back room of the Kirkstile Inn near Loweswater, almost lost in the lakes, hills and fells of the area, with Melbreak Mountain standing sentinel almost in the backyard. But the mix of stunning views, good beer, food and accommodation brought locals and visitors in droves to the inn, forcing Roger Humphreys to look for bigger premises and brewing equipment: the kit was designed and built in Kendal to fit with Roger's determination to support other local enterprises. At Esthwaite in 2009, he teamed

The casks are stamped with the brewery's name. They are proud of their Cumbrian heritage and there's no rush to go national

up with trained brewster Hayley Barton and they designed a range of beers that won plaudits in the Northwest and beyond, and mined gold in 2011 with the Champion Beer of Britain award. Much to Roger's disappointment, Hayley was head-hunted by Molson Coors and left in the summer of 2014 to work for Sharp's in Cornwall.

STAYING LOCAL

In spite of the success of the beers, Roger is not tempted to move to bigger premises. 'We're about the right size and we don't want to get bigger,' he says. 'We brew great beers for Cumbria – we don't want to go national with all the problems that can bring. 90% of our sales are in Cumbria.' Staying local doesn't mean thinking small, though. Roger and his team are constantly revising their beer list and designing new styles to meet current fashions. Recent additions to the range include American IPA using all-American hops, and Pacific Voyage that

"We're about the right size and we don't want to get bigger. We brew great beers for Cumbria – we don't want to go national with all the problems that can bring."

uses Kiwi varieties. The brewery has moved into the lager market with Buttermere Beauty, its take on a Pilsner, while Croglin Vampire, with a scary label, is a German-style strong Bock that bites your neck on the way down. Less esoteric needs are also met with LPA, a hoppy light bitter, while a traditional mild, Old Hall, has also been introduced.

The latest innovation came in 2014 with the addition of a bottling line that will allow Cumbrian Legendary to produce bottle-conditioned beers. That could mean the beers going national – but only in a small way.

Beers to try ...

Langdale, 4%
Brewed with Maris Otter, crystal and lager malts and hopped with English varieties. It has a tart and tangy orange-and-lemon fruit character, balanced by nutty malt and a long bittersweet, fruity finish.

Grasmoor Dark Ale, 4.3%
A rich and complex beer with a roasted grain and bitter hop character from chocolate and crystal malts. English hops add a fine balance of spice, pepper and pine wood.

Loweswater Gold, 4.3%
Fruit builds in the mouth but is balanced by juicy malt and cedar-like hops. The finish is bittersweet with lemon fruit vying for attention with bitter hop resins, butterscotch and creamy malt.

The brewery is situated on the shores of Esthwaite Water, and their pumpclips showcase Lake District scenery

Established: 2007

Founder: John Costello

Beers: Little Bollington Bitter, Chocolate Cherry Mild, Dunham Dark, Dunham Light, Mildly Ginger, Big Tree Bitter, Obelisk, Dunham Milk Stout, Landlady, Green Hop Beer, Ruby Sunset, Treacle Treat, Dunham Damson, Dunham Stout, Stamford Bitter, Duerr's Blossom Honey Beer, Summer Meadow, Deer Beer, Cheshire IPA, Altrincham Pilsner, Dunham Spice, Dunham Brown Ale, Dunham Porter, East India Pale Ale, Winter Warmer, Dunham Gold, Vintage Red, Vintage White

Website: www.dunhammasseybrewing.co.uk

DUNHAM MASSEY

Altrincham, Cheshire

Dunham Massey is a jaw-dropping success story. John Costello opened the brewery in 2007 and within the space of just seven years it has grown to such an extent that John has launched a second specialist micro-plant in Lymm with its own bar and has two other pubs in the area, including in the major town of Altrincham. Along the way he has picked up a fistful of awards for his beers at festivals as far away as Aberdeen and in 2014 he won the highly-prized Champion Winter Beer of Britain award for his Dunham Porter.

John worked for Tetley-Walker in Warrington for many years and developed a passion for beer, real ale in particular. When the Warrington brewery closed as a result of the break-up of Allied Breweries, John was determined to carry on brewing. He needed a suitable site and one arrived courtesy of the National Trust, which offered him a barn on a farm in the village of Dunham Massey. The building was badly run-down but John saw it had potential as a result of its size and its proximity to farmland. He is keen to use English ingredients in his beer and to help the environment. At Dunham Massey, he's been able to supply both grain and hops as animal feed and natural land fertiliser.

John, with family and friends, threw himself into converting the barn into a brewery and in the autumn of 2007 he launched his first beers, Big Tree Bitter (3.9%) and Stamford Bitter (4.2%), followed by 6.6% Winter Warmer.

The range of beers has blossomed, with more than 12 regular brews and a rolling programme of seasonals. Range is the fitting description as the beers include a traditional Northwest dark mild, a light mild, an immensely complex chocolate cherry mild, and two stouts, including a rare example of a milk stout made with the addition of lactose or 'milk sugar' that delivers a smooth, creamy palate. East India Pale Ale at 6% is a fine example of the style and is close to the strength of the original beers of the 19th century, while Dunham Gold at 7.2% is not just another golden ale but John's interpretation of a strong, straw-coloured Belgian beer, of which Duvel is the best-known example.

NATIONAL SUCCESS

In February 2014, Dunham Massey sprang to national attention when its Porter won CAMRA's winter champion beer award, a coveted prize that can open pub doors throughout the country. The beer is brewed with pale, crystal, black, brown and chocolate malts and is hopped with Fuggles.

As a result of the clamour for his beers, John and his small staff are brewing 30 barrels a week and are at full capacity. This explains the addition of the micro-plant in Lymm, which allows John to make small run beers there, many of which find their way on to the bar of two brewery taps and Costello's Bar in Altrincham.

The brewery is based on a farm, enabling John Costello to supply spent malt and hops to the farmer

Beers to try ...

Chocolate Cherry Mild, 3.8%
Packed with flavours of chocolate and coffee from the use of heavily-roasted dark malts and a dry, fruity palate and bittersweet finish from the addition of fruit. It has won five gold awards at beer festivals.

Big Tree Bitter, 3.9%
A full-bodied beer for its strength, with a rich biscuit malt note balanced by tart fruit and a powerful blast of spicy hops on the aroma and palate.

Dunham Porter, 5.2%
A massive aroma of bitter chocolate and espresso coffee, with liquorice and molasses building in the mouth, with hops adding a peppery note to the long, dry finish.

Top: Head brewer Matt Clarke and his team in the brewhouse. **Bottom:** Hawkshead's gleaming custom-built brewing vessels can be viewed from their Beer Hall

Established: 2002

Founder: Alex Brodie

Beers: Windermere Pale, Bitter, Red, Lakeland Gold, Dry Stone Stout, Great White, Brodie's Prime, Cumbrian Five Hop, Lakeland Lager, NZPA, IPA, Imperial Stout, Brodie's Prime Export

Website: www.hawksheadbrewery.co.uk

HAWKSHEAD

Staveley, Cumbria

Alex Brodie's route to success is the result of throwing away the rule book. 'For years, craft brewers followed the big brewers and made the same styles of beer,' he says. 'We don't do that any more.' He proves the point by listing just a few of the 18 beers he produces, including – controversially – a 'black IPA' for Booths' supermarkets, a strong ale aged in American Bourbon casks and an 'Oat Wine' with 40% oats in the recipe.

Brodie is that rare species – a journalist with a head for business. He worked for the BBC for many years and was the corporation's Middle East Correspondent before becoming one of the presenters on the flagship Radio 4 *Today* programme. But he wanted to settle down and spend more time with his wife, Anne. So he turned to his second love: beer. He was a long-standing CAMRA member and, with a journalist's skill in sniffing out an opportunity for a good story, opened a small brewery in 2002 in an ancient barn in Hawkshead, an area of the Lake District rich in Beatrix Potter associations. The success of his Bitter, Lakeland Gold and – a neat literary allusion – Brodie's Prime forced a move in 2006 to a custom-built plant at Staveley that he called the Beer Hall. As well as a brewery with custom-built German kit, there's a visitor centre, restaurant and observation hall where the brewing process can be watched at first hand. The food menu includes a good selection of tapas to complement the brewery's beers.

KIWI INFLUENCE

'When I started there was only me,' Brodie says. 'Now the place is full of enthusiasts.' They include head brewer Matt Clarke from New Zealand who has fashioned an impressive range of beers, including both an NZPA (New Zealand Pale Ale) – using such Kiwi hops as Nelson Sauvin, Motueka and Green Bullet – and a junior partner called Iti (the Maori for 'little') which is low in strength but packed full of fruity hop character.

The Lakeland range includes Lakeland Gold, brewed with Fuggles, Goldings and Cascade, which has won many plaudits, including CAMRA Champion Beer of Cumbria 2009 and 2012. Cumbrian Five Hop has gone down so well in the area that it was named CAMRA Champion Beer of the North West in 2013. As the name suggests, it bursts with hops and the varieties include Amarillo, Bramling Cross, Citra, Fuggles and Goldings.

DEFYING CONVENTION

Brodie and Clarke are prepared to defy convention. Their Dry Stone Stout is brewed with untreated, soft Lakeland water, whereas historically porter and stout, originating in London, used hard water rich in chloride from a chalk base. The end result is a beer with good roasted grain character backed by a solid hop base. A number of beers are the result of collaborations with other craft breweries, including Buxton and Magic Rock. There's a good sense of humour at work in the brewery: two beers aged in American Bourbon barrels are called Jack and Jim, with no prizes for guessing the distilleries that supplied the casks. Both beers are based on a souped-up version of Brodie's Prime called Export.

Production is running at 7,000 barrels a year and Brodie and his team almost had to remove the roof of the brewery to squeeze in an additional fermenting vessel. They're brewing to capacity and may eventually outgrow the present site.

As for black IPA, Alex Brodie agrees the name is something of a misnomer but it was brewed specifically for Booths' supermarkets and the company was keen on the style. Brodie wanted to call it Contradiction in Terms but there wasn't room on the label.

Visitors can relax with a glass of one of Hawkshead's many beers in their Beer Hall

Bitter, 3.7%

A conventional beer, for the brewery, using Maris Otter pale malt, crystal malt and First Gold and Styrian Goldings hops. It has a glowing copper colour, with a big aroma and palate of peppery hop resins, nutty malt and tart fruit.

Lakeland Gold, 4.4%

A pale bronze beer with a fruity/citrus nose, and earthy/peppery hops. Orange and lemon fruit build in the mouth with juicy malt and spicy, peppery hops in the finish.

Cumbrian Five Hop, 5%

Massive tropical fruit on nose and palate, with orange marmalade and herbal and grassy hops, and a long, complex finish combining biscuit malt, tart fruit and fruity hops.

"When I started there was only me. Now the place is full of enthusiasts"

Hawkshead has been inspired to brew a range of beers showcasing Kiwi hops

The final stage...
CASK TO GLASS

The pub licensee needs to be a person of many talents: a host at the bar; a hirer and trainer of staff (and occasionally firer); an accountant and stock-taker, a beer expert and sometimes a chef and/or brewer.

Not content with taking on these particular roles, the licensee must also be an expert dedicated to the quality of his/her beer cellar. If the beer is of poor quality, customers will vote with their feet and leave, or even start thinking that all cask beer is of a similar ilk.

The cellar is the out-of-sight engine room of the bar, the place where cask beer continues the journey that began in the brewery and ends in the drinker's glass. There's almost a secret society-like mystery about the art and science of good cellar management – words such as 'spile', 'fob' and 'ullage' suggest the arcane language of a lost tribe, while the process of getting beer in the cellar ready for service has a hint of the alchemical.

So it goes without saying that it's an absolute necessity for a successful licensee (and staff) to know how the cellar works, especially as many on the other side of the bar-top claim to be a beer expert these days. Times have also changed when it comes to tricks of the trade: no longer is tonic water tipped into the cask to help beer clear faster or slops poured back into the mild.

So what are the secrets of good cellar management, that allows drinkers to enjoy a glass of perfectly kept cask? Three experts spill the beans.

Manchester beer festival is held at the city's Velodrome and showcases over 500 beers

Becky Newman, landlady of the Bricklayers Arms, Putney, London

As with all things to do with food and drink it's hygiene, hygiene, hygiene. Running a pub/cellar is just extreme housework when you get right down to it. Lines should be cleaned and cellar floors scrubbed at least once a week. This will minimize the risk of yeast infections in the beer. You should also keep the cellar clutter free. It should be as pleasant a working environment as possible especially if you need to spend an entire morning down there getting organised before opening time!

Stuart Chapman-Edwards, landlord of the Albion Ale House, Conwy, North Wales

Once a beer is connected to the line and being served, air is drawn into the cask, which starts the deterioration of the product. This will take 3-4 days max. The whole cask needs to be served within this time frame. This is where some pubs get it wrong by using bigger casks than they can empty in this time, or by having too many real ales on their bar for their amount of sales. Therefore a good cellar-operative will always be thinking three days in advance. In a pub such as ours, which can easily have 40 different ales a week, this is the head-scratcher.

Peter Alexander, deputy organiser of the Manchester Beer and Cider Festival

There are simple rules for good cellaring. Keep it all clean and maintain your cask beer in the cellar at or around 10°C. Clean lines frequently, at least once a week and remember that all cask beers aren't the same so be guided by what happens when you vent. Use a porous hard spile wherever possible and test the beer frequently for clarity, smell, temperature and condition. Hard peg the beer at the end of each session with a non-porous hard spile and use a race spile if possible. The greatest joy for all this work is the perfect pint and people saying "that beer was spot on". Praise from customers is the best thing you can ask for.

> *"Running a pub/cellar is just extreme housework when you get right down to it. Lines should be cleaned and cellar floors scrubbed at least once a week. You should also keep the cellar clutter free. It should be as pleasant a working environment as possible"*

Established: 2009

Founder: Mark Hensby

Beers: Cascade, Iron Men, Joseph Williamson, Liverpool Pale Ale, Styrian, Jade, Bier Head, Best Bitter, 24 Carat Gold, Cambrinus Deliverance, Cambrinus Endurance, Liverpool Stout, William Roscoe, Honey Blond, Josephine Butler, Kitty Wilkinson, Liverpool Pilsner, Simcoe, Stella Gold, Cambrinus St Antonys, Empire Ale, Shipwreck IPA, Imperial Russian Stout

Website: www.liverpoolorganicbrewery.com

LIVERPOOL ORGANIC

Liverpool, Merseyside

Liverpool Organic takes a stand and sources only organic materials for its beers. According to the brewery's founder and managing director Mark Hensby, the reason for going organic is simple – he'd rather use malted barley that hasn't been sprayed with chemicals, even though organic malt is 50% more expensive than the conventional variant. There is a passionate desire to be more natural and sustainable with the beer that his company makes. A focus on the natural and sustainable is another feature that many of those at the forefront of Britain's brewing revolution have in common: it's not just about the hops and snazzy graphics (though popular hop varieties such as Citra and Cascade are frequent guests in Liverpool Organic's hop store).

ORGANIC FOCUS

First of all though, let's think about the brewery's

organic status: everyone likes a food and drink hero, but using organic materials is no guarantee of good beer. You might feel you're helping to save the world with the glass in your hand, but you still want to have a good beer inside it as well. The first wave of organic beers at the end of the 1990s was very much a ragtag army of good causes with several decent beers and a lot of indifferent ones. So it's good to report that Liverpool Organic tick all the boxes. Their beers are exceptional: a melodious mixture of bright bitters and briskly hopped pale ales and IPAs; on the dark side there's a perky Liverpool Stout in the company of the powerful and complex Imperial Russian Stout.

'Personally I like popular easy drinking beers like our 24 Carat Gold but I would say that we brew something for everyone,' says Hensby who jumped ship from the financial services world to found the brewery in the Liverpool suburb of Kirkdale in 2008 (it started trading a year later.) You could say that setting up the brewery was a bit of a lifestyle change. 'However, I also realise the demand for more overtly hoppy beers and I would place a lot of our beers at the predominantly high hop end.' He also says that there are plans to barrel-age some of the beers in oak barrels that previously held rum and Bourbon.

This is a brewery with a sense of its own mission. It is also a brewery that is comfortable celebrating its home city, with its 'Heroes of Liverpool' series of beers named after local notable figures. William Roscoe is a floral bitter celebrating one of the great anti-slavery campaigners, while Kitty Wilkinson was active in the fight against cholera in the 19th century and is remembered with a chocolate and vanilla stout. The brewery also dabbled in the historic beer recreation game in 2011 when they released their version of the city's historic Higsons Best Bitter, with the aid of Stewart Thompson, who was Higsons brewery chemist when it closed in 1990. The beer has since been renamed as Bier Head, but it retains the Higsons Liver Bird logo.

Beers to try ...

Liverpool Pale Ale, 4%
Pale and winsome in the glass with a beneficent blast of grapefruit on the nose; there's a bracing bitterness on the palate, more citrus and a lasting bittersweet finish.

Liverpool Stout, 4.7%
Midnight in the glass with a mixture of berries and liquorice on the nose; the mouthfeel is full-bodied and dark, with a brisk cascade of hoppy notes and coffee bean dryness in the finish.

Great tasting beer, a sustainable outlook and a joyous sense of community: it's time Liverpool Organic were inducted into their own 'Heroes of Liverpool' hall of fame.

Visitors to Liverpool Organic can enjoy a brewery tour, and sample the ales in a bar in the main brewing room where beers are served by members of the brewery staff

organic

LAGONDA IPA

ALC. 5% VOL.

MARBLE BEERSLTD

organic

CHOCOLATE MARBLE

ALC. 5.5% VOL.

MARBLE BEERSLTD

organic

TAWNY No3

ALC. 5.7% VOL.

organic

GINGER '6'

ALC. 6% VOL.

MARBLE BEERSLTD

MARBLE BEERSLTD

Established: 1997

Founder: Vance Debechval

Beers: Ade, IALE, Marble Squared, Draft, Pint, 'Stouter' Port Stout, Manchester Bitter, Best, Ginger Marble, Summer Marble, Spring, La Petite Toulousaine, Stout, Off to the Match, Choc Ginger, Lagonda IPA, Ginger 5.1, Chocolate Marble, Dobber, Earl Grey IPA, Emancipation, Farmhouse IPA, Black Marble, Vurr & Vlam, Bennett's Progress, Dubbel, Decadence, Saison, 125 Imperial Stout, 125 Barley Wine

Website: www.marblebeers.com

MARBLE

Manchester

Even though it's got tea in it, at 6.8% you wouldn't call Marble's Earl Grey IPA a breakfast beer. There is an element of mid-afternoon luxury about it, with the tannins from the Earl Grey (which is added in the shape of tea bags during fermentation) giving it a brisk, rousing bitterness at the end of the palate, while pleasing mid-palate notes of lemony style bergamot link arms with orange/tangerine and hints of almond nougat. Originally brewed in collaboration with Emelisse, one of the more thrusting and innovative Dutch craft brewers around, this is now one of Marble's regulars, which, according to head brewer Matthew Howgate, 'is one of our most popular beers and we cannot keep up with demand'.

Of course, if you're not a tea drinker, you can always settle for chocolate, in the shape of Chocolate Marble, another favourite beer of this Manchester brewery. Despite the name, there's no chocolate added during the brewing process. Cocoa used to be chucked in when the beer was first brewed in 2000, but the then head brewer James Campbell switched to chocolate malt to give the beer its silky, creamy note.

Marble brew beers for every taste: the classic Manchester Bitter, the citrusy Lagonda IPA and the rich and spirituous Belgian-style Dubbel. After nearly 20 years, the spirit of brewing adventure remains alive and well at Marble.

'Our philosophy has always been to brew beers that we enjoy ourselves,' says Howgate, who joined the company from AB-InBev at the start of 2014. 'By doing so we are confident that others will enjoy them. The brewery itself has always had a reputation for using new world hops to produce hop-focused beers. The changing of the market towards these styles of beers has made it our job to create beers that accentuate these flavours.'

Top: The Marble Arch is a listed building and used to be home to the brewery. **Bottom:** The Beer House in Chorlton serves seven of the brewery's beers in a relaxed atmosphere

"Our philosophy has always been to brew beers that we enjoy ourselves. By doing so we are confident that others will enjoy them"

MANCHESTER ICON

Marble emerged into the Mancunian beer scene in 1997 when Vance Debechval bought the Marble Arch Inn, a pub on the Rochdale Road that had seen better days. The Inn is a stunning survivor of the late Victorian/early Edwardian age of pub splendour. Apparently, he wasn't sure whether to put in a brewing kit or install a karaoke room. Thankfully for the beer world he went for the former. In 2011 the brewery moved to larger premises in a nearby railway arch and began brewing with a 12-barrel plant.

'The brewery has a weekly capacity of 100 hectolitres,' says Howgate, 'and we are running flat out producing seven core beers as well as regular one-offs and seasonal brews. All the beers that we produce are vegan. This means we don't use any finings, so we have to have very tight control on the quantity of yeasts we pitch, crop and leave for final products to ensure we achieve a level of clarity that the customer is happy with.

'The folk of Manchester know what they want and what they like. We try to make beers that the people of the city enjoy. If we get it wrong they tell us and stop drinking it.'

He pauses. 'Just look at what happened with Boddingtons for example.'

Manchester Bitter, 4.2%
There's a buzzsaw of northern bitterness on the palate of this straw gold-coloured best bitter; there's also a sprightly bittersweet character, citrus, a bracing graininess and a long dry finish.

Lagonda IPA, 5%
A big bold aroma of grapefruit alongside a waft of floral notes emerges from the glass after this light golden beer has been poured. The palate is more grapefruit, some tropical fruit, a malt-accented spine before it finishes with a dry, bitter and fruity flourish.

Head brewer Matt Howgate joined the company in 2014

Established: 2010

Founder: Toby McKenzie

Beers: Endless, Headless, Mirthless, Feckless, Directionless, Wreckless, Heartless, Fathomless, Sleepless, Peerless, Smokeless, Ageless

Website: www.redwillowbrewery.com

REDWILLOW

Macclesfield, Cheshire

One of these days beer-lovers will erect a memorial to the home brewer, commemorating the fact that – just like in the USA during the 1980s – this humble artisan is one of the driving forces behind Britain's brewing revolution.

Those who have stepped up to the brewing plate include Kernel's Evin O'Riordain, Beavertown's Logan Plant and Purple Moose's Laurence Washington. Here's another name to conjure with, RedWillow's founder Toby McKenzie who took the big step from amateur to pro in 2010, when he merged the middle names of his young son (Red) and older daughter (Willow) for the brewery name.

'In a nutshell, I thoroughly enjoyed brewing at home,' he explains, 'and I liked flavour in all formats (food, wine, beer) and wanted to move away from a very intangible job to actually making something.'

MAKING SOMETHING

This 'making something' has involved a collection of award-winning beers, many of which have taken a deep plunge into the American hopsack and resurfaced glistening with bright and bravura flavours. Wreckless, which was made the champion beer of Cheshire scarcely a year after it was first brewed, is a brisk pale ale loaded to the gunnels with Citra and Amarillo. Further up the alcoholic scale at 7.2%, we come across Ageless, the brewery's high-five hit on the US-style IPA – take a sip and you're in a deep fruit bowl of ripe mango, lychee and pineapple, while the lasting bitter finish adds an appetising contrast.

'What I look for in our beers varies,' says McKenzie, 'but in general they should fit into a style. i.e. a session beer should be just that, a beer that you drink. I think that's nice and you can ignore what you're drinking and concentrate on talking to your friends. At the other end of the spectrum beers should be fun and interesting, but still balanced and drinkable.'

And to demonstrate that RedWillow isn't just about stuffing hops into the brewing kettle, how

"I thoroughly enjoyed brewing at home. I liked flavour in all formats (food, wine, beer) and wanted to move away from a very intangible job to actually making something."

Toby McKenzie founded RedWillow in 2010, creating the name from the middle names of his children

about Smokeless, which despite its name is a smoked porter. To make things more interesting, McKenzie adds chipotle chillies after it's been brewed, helping to ramp up the smokiness, which is then balanced by the heat.

'I think that this beer best represents what we are trying to do with RedWillow,' he says, 'as it combines traditional and non traditional ingredients and it is very drinkable (plus it goes really well with and in food).'

EXPERIMENTAL BREWING

This philosophy also incorporates a sense of experimentation with a range of beers produced under the Faithless label. These have included that most divisive of beers, black IPA, plus a well-hopped Bavarian Weisse and a gooseberry saison. It hasn't always gone right though: Faithless 23 had to be poured away as McKenzie explained on his blog. 'A decision to try and use up a large amount of Summer, Stella and Summit hops I had lying around but did not use in any of our core beers went badly wrong and was way too bitter'. He kept three casks and a couple of cases of bottles to see if time would mellow the bitterness. The failure didn't dim his future plans, which also include barrel-ageing and experimenting with sours and *Brettanomyces* yeast.

The beer names may have a theme of less, but less is definitely more at RedWillow.

Beers to try...

Directionless, 4.2%
Classic best bitter that turns up the hoppy volume with a sprightly fresh nose of grapefruit and lemon, while the palate tingles with more citrus fruitiness alongside a frisky grainy malt character before a dry, juicy finish.

Heartless, 4.9%
Winter months are warmed with this luxurious seasonal chocolate stout using high quality Columbian chocolate: the mouthfeel is soothing, while the finish has a pronounced coffee-like dryness and bitterness.

BEER DESTINATIONS

PHILHARMONIC
Liverpool, Merseyside
www.nicholsonspubs.co.uk

It's worth going to 'the Phil' just to visit the Gents – ladies are welcome but they have to ask first to ensure there are no embarrassing confrontations. It's luxuriantly decked out with marble and tiled urinals and washbasins. But then the entire building is a shrine to marble, tiles, cut and etched glass and wrought iron. It's part of the Nicholson's chain of historic and architecturally important pubs and stands opposite the Philharmonic Hall. The beers include Nicholson's house beer, Pale Ale, with a big range of ales from independent breweries, including Black Sheep. The stupendous Art Nouveau exterior resembles a French chateau with gables, turrets and parapets.

ROSCOE HEAD
Liverpool, Merseyside
www.roscoehead.co.uk

Landlady Carol Ross previously ran the Philharmonic and it was a major culture shock to come to such a small and unassuming pub close by. The Roscoe is all about good beer. Six handpumps dispense Jennings Cumberland Ale and Tetley Bitter and an ever-changing range of guest beers. The Roscoe enjoys iconic status in Liverpool: it's one of only a handful of pubs throughout the country that's featured in every edition of the *Good Beer Guide* since 1974. The main wood-panelled bar and snug are designed for conversation. Carol Ross took over when her parents Nicholas and Margaret hung up the bar towels: the pub has been in the same family for more than 30 years. It's named after William Roscoe, a local campaigner against the slave trade.

CROWN & KETTLE
Manchester
0161 236 2923

Stop on your way in and admire the Crown & Kettle's ceiling: all recessed tiles and chandeliers with some Art Nouveau flourishes. The pub has a long bar running almost the entire length of the main room and offers many beers from Ossett brewery, with other Northwest brewers also represented. It started life as a stipendiary court, which accounts for the crown in the name though nobody knows where the addition of kettle comes from. A stupendous wall mirror is embossed with the name and a royal crown. For many years, the pub was next door to the Manchester office of the *Daily Express*. It's Grade-II listed and said to be haunted by a former judge who held court here.

MARBLE ARCH
Manchester
www.marblebeers.com/marble-arch

This 1880s red-brick, street-corner pub is a listed building and was the first home of Marble brewery, which has moved nearby to a bigger 12-barrel plant. The pub is a shrine to Victorian grandeur, with a notoriously sloping tiled mosaic floor embossed with the red rose of Lancashire, leather wall settles, open fireplaces and large mirrors on the walls. Look up to admire what architectural guru Sir Nikolaus Pevsner described as 'an unusual jack-arch ceiling with cast-iron beams supported by tile-clad brackets'. The large bar at the rear has a canopy listing snacks available but food also comes in full measure from a tiny kitchen where chef Justin Berry and his team knock out such delights as aubergine and wild mushroom risotto, lobster and mushroom raviolis in tarragon butter, and lemon sole and cockle chowder. Marble is dedicated to organic materials wherever possible with several beers and dishes suitable for vegans.

BEER HALL
Staveley, Cumbria
www.hawksheadbrewery.co.uk

Ernest Hemingway would approve of the Beer Hall as it's a 'clean, well-lighted place'. The glass and steel building tucked away in a small Cumbrian village offers good beer, good cheer and good food. It's the second home for the fast-growing Hawkshead brewery and founder Alex Brodie and his team have created a visitor centre where you can watch beer being made as you tuck into food from a menu with beer-matching suggestions. A large bar dispenses the full range of Hawkshead beers, which can be supped from the comfort of large sofas. The on-site shop has a range of 60 or more foreign beers and you can also buy Hawkshead's brews in bottle to take away. There are spring and summer festivals where as many as 70 beers are available and the Beer Hall frequently rocks to live music.

Staveley

Manchester

Liverpool

The Roscoe Head is famous for its cask beer: it's one of only a handful of pubs in the UK to have featured in every *Good Beer Guide*

YORKSHIRE

EAST YORKSHIRE, NORTH YORKSHIRE, SOUTH YORKSHIRE, WEST YORKSHIRE

Yorkshire. So many breweries, so many beers, so little time. Ranging from the Pennines to the North Sea and the Humber, taking in the northern edge of the Peak District plus the Dales, the Yorkshire brewing scene is vibrant and voluminous, as are its pubs and bars – whether hidden away in a remote Dales village or brassy and bold on a buzzing city high street. However, there's a question that needs to be asked. Is it possible to describe a Yorkshire beer?

TRADITIONAL ALES

How about Black Sheep Bitter – creamy, flinty, bittersweet, dry in the finish, with an appetising bitterness – the kind of beer that sessions are made for, the kind of beer that takes you straight to the small town of Masham. While we're still in Masham it would be remiss not to try a pint of Old Peculier – brewed down the road from Black Sheep at Theakston's – a rich malty concoction of toffee, caramel, smoke, coffee, ripe dark fruit and a long dry finish.

Both breweries are also unique in that they ferment their beers in Yorkshire squares, a method of fermentation that was once very common in the area. This works with the top of the square acting as a yeast collector, which separates the fermenting beer from the rigorous yeast head that

BEER DESTINATIONS
> go to page 232

Little Valley: Hebden Bridge, West Yorkshire

Black Sheep: Masham, North Yorkshire

Theakston: Masham, North Yorkshire

Rudgate: York, North Yorkshire

Masham

York

Shipley

Saltaire: Shipley, West Yorkshire

Hebden Bridge

Leeds

Elland

Huddersfield

Sheffield

Magic Rock: Huddersfield, West Yorkshire

Elland: Elland, West Yorkshire

forms on the top of the liquid; it is said to soften the beer's taste.

Maybe we need to swap towns and head to Keighley and take a pint or two of Timothy Taylor's Landlord, a marvellous pale ale that sings with zestful and tangy citrus and floral notes on the nose, while the palate is a lively whirl of orange fruit, nutty maltiness and a long and loving bitterness. The same brewery's Boltmaker was awarded Champion Beer of Britain in 2014.

When learned drinkers talk about Yorkshire beer these three are never far from their thoughts, while the so-called 'Burton of the north' Tadcaster also gets a look in. But in this great age of brewing diffusion when brewers' influences are pan-global rather than parochial, it's getting harder to pin down what a Yorkshire beer is – especially as the iconic Tetley's has now left the field to be brewed in the Black Country; Tetley's for many was Yorkshire beer made flesh, Geoffrey Boycott in a glass.

A NEW GENERATION

They may be synonymous with Yorkshire, but you'd be wrong to think Yorkshire beer is solely typified by these traditional ales. Cast your eye over a bar in Leeds or York and you're just as likely to see something by Magic Rock from Huddersfield, whose big colourful beers – influenced by the American brewing revolution – are crafted by Stuart Ross, who some say is one of the most accomplished brewers in the country, never mind just Yorkshire.

Or the lubricious, so-laidback-it's-horizontal Triple Chocoholic Stout from Shipley-based Saltaire, a luscious and luxurious chocolate stout that uses chocolate malt, real chocolate and chocolate syrups. Yet, despite all this chocolate it's not a sweet beer, being more like a hot chocolate with a creamy, soothing mouthfeel while a judicious hop bitterness keeping everything from toppling over into a tooth-jangling nightmare. Awards stick to it like flies to flypaper.

Then there is Cohort from Summer Wine: a double black Belgian rye IPA. Meanwhile 2013's CAMRA champion winter beer and overall champion was Elland's 1872 Porter, a complex-flavoured and well-considered beer, with notes of chewy toffee, horse saddle, mocha coffee and milk chocolate rising from the glass.

Other breweries worth noting include Acorn in Barnsley, whose Barnsley Bitter is an intensely

Yorkshire is proud of its breweries, both old and new, and craft beer bars are springing up where you can enjoy their beers

bitter delight (we're probably looking at a classic Yorkshire beer here), and sits comfortably in the range alongside the full-bodied Gorlovka stout and a series of IPAs using different hops. There's also Kelham Island in Sheffield, founded by the late Dave Wickett, and whose Pale Rider won Champion Beer of Britain in 2004.

If we travel over to Harrogate we find Roosters, which was a truly trailblazing and revolutionary brewery in the 1990s when its then brewer (and founder) Sean Franklin was a devotee of American hops; he'd formerly worked in wine and brought over his enthusiasm for the grapes and what they could do to wine to hops. Perhaps it was Franklin more than any other brewer who changed the way Yorkshire beer was viewed when he introduced Yankee to local pubs. This was a pale ale where American Cascade hops were (and still are) used to produce a stunning array of tropical fruit aromas (think lychee and even papaya), while the palate has a soft and caressing bitterness that is almost creamy. This was (and remains) a Yorkshire beer.

MORE THAN JUST BITTER

In simpler days it was easy to say what a Yorkshire beer was. Bitter came first to people's thoughts, bitter with a creamy head, served through a sparkler as Tetley bittermen queued up in their thousands to grab a glass of this beneficial benediction. Then there was dark mild in some industrial areas, lighter mild in others (Timothy Taylor's Golden Promise is a rare survivor of this style). There was also Yorkshire Stingo, a strong barley wine, which Alfred Barnard, author of *The Noted Breweries of Great Britain and Ireland*, wrote about when he visited Tetley's in Leeds: 'we found [it] very luscious, full of body, and well flavoured without being heady.' Since 2008, Samuel Smith has brewed a Yorkshire Stingo, which is 8% and bottle conditioned.

Yorkshire. So many breweries, so many beers, so little time.

Insider's view...

Zak Avery
www.thebeerboy.co.uk

There can be no doubting the influence of Yorkshire on the global brewing scene. Over the years, I've been lucky enough to talk to many of the leading lights of the American craft brewing scene, and the touchstone they return to again and again, the brewery that made them rethink what beer was, is Samuel Smith's of Tadcaster.

The legalisation of home-brewing under the Carter administration coincided with the first wave of imports in the late 70s and early 80s of Smith's bottled beers. These two events, perhaps more than any others, are responsible for the first generation of American craft brewers making British-style ales from local ingredients.

Not only does Yorkshire claim an influential past but its present is equally dominant. Pop into any great beer bar in London, and you will see the evidence – Magic Rock, Roosters, and a host of others. And the alumni of Yorkshire breweries, from when the traditional route into brewing was a long apprenticeship rather than early retirement from IT, perhaps have more influence over the UK scene than any other county.

Zak Avery is a former Beer Writer of the Year, author of 500 Beers and co-owner of Leeds-based wholesaler Beer Paradise and online retailer and shop Beer Ritz

Top: Black Sheep brewery. **Left:** Theakston employs cooper Jonathan Manby. **Right:** Theakston's iconic Old Peculier

BLACK SHEEP

Established: 1992

Founder: Paul Theakston

Beers: Best Bitter, Golden Sheep, Ruddy Ram, Black Sheep Ale, Riggwelter

Website: www.blacksheepbrewery.co.uk

THEAKSTON

Established: 1827

Founder: Thomas Theakston

Beers: Traditional Mild, Best Bitter, Black Bull Bitter, Lightfoot, XB, Old Peculier

Website: www.theakstons.co.uk

BLACK SHEEP & THEAKSTON

Masham, North Yorkshire

Is it something about Yorkshire families? In Tadcaster, John Smith and Sam Smith had a row and set up rival breweries. Something similar happened in the otherwise sedate old market town of Masham, where members of the same family have competing breweries separated by only a few hundred yards. In the case of Black Sheep and Theakston it wasn't so much a row as a matter of principle for one member of the family.

Theakston has been around since 1827 and the brewery is deeply rooted in tradition. It employs a cooper to make and repair oak casks as many of the publicans it supplies prefer 'beer from the wood'. While it has vigorously expanded its beer range in recent years, its world-wide fame is based on the legendary Old Peculier strong ale.

As sales of cask beer took off in the 1980s, Theakston had the misfortune to be head-hunted by bigger brewers whose own real ale credentials were poor. In 1984 the Masham brewery was bought by Matthew Brown of Blackburn and three years later Brown was taken over by national giant Scottish & Newcastle. S&N promptly closed Brown's: its only interest was in acquiring Theakston and its renowned ales, which it made available throughout the country. It grew sales of Best Bitter to such an extent that it moved production to other plants outside Yorkshire, which did little for Theakston's reputation.

NEW START

Paul Theakston, managing director of the family firm, was offered a top job and big salary in the S&N empire but he walked away. As he says, 'I wanted to make real beer in the time-honoured fashion'. That meant, if possible, staying in Masham. He licked

Left: Theakston still brew in their original brewery.
Right: Black Sheep's copper, mash tun and hop back were rescued from the closed Hartley's brewery in Ulverston, Cumbria

Paul Theakston set out on an unusual marketing route of relying entirely on the free trade, without owning a single pub

his wounds and looked around for premises, which he found in an old maltings that had belonged to Lightfoot's brewery, taken over and closed by Theakston in 1919.

Paul scoured the country looking for suitable brewing equipment. Copper, mash tun and hop back were rescued from the closed Hartley's brewery in Ulverston, Cumbria. He was determined to use traditional 'Yorkshire Square' fermenters: they are the northern version of the Burton Union system, two-storey vessels where rising yeast is trapped

in the top storey, ensuring a clear, creamy and sparkling finished product. He found three in the unlikely setting of Hardy's & Hanson's brewery in Nottingham and rescued three more from Darley's brewery in Thorne just as the wrecking ball was about to demolish the site.

By 1992 Paul Theakston was ready to brew. All he needed was a name for his brewery as he couldn't use the family one. His wife Sue, looking across to the Dales dotted with black-faced sheep, said, 'You'll be the black sheep of the family when you start brewing' and a legend was born. The name created great interest when the first casks of Black Sheep Best Bitter rolled out of the brewery and it's a name that has imbued the entire enterprise with a wry sense of humour: visitors are invited to enjoy a ewe-nique dining experience in the Baa..r and Bistro and then take a Shepherded Tour of the site.

Paul Theakston set out on an unusual marketing route of relying entirely on the free trade, without owning a single pub. Using pure Dales water, the finest Maris Otter malting barley and English hops, he has built a portfolio of beers that are distributed far and wide, with Best Bitter named the official beer of Yorkshire County Cricket Club. The brewery has expanded frequently and now has a capacity of 80,000 barrels a year. 'Don't dare call me a micro,' Paul Theakston says firmly. After 21 years of exhilarating success, he has now taken a well-earned back seat and handed over the daily running of the business to his sons Rob and Jo.

On the other side of the wall, four brothers – Simon, Nick, Tim and Edward Theakston – planned their own revolution. After years of painstaking negotiations, they finally wrung ownership back from S&N. It took several more years to get S&N to relinquish control of Best Bitter but once the brothers owned the flagship brand they were able to bring it back to Masham and restore its good name.

POWERFUL TRADITION

Like their noisy neighbours, they have expanded the beer range and extended the brewery, removing the roof to lower in additional fermenters that have tripled capacity and allowed a range of 15 beers to be brewed. A visitor centre includes the cooper's shop where Jonathan Manby is seen fashioning oak casks with awesome skill. In their different ways, both sides of the brewing family have maintained a powerful brewing tradition in Masham... and given greater recognition to sheep from the Dales.

Beers to try ...

Best Bitter, 3.8%
This beer belies its modest strength with a big malty and fruity character, with a solid hop base created by English varieties. The finish is long, complex, bittersweet and ends finally dry and hoppy.

Best Bitter, 3.8%
Also 3.8%, Theakston's version has a pale bronze colour and an intense spicy hop note from Fuggles, balancing juicy malt and tart fruit. Malt, hops and fruit combine in the lingering bittersweet finish.

Old Peculier, 5.6%
Takes its name from the medieval time when Masham was a 'Peculier' – outside the control of the bishop in York. It was originally a stock ale, used for blending with other beers but now stands on its own feet: robust and roasty, with delicious hints of caramel, coffee and liquorice.

Established: 2002

Founder: Dickie Bird, Mark Smith, Fiona Smith, Andy Parker

Beers: Bargee, Best Bitter, Beyond the Pale, Eden, Nettlethrasher, 1872 Porter

Website: www.ellandbrewery.co.uk

ELLAND

Elland, West Yorkshire

A quiet toast turned in to a rip-roaring celebration at Elland brewery in August 2013. The employees were preparing to raise a glass to their 2,000th brew since the company was launched 12 years before when the news came through that they'd won the most prestigious award in the brewing industry: Champion Beer of Britain at CAMRA's Great British Beer Festival in London. The beer that had so impressed the judges at London Olympia was 1872 Elland Porter, which had already walked off with the title of Champion Winter Beer of Britain in January that year.

And just to add to the joy of the moment, the beer that was being brewed at Elland when the victory was announced was... 1872 Porter. It's a special beer. Dave Sanders, who ran the West Yorkshire brewery that merged with Barge & Barrel to form Elland, discovered the recipe in an old brewery book from the late 19th century. It's an authentic example of a Victorian porter, the style that helped create the commercial brewing industry and which spawned its stronger brother, stout porter, shortened to just stout.

The brewery is based in a spacious building measuring 3,200 square feet, with plenty of room for expansion. The 10-barrel kit is based around a wood-clad mash tun and copper that came from a former Firkin brewpub in Birmingham. They feed five fermenters, including one giant 10-barrel vessel built in Bavaria.

Following the merger that formed Elland, the brewery has been owned by four partners, one of whom is Dickie Bird. Dickie says he's the genuine article, as the famous former cricket umpire of the same name was christened Harold, whereas Dickie at Elland is a true Richard.

The brewery's main brand is Bargee, a firmly traditional English bitter, brewed with Maris Otter pale and crystal malts and hopped with Challenger, First Gold and Progress varieties. The brewery team, led by head brewer Michael Wynnyczuk, are keen to use as many English malts and hops as possible, although Best Bitter does have some American Cascades as well as domestic Progress. Some drinkers have criticised Elland for making Best Bitter exceptionally pale but Bird and Wynnyczuk

Dickie Bird and Michael Wynnyczuk celebrate winning Champion Beer of Britain with their 1872 Porter

think they have short memories. Down the road in Sheffield, Stones Bitter is fondly recalled as a golden bitter popular long before golden ales were developed. And over the hills there was once a straw-coloured bitter called Boddingtons that made Mancunians weep for joy.

For a true golden ale from Elland you have to turn to Beyond the Pale, which has a touch of Munich malt blended with pale malt and just one hop, Cascade. Nettlethrasher is distinctively different in colour, burnished copper, and its odd name comes from the fact that John Eastwood, who ran the Barge & Barrel brewery and first brewed the beer, was aware that he shared his name with the small town in Nottinghamshire where D H Lawrence was born. One of Lawrence's many odd practices was to thrash himself with stinging nettles: it's claimed he may even have indulged the practice on other people. The beer may not include nettles but, as hops come from the same plant family, Bramling Cross, Challenger and Progress add a resinous character that should appeal to sons, lovers, aristocratic ladies and their gardeners.

Elland's beers go to Manchester in the west and as far as Hull and Scarborough in the east. The beers reach as far south as Peterborough and Scunthorpe. And a special beer appears from time to time, 1872 Porter aged for 12 months in Scotch whisky casks. This warming version of the beer, with tannins and vanilla from the wood, can be found in the Junction pub in Castleford, and the tapping of a barrel is an event not to be missed.

Beer trends...
BREWSTERS

Women are back doing what they originally did – making beer. There are a growing number of 'brewsters' playing a key role in not only making beer but also developing new styles that appeal to drinkers; women in particular.

For centuries beer was made in the home and women made beer and bread side by side, using the same grain to fashion the basic staples of life. The women who made the best beer in a community were singled out for praise and were given the title of brewster. Their homes became rudimentary alehouses where villagers met to drink the beers in return for a small payment.

From these humble beginnings, alehouses, inns and taverns developed, many of them run by women – immortalised by Shakespeare's Mistress Quickly at the Boar's Head in London's Eastcheap.

When brewing moved out of the house or the pub cellar into big commercial breweries from the 18th century onwards, women were sidelined and brewing became a male preserve. Pubs, too, became 'blokeish' and women began to drink less beer, stayed at home and turned to wine as their preferred tipple.

Now women are calling the shots again, ordering the malt and hops, and conjuring forth fine-tasting beers from their mash tuns and coppers. The High Priestess of modern female brewers is Sara Barton: her Brewster's brewery opened in 1998 in the Vale of Belvoir in Lincolnshire and as well as producing traditional beer styles – from pale, through amber to stout – she also developed a Wicked Women range with such titles as Andromeda, Galaxy, Sadie the Goat, Sexy Sadie and Stella.

Sara lit the blue touch paper. Today there are around 30 brewsters adding to the pleasure of beer drinking. Some of them are in large and once deeply conservative companies where women worked as secretaries or made the tea. Georgina Young is manager of brewing at Fuller's in west London, Belinda Jennings partners Fergus Fitzgerald at Adnams in Suffolk and Michelle Holden is a brewer with the major Northwest family brewer, Thwaites of Blackburn.

Bigger brewers are aware of brewsters' potential. Hayley Barton was so successful at Cumbrian Legendary Ales, where she won many prizes for Loweswater Gold, that she was headhunted by global giant Molson Coors and now brews at their specialist Sharp's ale plant in Cornwall.

And arguably the most influential brewer in Britain today is a woman. Emma Gilleland was head brewer at Marston's in Burton upon Trent but has been promoted to oversee production and quality control at all the group's breweries, including Banks's, Brakspear, Jennings, Ringwood and Wychwood. Brewing today is truly an egalitarian business.

Sara Barton

Her success could be described as stellar. She has been featured in both Country Living magazine and the Daily Telegraph as an example of a thriving businesswoman and in 2012 she was named Brewer of the Year by the British Guild of Beer Writers. To keep up with demand, she has moved to a bigger site in Grantham, which happens to be the birthplace of Britain's first woman prime minister.

Claire Monk

Quite what Belgian Trappist brewers would make of a woman called Monk brewing in an abbey is not known – and they're not likely to say – but Claire Monk has built a fine reputation for beers sold both to pubs in the Midlands and for Welbeck Abbey's school of cuisine near Worksop.

Petra Wetzel

German-born Petra Wetzel has brewed up a storm in Glasgow with WEST, a Bavarian-style beer hall and brewery where she brews wheat beer and her lager adheres strictly to the Reinheitsgebot, or German Beer Purity Law.

Wim van der Spek learned his brewing skills in his native Netherlands before moving to the Yorkshire Dales to make organic beer

Established: 2005

Founder: Wim van der Spek and Sue Cooper

Beers: Withens Pale Ale, Ginger Pale Ale, Cragg Vale Bitter, Hebden's Wheat, Stoodley Stout, Tod's Blonde, Moor Ale, Python IPA, Ampleforth Abbey Beer

Website: www.littlevalleybrewery.co.uk

LITTLE VALLEY

Hebden Bridge, West Yorkshire

There's a quiet determination at Little Valley to not only brew great beer but also to 'put something back' and aid the environment. Head brewer Wim van der Spek and his wife Sue Cooper are dedicated to using the best-possible organic malts and hops, grown without 'agri-chemicals'. As a result, the substantial range of beers has Soil Association and Vegan Society accreditation and appeals to the growing number of drinkers who are concerned about how and where drinks are made. The draught beers don't contain isinglass – made from fish swim bladders – as a clearing agent: instead they use carrageen, also known as Irish moss, an edible seaweed.

The husband and wife team are based on a former farm near Hebden Bridge, high in the Yorkshire Dales and with superb views over to Lancashire: it's rumoured you can even glimpse the Isle of Man on a clear day. They use crystal-clear Dales water for brewing while power comes from a wind turbine that feeds both the brewery and other industrial units on the site. Wim van der Spek is from the Netherlands and brewed his first beer at 18. It was called De Gustibus est Disputandum, which translates either as 'drink and discuss' or 'get p*****d and fight'. He worked with a leading Dutch brewery, Gulpener, and then studied to become a master brewer in Munich.

He met Sue Cooper while they were both cycling in Tibet: van der Spek was searching for the world's highest brewery while Cooper was working for Voluntary Service Overseas. Downsizing from the Himalayas, they set up Little Valley in 2005 and have achieved local, national and even international sales with draught and bottle-conditioned beers: Vanilla Porter was specially commissioned by a company in Finland and it was followed by a cask version for Britain.

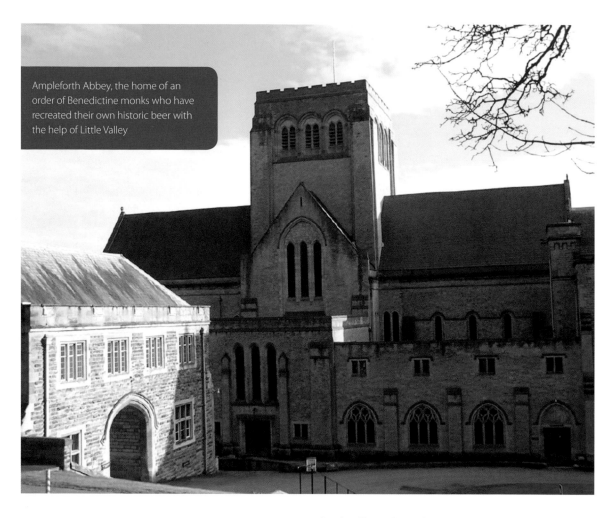

Ampleforth Abbey, the home of an order of Benedictine monks who have recreated their own historic beer with the help of Little Valley

One of the brewery's most popular beers is Ginger Pale Ale. At 4% alcohol, it should not be confused with ginger pop, even though it has a big hit of Fairtrade ginger. It's a warming beer and has a fine balance of hops – Cascade and Pacific Gem – and cookie-like malt. The addition of Fairtrade sugar adds to its ethical credentials.

Vanilla Porter is another beer with an unconventional ingredient, with vanilla pods ground into a powder and added to the copper boil with the hops.

Python IPA is the brewery's leading brand and, to give it an authentic Indian twist, is named after the deadly snake. It has no connections with the Monty Python team but when he heard about it Terry Jones, a great beer lover, ordered a case for the reunion in London in 2014. The Ministry of Silly Walks sketch had an added kick…

HOLY BEER

Little Valley has been at the centre of a fascinating recreation of a historic beer style. The Benedictine monks at Ampleforth Abbey in Yorkshire were keen to restore a brewing tradition that dates from the 17th century. Expecting persecution, they fled to France when Elizabeth I came to the throne. They

Father Wulstan, a leading monk at the Abbey today, was keen to create an Ampleforth beer and, following years of painstaking research, managed to unearth the original recipe from the monastery in Lorraine

settled in Lorraine and brewed a strong brown beer that created great interest in France where it was called *La Bière Anglaise*.

The monks returned to England following the French Revolution and were granted land at Ampleforth, where they built an abbey. Father Wulstan, a leading monk at the Abbey today, was keen to create an Ampleforth beer and, following years of painstaking research, managed to unearth the original recipe from the monastery in Lorraine. He followed this with a tour of Belgian Trappist breweries with Wim to study the styles and brewing methods of the monks there. Wim and Father Wulstan settled on the style known as Dubbel or Double, a strong brown ale. The first batch of the 7% bottle-fermented beer went on sale in 2012 and within six months had sold 30,000 bottles. A golden Tripel ale may follow.

Wim and Sue brew 1,500 barrels a year and are happy with that capacity: growing bigger would not fit with their green credentials. But they're not standing still. In common with a number of Yorkshire breweries, they produced a special beer to celebrate the Tour de France starting in the Dales in 2014. It was called Stage Winner but, wearing their environmental hats, surely it should have been On Yer Bike?

Beers to try ...

Hebden's Wheat, 4.5%
Wim's take on a Belgian spiced beer. The beer has a spicy and lemon character with hints of herbal hops and bubblegum from the special yeast culture. Peppery hops and tart fruit build in the mouth with honeyed malt while the finish is full of lemon zest and spices.

Python IPA, 6%
It has a bright gold colour with spicy hop resins, orange fruit, honeyed malt and a hint of butterscotch on the aroma. Tart citrus fruit and bitter hops dominate the palate while the finish is long and complex with spicy hops, tart fruit and toasted malt.

Ampleforth Abbey Beer, 7%
Brewed with pale and wheat malts and three darker grains: chocolate, crystal and Munich. Soft brown sugar, in the Belgian Trappist tradition, is also added. The beer has a spicy and peppery aroma from the hops, backed by roasted grain, chocolate and sultana fruit. Rich fruit and malt dominate the palate, balanced by spicy hops while the finish is bittersweet with dark fruit, roasted grain, chocolate and hop resins.

Established: 2011

Founder: Richard and Jonny Burhouse

Beers: Ringmaster, Rapture, High Wire, Dark Arts, Cannonball

Website: www.magicrockbrewing.com

MAGIC ROCK

Huddersfield, West Yorkshire

Magic Rock seems to be home to all manner of fairground folk and crazy-looking characters with the air of the American carnival about them; we're talking strongmen, bearded ladies, ringmasters and human cannonballs. Considering the bottle and pump clip labels on which said folk appear you might think the universe that Magic Rock inhabits is a slightly surreal one, but just one swig of their beers will plant your feet (and palate) firmly on the ground. Maybe that's the effect of being based in sensible Huddersfield. Yes, the beers are brightly flavoured and boldly hopped, but there's an authority about their character, a firmness in their appeal to the senses.

Head brewer is Stuart Ross, a softly-spoken Yorkshireman who, since starting brewing in 2004, has worked at three different breweries, including

"we would like people to try our beer and always want to come back for more"

the well-regarded Kelham Island, plus a brewpub; the latter job gave him the chance to experiment (smoked Oktoberfest anyone?). However, it was US beer that crystallised everything for him after he was asked to join with brothers Richard and Jonny Burhouse when they began Magic Rock in 2011.

INSPIRED BY THE US

'The idea behind Magic Rock's beers,' says Ross, 'was to bring the wonderful fresh flavours of the US West Coast IPAs and pale ales to the UK. We had tasted fresh beer brought in by friends and then tasted the beers that had been imported which had suffered the test of time. We brew a range of hop forward, bold and exciting beers and one of the most important things for us is making sure the beers stay drinkable; we would like people to try our beer and always want to come back for more.'

Cannonball IPA is the standout Magic Rock beer, the signature beer, the beer that says 'here we are, we are Magic Rock'. At 7.4% it's not exactly a session beer but it's still an eminently drinkable hop bomb, with a nose that's a primeval rush of passion fruit, grapefruit and pineapple, while the palate is velvety, ripe orange skin, grapefruit, and the blast of alcohol, and a slap of dryness and malt sweetness keeps everything in place.

Then there's the limited version Unhuman Cannonball IIIPA, an 11% version of Magic Rock's talisman beer, which, according to Ross, was inspired by a beer from Alpine Brewing in San Diego. This is a beer that – understandably – gets the beer geeks going delirious.

'At 11% the Alpine beer was big on ABV and massively hopped, but was very clean and drinkable. We wanted to make something like it. Brewing a beer like this could almost be compared to making a lager. It takes a lot of time to do; the dry hop has to be added in multiple stages to add depth and to give the hop character time to be absorbed. So we couldn't make this beer all the time because it would take up a lot of our brewing capacity so we decided to brew it once a year when the US hops are at their freshest.'

Magic Rock is a brewery at the top of its game, an inventive and innovative brewery that enjoys playing with recipes – as the Gose-style Salty Kiss with added gooseberries demonstrates – a brewery that understands both brewing and branding, with Ross

Beers to try...

Rapture, 4.6%
Red ale with a blast of zesty grapefruit on the nose, while the palate has a powerful surge of grapefruit citrus plus apricots, lychees and papaya all balanced by toasty grainy notes and a dry, bittersweet finish.

Dark Arts: Surreal Stout, 6%
So-called 'surreal stout' with roast notes, charred wood, ripe berries and chocolate on the nose; the mouthfeel is initially smooth and luxuriant before liquorice, chocolate and dark fruits make an entrance. The finish is appetisingly bitter and smoky.

one of the most accomplished brewers working in the UK. Not that he's sitting on his laurels.

'It's always a great feeling when someone tells me they love the beers,' he says, 'it always keeps me motivated to brew more and keep working to make great beer.'

Established: 1992

Founder: Craig Lee

Beers: Jorvik Blonde, Viking, Battleaxe, Ruby Mild, Volsung, York Chocolate Stout, IPA

Website: www.rudgatebrewery.co.uk

RUDGATE

York, North Yorkshire

If your brewery is based in or close to York, you can't ignore the history. York's Roman and Viking past is engrained in its history and architecture, and Rudgate underscores this by taking its name from the old Roman road where the brewery stands. The city's history is also reflected in the beer names: Viking, Battleaxe (no Les Dawson jokes, please), Jorvik and Volsung. Jorvik is the Viking name for the city while Volsung was a Nordic 'dragon priest'.

The brewery's base in a tad more modern but still has warrior status. It's at RAF Marston Moor – home of Halifax bombers in World War Two – in the Vale of York, and was originally in an old ammunition building, though it moved to bigger premises in 2010. The need to expand was driven by Rudgate's success the previous year when it won the Champion Beer of Britain award for its Ruby Mild. Founder Craig Lee says the award not only boosted sales of the Mild but had a 'bumper effect' on his beers, prompting the move to bigger premises and the installation of an additional fermenting vessel. Production has grown from 15 barrels to 30 barrels per brew.

Craig Lee launched Rudgate in 1992 and it's one of the longest-standing craft breweries in Britain. While the bulk of its sales are confined to Yorkshire, cask beers cross the Pennines into Lancashire and can be found as far south as Essex while bottled beers are taken by most major supermarkets.

REVITALISING MILD

When Lee and head brewer Jamie Allen picked up their plaque for Champion Beer of Britain in 2009 they helped restore interest in mild ale, a style that had been in the doldrums for decades and has only found favour again due to the efforts of craft brewers. Ruby Mild also emphasises the fact that mild doesn't have to be low in alcohol: the Rudgate beer is 4.4% and in its heyday in the 19th and early 20th centuries the style reached strengths of 5% or more. Rudgate Ruby has 32 units of bitterness, high for the style and, ironically, bitterer than some bitter beers.

As well as a core range of six beers, additional brewing capacity has enabled Rudgate to produce four seasonal beers every month of the year, a remarkable collection.

Head brewer Jamie Allen and founder Craig Lee celebrate Ruby Mild's victory in the Champion Beer of Britain competition in 2009

Beers to try...

Jorvik Blonde, 3.8%
A delightful, nose-tingling aroma of melon and tropical fruits, with honeyed malt and crisp hop resins. Bittersweet fruit, hop resins and juicy malt build in the mouth, followed by a lingering finish that's well balanced between malt, fruit and hops.

Ruby Mild, 4.4%
There's roasted grain, chocolate, burnt fruit and hop resins on the nose, with chocolate and roast moving on to the palate. The finish has a delicious creamy malt note with continuing chocolate, dark fruit and hops.

Volsung, 5%
A gold/bronze beer with honeyed malt and tart, lemon fruit on the nose. Juicy malt, lemon fruit and tangy hops dominate the palate, followed by a long finish that starts bittersweet but becomes dry, hoppy and fruity.

Established: 2006

Founder: Tony Gartland and Derek Todd

Beers: South Island Pale, Rye Smile, Pride, Blonde, Cheeky Kriek, Elderflower Blonde, Raspberry Blonde, White Christmas, Blackberry Cascade, Cascade Pale Ale, Cascadian Black, Triple Chocoholic, Winter Ale, New World Red, Smoked Porter

Website: www.saltairbrewery.co.uk

SALTAIRE

Shipley, West Yorkshire

Saltaire brewery isn't in Saltaire. Founders Tony Gartland and Derek Todd wanted to set their brewery in the Unesco World Heritage site, a model village created by Thomas Salt in the 1850s for wool workers. But the worthy burghers who run the site, which is home to a museum that houses a collection of David Hockney's art, felt a brewery was 'inappropriate'. Local man Hockney would almost certainly disagree.

![Saltaire's gleaming brew kit can be viewed on one of their monthly beer nights when visitors fill the brewery]

Saltaire's gleaming brew kit can be viewed on one of their monthly beer nights when visitors fill the brewery

So Tony and Derek set up their brewery in Shipley in 2006 in a building that was once a power station. In the 19th and 20th centuries, trams struggled to climb the steep streets in Shipley and needed a boost of electricity from the power plant. It's the ideal base for a brewery, with thick, sturdy walls and steel joists and beams. There's a spacious loft that houses a bar and tables where visitors can sample the beers and watch the brewing process. A Beer Club meets there on the first Friday of the month: Gartland says 'it's important to get drinkers in and see the operation. It builds brand loyalty.' That loyalty was emphasised when a beer festival at the site attracted 5,300 people.

BREWLAB GRADUATES

Gartland and Todd met on a Brewers' Laboratory course in Sunderland and set out to create their own company based on a wide portfolio of ales. They have had to tear up the first business plan due to the clamour for their beers. The original 20-barrel kit has been replaced by a custom-built Moeschle plant that allows them to brew 12 times a week with

Dave Sanders (left)
with the Saltaire
brewery team

a brew length of 22½ barrels. While the equipment is German-built, it's designed along English lines, with mash tuns and coppers feeding a mix of square and conical fermenters. Three more fermenters were on order in 2014 as demand for the beers is insatiable.

Beer is supplied to Manchester, York and Sheffield, with Wetherspoons taking it further afield. Saltaire also has substantial sales for its bottled beers: production of draught and bottled is evenly split. The runaway best-seller is Blonde, 4%, which accounts for half the brewery's production. As well as the regular beer, there are versions made with the addition of elderflowers and raspberries. Gartland, Todd and their team aren't afraid to try out unusual ingredients: their Triple Chocoholic has won top awards from CAMRA and SIBA and is brewed with chocolate and cocoa, while Hazelnut Porter has crushed nuts alongside malts and hops.

Saltaire has a solid core of 10 to 12 regular beers and great use is made of local ingredients, with some hops coming from a farm underneath the Humber Bridge. The brewery is now so busy that it has a workforce of 20. And who is that beavering away in the brewhouse – none other than Dave Sanders, creator of Elland 1872 Porter. Yorkshire brewing is a tight community.

Beers to try ...

Blonde, 4%
Brewed with just Czech Saaz hops, with a touch of caramalt blended with Maris Otter pale. It has a grassy hop nose with creamy malt, tart fruit in the mouth balancing herbal hops, with a dry, fruity and hoppy finish.

Cascade Pale Ale, 4.8%
In spite of the name, this is brewed with both Cascade and Centennial hops. Pale malt is blended with a touch of pale crystal. It has a pronounced biscuit malt aroma with fruity hops, followed by rich malt in the mouth balancing hop resins and citrus fruit, with a dry, bitter and fruity finish.

Smoked Porter, 6%
Brewed with pale, dark crystal, cara and oat malts and hopped with Hersbrucker and Magnum varieties. It has a big smoked malt and burnt fruit nose, with dark vinous fruit and floral hops in the mouth, followed by a dry, complex finish with liquorice, burnt fruit and bitter hops.

BEER DESTINATIONS

EAST YORKSHIRE, NORTH YORKSHIRE, SOUTH YORKSHIRE, WEST YORKSHIRE

GROVE
Huddersfield, West Yorkshire
www.groveinn.co.uk
01484 430113

This beer paradise is situated in a sandstone corner pub that has been around since the 1850s when Huddersfield was in the throes of the Industrial Revolution. There are nearly 20 cask beers (and nearly the same amount of craft keg lines) at this lively and comfortable pub (and let's not forget the bottles either) – a pub that bridges the divide between thrusting craft breweries and more established family firms. This means that beers from the likes of Arbor, local heroes Magic Rock, Thornbridge and Harbour sit happily alongside Taylor's Landlord and something from Fuller's. As the saying goes: so many beers, so little time.

KELHAM ISLAND BREWERY
Sheffield, South Yorkshire
www.kelhambrewery.co.uk

The brewery was founded by a Sheffield legend, Dave Wickett. He was a university lecturer but his love of good beer encouraged him to take over a rundown pub and re-open it as the Fat Cat in 1981. Devoted to real ale, the pub drew hordes of drinkers in Steel City. In 1990 Wickett added Kelham Island brewery next to the pub, which was an immediate success. To keep pace with demand, a bigger brewery was built just a few yards away and, with its Loft Bar, offers a wide range of brewery tours for parties of 10 or more, with meals and beer tastings as added attractions. After the tour, visitors can sample the Kelham Island beers, including Best Bitter,

Pride of Sheffield and Pale Rider, which are also available in the Fat Cat. Bottled versions can be bought in the brewery shop. Dave Wickett died in 2012 but his son Edward keeps the family flag flying.

NORTH BAR
Leeds, West Yorkshire
www.northbar.com

From the outside, North is a bit of an enigma. Its façade is a lattice of big open windows reaching up from the pavement, suggesting a fashionable café bar. Step inside and there's a long, lean bar, with polished wooden floors and framed posters and photos decorating the wall (they also have regular art exhibitions). Wine bar perhaps? Look closer and the gleaming, stainless steel taps, ramrod straight hand pumps and fridges full of brightly labelled bottles from all over the world loudly proclaim that beer in all its beautiful varieties is king here – cask is local where possible, which means the likes of Ilkley, Kirkstall and Roosters. You could argue that North was the northern axis of the craft bar pioneers (the White Horse was the southern one) when it opened in the 1990s, and since then it's become a gleaming, sturdy, bounteous trailblazer for good beer that attracts male and female and old and young.

YORK BREWERY
York, North Yorkshire
www.york-brewery.co.uk

The brewery is a short walk from the station and castle and is based in the former city morgue: no jokes about it being a good place for a stiff drink. It

opened in 1996 and was the first new brewery opened within the city walls for 40 years. It's now owned by Mitchell's of Lancaster, which closed its own brewery in 1999 but then got an itch to brew again. You can tour the compact brewery with its 20-barrel plant then clamber up narrow stairs that lead into a surprisingly spacious Tap Room with tables fashioned from wooden beer casks and decorated with brewery memorabilia. The bar serves the brewery's three regular beers, Guzzler, Yorkshire Terrier and Centurion's Ghost as well as monthly specials.

YORK TAP
York, North Yorkshire
www.yorktap.com

Off the train and straight into the pub! What better way to start a visit to York. The York Tap, entered from the platform, with its restored Edwardian design, is breathtaking. The original bar closed after World War Two and for many years it was a model railway museum. It's been restored by the Pivni Group, which runs similar station taps at London Euston and Sheffield. The York Tap is dominated by a large circular bar with a central gantry and has a marble floor, large windows with views of the city to one side and the station to the other, and comfortable leather chairs and chesterfields. There are many Art Nouveau touches, including lampshades and an impressive stained-glass cupola in the ceiling. No fewer than 20 handpumps dispense a big range of Yorkshire beers and you may find Roosters, Tapped Brew Co and Wold Top, plus Thornbridge's Jaipur from Derbyshire.

The York Tap can be accessed straight from the platform of York Station and serves beers from Yorkshire and further afield from 20 handpumps

NORTH EAST ENGLAND

DURHAM, NORTHUMBERLAND, TYNE & WEAR

The Northeast of England was once synonymous with coal mining, shipbuilding and Newcastle Brown Ale. Sadly all the mines have now closed, ships aren't built on the Tyne, Wear or Tees, and Newcastle Brown Ale is no longer brewed in Newcastle, but has been moved to Tadcaster.

In the early 1980s, the region's brewing scene was dominated by large Victorian breweries: Scottish & Newcastle appeared to run every pub on Tyneside and in Northumberland with keg Exhibition and McEwans Scotch on the bar, Sunderland-based Vaux ruled the roost on the Wear, and the northern outpost of the Whitbread empire, Castle Eden, supplied pubs in County Durham and beyond.

GASSY KEG

Working men's clubs were supplied with cheap, gassy keg beer from the Federation brewery: but the clubs have declined and the brewery no longer exists, having been sold to S&N in 2004. Of them all, the only large-scale brewery still standing is Hartlepool's Lion brewery, established by Camerons in 1865. It changed ownership several times and became independent again in 2002.

But the indomitable spirit of the Northeast has seen a resurgence in brewing. The first seeds of the Northeast's

BEER DESTINATIONS
> go to page 252

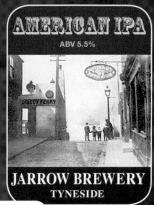

Jarrow: Jarrow, Tyne & Wear

Tynemouth
Newcastle
Gateshead **Jarrow**
Sunderland

Houghton le Spring

Durham

Maxim: Houghton le Spring, County Durham

Durham: Bowburn, County Durham

microbrewing revolution were sown by Big Lamp, formed in 1982 just outside Newcastle city centre. It relocated in 1996 and built a new brewery in an old water pumping station at Newburn, where urban Newcastle meets rural Northumberland and the river Tyne enters Tyneside.

MICROBREWING BOOM

In the early 1990s several more microbreweries joined Big Lamp. Hexhamshire brews in a former milking parlour on an upland farm. Durham brewery was founded by two music teachers in 1994 and has gone on to brew many award-winning beers, gaining national recognition for its bottled beers. Mordue brewery was created by two brothers in 1995, picking the name after the brothers learned there had been a successful brewery of that name based locally in the nineteenth century. Gary and Matthew Fawcett surprised everyone – including themselves – when after only two years their Workie Ticket won the Gold award in the strong bitter category of the Champion Beer of Britain competition. This was the first of many prestigious awards, including CAMRA's Champion Best Bitter of Britain in 2013.

Throughout the 21st century each year has seen the formation of new breweries creating high-quality beers. Some of the breweries have relocated to larger premises with greater capacity. Hadrian Border started as two small breweries and has moved on and built a much bigger plant. When Hadrian Border moved out, Julia Austin, who had been searching for a location for her new start-up Tyne Bank brewery, moved in. In Tyne Bank's first three years it has won a number of awards and succeeded in selling its beer nationwide.

SNUG IN A PUB

Jarrow has grown from a tiny brewery in a pub's snug to a purpose-built brewery in a dairy and has recently built a new site as demand for the beers has grown. Wylam brewery has also had to redevelop and built a larger brewery, but has remained in the same rural location in the Tyne Valley.

Maxim brewery, established in 2007, has rescued Vaux's famous Double Maxim and other historic beers. It has also created a number of new beers that are sold widely in pubs and supermarkets but its main success lies in restoring the Northeast's famous strong brown ale tradition.

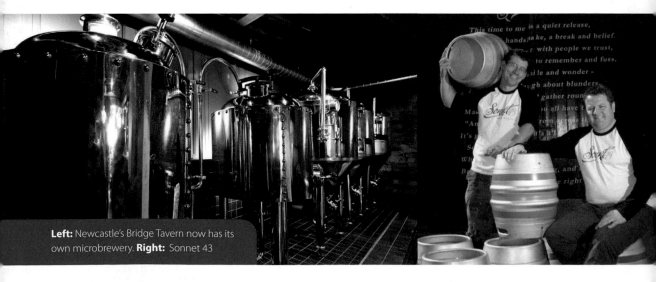

Left: Newcastle's Bridge Tavern now has its own microbrewery. **Right:** Sonnet 43

BREWING ACADEMY

The Northeast plays an important role in the development of breweries throughout the British Isles and globally. Sunderland's Brew Lab, which started in Sunderland University, is now independent and is one of the few places where people can study brewing in depth. The courses range from short courses aimed at serious enthusiasts to in-depth programmes that enable students to start a career in brewing or set up their own production units. Countless craft brewers owe their existence to the work of the laboratory.

A number of breweries that have been launched in the past few years have rapidly achieved success, in particular Sonnet 43 based in County Durham and Anarchy in Northumberland. The Ouseburn area of Newcastle is a focal point for real ale, with a cluster of pubs supporting local breweries. It's also the home of Tyne Bank and Out There Brewing Company. In 2012 the then Bishop of Durham, Justin Welby, officially opened Black Paw Brewery in Bishop Auckland. Justin Welby is now the Archbishop of Canterbury and Black Paw Brewery is flourishing, proving perhaps that God and Mammon can co-exist.

Temptation is another recent start-up, brewing American-inspired ales using ingredients from the US. The Workers Education Association in 2002 ran a course on traditional home brewing and people who attended formed the Darlington Traditional Brewing Group. One of their members, Pete Fenwick, went on to set up Mithril Ales, which supplies free houses in the Darlington and Richmond areas.

There has also been a growth in brewpubs producing beer solely for consumption in-house. The Ship at Low Newton is a picturesque producer of ales while in Newcastle upon Tyne, the Trent and the Bridge Tavern also brew on the premises.

With more and more pubs championing locally-produced beer, there has never been a better time for drinkers in the Northeast, free at last from the grip of giant breweries producing industrial fizz.

Insider's view...

Tony Brookes

Until the 1980s, Northeast beer lovers had to put up with just a handful of pubs serving real ale. Things started to change, with the opening of the first Legendary Yorkshire Heroes real ale off-licence in Newcastle and the associated beer agency in 1980. More pubs started to stock real ales, with Sir John Fitzgerald pubs at the forefront. The Government's Beer Orders in 1990 – which restricted the number of pubs owned by big breweries and forced them to serve guest beers from other breweries – led to a burst of new real ale outlets and it was clear the old order had gone forever.

While the decimation of the old order was going on, scores of new breweries sprang up to take their place: in Darlington in 1979, Kelly's Real Ale brewery; in Newcastle, Big Lamp started in 1982, followed by Hadrian in 1987. Then the floodgates opened and now there are more than microbreweries in the region – the biggest being Durham, Maxim, Mordue and Wylam.

Brewpubs are being established at a fast rate, with Newcastle due to have five open by 2015. The ale drinker in the Northeast now has a great choice, from breweries near and far.

Tony Brookes founded the specialist beer group Head of Steam, which had its head office in Newcastle. The pubs were bought in 2014 by Camerons. Tony remains a consultant to the brewery

Established: 1994

Founder: Steve and Christine Gibbs

Beers: Magus, John Duck, Apollo, Black Velvet, White Gold, White Amarillo, Cloister, Evensong, St Cuthbert, Bombay 106, White Stout, Benedictus, Bede's Chalice, Redemption, Diabolus, Temptation

Website: www.durhambrewery.co.uk

DURHAM

Bowburn, Durham

If you ask Durham's brewer and co-founder Steve Gibbs what he looks for in his beers, his reply makes it relatively easy to guess what he used to do before he started brewing.

'Classic art and music have poise and balance,' says the former music teacher, 'while intensity and passion are key ingredients. I believe that beer is an art form which, at its best, displays these qualities. Its component parts must be integrated and balanced. It should be satisfying and enjoyable.'

You can see what he means by the beers he brews. They possess an appetising drinkability: Magus is a light golden ale, refined and refreshing with plenty of bright citrus notes, it's a popular session beer and one of the brewery's best sellers; Evensong is a more sombre number, darker in colour and based on a beer brewed in the 1930s

by then thriving Halifax brewers Whitakers. This is described by Gibbs as a 'cross between bitter and old ale', and was CAMRA's Champion bottle-conditioned beer in 2005.

On the other hand, if we want to talk about the sense of innovation that has drives Durham along it creative path, then grab a glass of White Stout, an aromatic, complex and earthy beer released in 2011. Its name caused a lot of head scratching, even among drinkers who had readily accepted the controversial black IPA, a beer style that Gibbs has strong views on.

'Personally, I found the term ridiculous,' he says. 'How can there be a black pale ale? The link with IPA is through extreme hopping of an American nature... but black? The style is new, and rather than using double-think why not invent a new name?'

"Intensity and passion are key ingredients. I believe that beer is an art form which, at its best, displays these qualities. Its component parts must be integrated and balanced. It should be satisfying and enjoyable"

Durham's expanding portfolio of beers range from wheat beer to stout, and are all brewed on their gleaming kit

"Personally, I found the term ridiculous. How can there be a black pale ale?... The style is new, and rather than using double-think why not invent a new name?"

Yet you could argue that he's not prone to a bit of stirring with White Stout, which was introduced in 2011, but as he calmly points out the term has historic precedent. 'Before stout porter stole the word "stout" and placed it firmly in dark territory,' he says, 'stout was used to denote strong beers. Pale stouts and brown stouts were commonplace. Our White Stout is a modern pale stout at 7.2%, though not to be confused with an IPA. IPA should be fairly dry and well attenuated. White Stout has a fuller body. It is bitter but not greatly so, concentrating on a rich body and hop aroma.'

EXPANDING HORIZONS
Steve Gibbs had been a keen home-brewer since his teens, first of all starting with basic kits and then moving onto full-mash brewing. When he and his wife Christine were made redundant from their teaching jobs in 1994, he felt it was time to do something about his love of beer and Durham Brewery was the result. The legendary Sean Franklin at Roosters brewery was an early influence.

'I started to make very pale beers with complex flavours,' recalls Gibbs. These were joined by beers that looked beyond the British Isles for their influences, such as the full-flavoured and lubricious Belgian-style Tripel Bede's Chalice.

'In recent years, we have been innovating in more unusual ways,' he says. 'Diabolus is our Imperial Russian stout Temptation refermented and aged with gueuze yeast. The first aim was to make a Russian stout with *Brettanomyces* yeast

but there were already a number of these about using English *Brett*, so I gave Diabolus a Belgian sourness instead. Raspbeery Saison uses dark malts - which are unusual for a saison - saison yeast, and raspberry juice.

'This was a risky experiment that has exceeded all our expectations. The components all give distinctive characteristics to the beer. The spice of saison, plus chocolate from the malts, and the fruity acidity of the raspberry combine in a beer which comes close to a red wine and is excellent with food.'

Gibbs also produces fruit-flavoured Weisse beers, which see a classic Hefeweizen style fermented with natural fruit juice. He describes these as thirst-quenching with a difference. 'Not sweet like fruit beers normally are, but with the sugar fermented out. The Raspberry is acidic and tart like cider, and the Mango has gentle fruit qualities.'

UNDERAPPRECIATED BREWING TREASURE
Gibbs is a thoughtful brewer and dedicated to his craft. His brewery is not a noisy creature that lives on Instagram and Twitter (though it has embraced social media), and I have a sense that he's an underappreciated British brewing treasure. On the other hand, the musician in him brings a great sense of exploration to his brewing techniques, producing a variety of exceptional beers that readily chime with the revolutionary spirit of the current brewing age.

In 2014 the brewery celebrated its 20th anniversary and Gibbs marked it with a new 10% 'White Beer' called 1994 (the now defunct 'White Range' was a strand of beers he produced in the early days). It was based on White Stout with some being packaged in 750ml commemorative bottles.

'So, although the brewery has moved through many beer styles and new ideas, our anniversary beer came full circle, back to the "White Beers",' he says. 'I couldn't resist a tweak though. The beer was Trappist inspired and I added pink peppercorns.'

Casks of beer are racked by hand. Many of the beers are also available bottle-conditioned

Beers to try ...

Evensong, 5%
A traditional old school strong ale with plenty of citrus aromas and flavour notes, with a rich malty background. As it grows older in the bottle, it becomes more wine-like.

White Stout, 7.2%
Dark orange gold, an aromatic nose of ripe berries and freshly sliced red apple, while it's very complex in its fruitiness (ripe rich currants/plums perhaps?), soft rounded mouthfeel and an ambush of bitterness in the finish.

Bede's Chalice, 9%
Belgian-style golden Tripel with a crystalline citrus character on the nose, on the palate a Cointreau like fieriness along with white pepper before finishing dry and alcoholic.

Mikaela Finnigan is the head brewer at Jarrow. She started her brewing career early and, at 19, was the country's youngest brewster

Established: 2002

Founder: Alison and Jess McConnell

Beers: Bitter, Rivet Catcher, Joblings Swinging Gibbet, Caulker, Red Ellen, McConnell's Irish Stout, Westoe IPA, Isis, American IPA

Website: www.jarrowbrewery.co.uk

JARROW

Jarrow, Tyne & Wear

Jarrow brewery was launched in 2002 by CAMRA enthusiasts Alison and Jess McConnell who had run pubs for many years. Jess was born in Jarrow, the town on the south bank of the Tyne that's forever remembered as the starting point for the Jarrow Crusade when local people marched to London in 1936 to protest against unemployment.

Jess worked in industry and then as half of an award-winning comedy duo, the Jarrow Lads. His first pub, the Jarrow Lad, reflected his previous occupation. Alison McConnell was also born on Tyneside and before joining the pub trade worked in London in publishing. The pair teamed up to run pubs and they were travelling to York one day when their car broke down and they had to stop overnight at the Station Hotel in Easingwold. It changed the course of their career, for the pub had a small on-site brewery in former stables, which inspired Alison and Jess to set up their own pub brewery.

They booked a place on a brewing course in York and then bought the Robin Hood, a closed and burnt-out pub in Jarrow. They refurbished it and installed a small-scale brewing plant. The first brew was Jarrow Bitter, a light, golden session bitter that continues to be one of their most popular beers.

STRONG START

In the first year of operation, Jarrow brewery won five awards at CAMRA beer festivals. The most significant was for a beer that's become the brewery's flagship: Rivet Catcher. It's loosely based on Fenwick's Special, which was created by Darlington-based home brewers Pete Fenwick and Ian Jackson. The recipe was tweaked and developed for commercial brewing using Jarrow's yeast and stock ingredients. Rivet Catcher has won CAMRA's

Alison and Jess booked a place on a brewing course in York and then bought the Robin Hood, a closed and burnt-out pub in Jarrow. They refurbished it and installed a small-scale brewing plant

Alison and Jess McConnell were inspired to add a brewery to their pub when they visited the pub brewery at the Station Hotel in Easingwold

Champion Beer of the North, and both Silver and Bronze in the Golden Ales category of the Champion Beer of Britain awards.

Jarrow's policy is to name beers that reflect local heritage and traditions. Rivet Catcher is named for the riveters who were an important part of the shipyard trade while the stronger Caulker is named after tradesmen who made ships' joints watertight.

In the Northeast, Teesside with its steel industry has a tradition for strong ruby beers such as Samson and Strongarm, while Tyneside prefers lower strength beers and the Northern/ Scottish equivalent of mild, know as Scotch. The Northeastern taste profile is sweeter than southern England's. Red Ellen is a beer created with Teesside traditions in mind: strong, full bodied and a rich ruby red. Red Ellen was the nickname of Ellen Wilkinson, one of the first women MPs. She represented Jarrow in parliament and was also one of the leaders of the Jarrow March. The historic

event is further marked by Old Cornelius, named after the last surviving participant on the march, Cornelius Whelen.

EXPANSION AND GROWTH

In 2008 Jarrow brewery moved out of its small space at the Robin Hood to much larger premises and a 10-barrel plant built on the site of a former co-operative dairy, down river at South Shields. Above the brewery is the Maltings pub that was developed at the same time as the brewery. After a few years, demand for Jarrow beers meant Alison and Jess had to move to yet bigger premises and in autumn 2013 a new brewery started production in Jarrow. The Maltings site is still used for short-runs, new development and speciality beers.

Jarrow's new brewery has a 40-barrel brew length and is primarily used to satisfy demand for Rivet Catcher. It's very much a family brewery, run by Alison and Jess. Their youngest daughter

Mikaela is the head brewer – when she was 19 she was the country's youngest brewster – while siblings Lewis and Jannine provide support. The small brewing team is passionate about the beers, which are now available nationally. As the brewery slogan put it, they're beers you'd go a long way for. But the Northeast will always remain the central focus for Jarrow's customer base.

It's very much a family brewery, run by Alison and Jess. Their youngest daughter Mikaela is the head brewer – when she was 19 she was the country's youngest brewster – while siblings Lewis and Jannine provide support.

Beer trends...
BOTTLE CONDITIONING

Pasteurised bottled beer can taste cardboard-like and cooked, with the carbonation and alcohol (if it's strong) about the only thing that makes it stand out.

Filtered, un-pasteurised beers are fine, some are delicious, but to achieve the very best of beer in the bottle, many breweries, whether in the UK or further afield, swear by bottle conditioning (or as CAMRA calls its accreditation scheme, 'Real ale in a bottle'), where finished beer is bottled directly with remaining or added live yeast and allowed to naturally carbonate and further condition in the bottle. This is much the same as the secondary fermentation that real ale enjoys in cask.

Some brewers bottle-condition beer because the live yeast scavenges oxygen left in the bottle after closure, preventing oxidation and keeping the beer fresher (though hop character does mute over time). Others do it because the presence of the yeast helps to support an extra layer of complexity, while others believe it helps to give stronger beers better character during a longer maturation period (a similar argument that underlines the lagering of cold-fermented beers). Whatever the reason for bottle conditioning, it can result in some spectacular beers.

Back in the 1970s, famously there were only five bottle-conditioned beers available in the UK: Guinness Extra Stout, Courage's Russian Imperial Stout, Gale's Prize Old Ale, Worthington's White Shield and Thomas Hardy's Ale. Now only White Shield is bottle conditioned, although the rest of the beers – apart, sadly, from Thomas Hardy's Ale – are still being made.

The best bottle-conditioned beers continue to mature in the bottle, developing more rounded and deeper flavours. When one is on form you have a superb beer that is not only complex and engaging but is something to tantalise those drinkers who think that wine and whisky are the only drinks that improve with time.

> *"Bottle conditioning is, in my opinion, the best way to experience bottled beer. Flavour and body will be at their maximum and shelf life will be extended."*

Steve Gibbs, director and head brewer of Durham brewery

Bottle conditioning is, in my opinion, the best way to experience bottled beer. The key to really good bottle conditioning is to do as little to the beer as possible so that it can reach perfection naturally. The continued presence of yeast cleans by-products of the primary fermentation and scavenges any oxygen. Flavour and body will be at their maximum and shelf life will be extended.

Andy Smith, head brewer at Partizan brewery in London

We bottle condition partly out of necessity. I suspect that even if we were to grow and automate packaging, which would then give us more option to filter/force carbonate the beer, we would still choose bottle conditioning. The biggest benefit in my opinion is the oxygen scavenging properties of the yeast as beer is very prone to staleing. Yeast helps to keep beer fresher. Oxygen can also react with esters from fermentation to create unpleasant flavours like acetic acid or acetaldehyde. Generally these are all flaws in a younger fresher beer and can be in small quantities desirable in an older beer. Basically the yeast slows down the ageing so can help to keep young beers fresher but can also help with older beers to give a longer maturation period.

Stuart Howe, head of craft brewing and innovation at Molson Coors

At Sharp's we bottle condition our Connoisseur's Choice beers, Chalky's Bite and Bark and Cornish Pilsner. At Franciscan Well we bottle condition our Friar Weisse and Rebel Red and of course at Worthington's the White Shield is a classic of the style. I tend to think that stronger beers support higher yeast concentrations and a greater level of bottle fermentation. There is more substance to support the extra layer of complexity and more body and sweetness to control with the carbonation. Weaker beers are preserved better with low yeast counts and less bottle fermentation. It's up to the brewer to work with the bottling options as part of the recipe design. As with most brewing techniques some breweries make claims about flaws in a technique in order to justify their methods. There is no foundation to claims that bottle conditioning when done properly damages hop aroma and flavour.

Worthington's White Shield was once one of only a handful of beers still bottle-conditioned, but it's now been joined by myriad others, including those brewed by Sharp's, Durham and Partizan

Mark Anderson has helped to bring a Northeastern brewing icon back from the ashes to new success

Established: 2007

Founder: Mark Anderson, Doug Trotman and Jim Murray

Beers: Delilah, Lambton's, Stampede IPA, Black Maxim, Samson, The Great Escape, Ward's Best Bitter, Boxing Hare, Anderson's Best Scotch, Swedish Blonde, The Simcoe Kid, Space Hopper, Surf n Sup, Double Maxim, Stiff Tackle IPA, Santa's Soot, American Pride IPA, Maximus

Website: www.maximbrewery.co.uk

MAXIM

Houghton le Spring, County Durham

There's a large hole in the centre of Sunderland where the Vaux brewery once stood, tall and proud, a major employer in the town, until it was asset-stripped and closed in 1999. But senior managers from Vaux have restored the brewery's famous brands and brought pride back to Wearside.

THE PASSING OF AN ICON

Vaux was a mighty company. It rivalled Greene King and Marston's as a large regional brewer. It was famous for its Double Maxim brown ale, a Northeast speciality that predated Newcastle Brown by more than 20 years. Vaux owned Ward's in Sheffield and between them they brewed half a million barrels of beer a year and also had 888 pubs and Swallow Hotels – and it was the pubs and hotels that attracted the attention of City vultures.

The brewery was founded in 1837 by Cuthbert Vaux and passed through marriage to the Nicholson family. But Vaux became a public company in 1927 and by the 1990s chairman Sir Paul Nicholson and managing director Frank Nicholson controlled only two per cent of the shares and were in a weak position to fight the City institutions that owned the bulk of the business.

Vaux went into freefall in 1998 when a new chief executive and finance director were appointed and recommended that the breweries should close, with all the group's shares transferred to Swallow Hotels. Two senior executives at Vaux, Mark Anderson and Doug Trotman, put together a management buy-out that offered £75.5m for the breweries and 350 pubs but they were told their bid was £5 million short and in 1999 the breweries closed.

Vaux was famous for its Double Maxim brown ale, a Northeast speciality that predated Newcastle Brown by more than 20 years

Head brewer Glen Whale with the brew kit that Maxim purchased from the Scottish & Newcastle pilot plant

A NEW START

But Vaux has risen from the ashes. Mark Anderson, Doug Trotman and former head brewer Jim Murray were determined to resurrect Double Maxim, Samson, Lambton's and Ward's Best Bitter. They launched the Maxim Beer Company in 2000 and bought the rights to the brands from the owners. At first they were brewed under licence and only available in bottled form but they kept the names alive in pubs and supermarkets in the Northeast and Yorkshire.

There's now a substantial brewery based in spacious buildings at Houghton-le-Spring just outside Sunderland. Anderson, Trotman and Murray were able to buy the former Scottish & Newcastle pilot brewery plant in Edinburgh for

£70,000. A further £170,000 was spent on moving the kit to the new site and installing it, along with building work and electrics. The brewery opened and began brewing in 2008.

It says a lot about the relative size of national and small regional breweries that the S&N pilot plant, used by the big brewer for trial brews, enables Maxim to brew up to the cut-off mark for Small Brewers' Relief – 60,000 hectolitres a year – and pay lower rates of duty.

Jim Murray has now retired and the head brewer is Glen Whale, ex S&N and – mention it quietly – a Newcastle United supporter: Vaux was a long-standing sponsor of Sunderland FC and the club's shirts hang prominently in the brewery's bar and reception area.

Vaux has risen from the ashes. Mark Anderson, Doug Trotman and former head brewer Jim Murray were determined to resurrect Double Maxim, Samson, Lambton's and Ward's Best Bitter

Production is split between bottle and draught and Mark Anderson says the cask side of the business is growing. Maxim sells draught beer via Coors and also direct to Wetherspoon, Mitchells & Butlers and Punch pubs. The brewery's beers are available as far south as Sheffield and also in Durham, Hartlepool, Sunderland and York.

New beers, including Swedish Blonde and Maximus, a 6% stronger version of Double Maxim, have been added, along with seasonal beers. But Double Maxim remains the core brand in bottle and cask. It was launched in 1901 and named in recognition of Colonel Ernest Vaux who had led a Maxim gun detachment during the Boer War. It was increased in strength in 1938 and renamed Double Maxim to tackle the might of Newcastle Breweries and its Brown Ale on Tyneside. Its rival, the iconic Newcastle Brown Ale has lost its credibility – and an EU Guarantee of Origin – by being moved by Scottish & Newcastle to John Smith's brewery in Yorkshire.

Maxim has returned famous brands to Wearside. Back in the centre of Sunderland, the Vaux site was sold to Tesco for £13 million but the supermarket group's plans have stalled. The site is now being turned in to a road, leading no doubt to the graveyard of lost dreams. But in Houghton le Spring dreams have been turned into reality and Double Maxim is once again firing on all cylinders.

Beers to try ...

Samson, 4%
Brewed with Maris Otter pale malt, crystal and caramel, and all English hops, it has a creamy, honeyed malt nose with a good underpinning of peppery and spicy hops. Raisin fruit is evident in the mouth and the finish is bittersweet with earthy hops balancing the rich malt and dark fruit notes.

Swedish Blonde, 4.2%
A new addition to the range, brewed with pale malt and hopped with American Cascade and English First Gold. It has a juicy, light biscuit aroma balanced by tart fruit, with citrus building in the mouth, and a long, dry, fruity and hoppy finish.

Double Maxim, 4.7%
Brewed with pale and crystal malts with caramel and primed with sugar. It's a single hop beer, using Fuggles. It has a fruity – apricots and plums – aroma and palate, with earthy hop notes. The finish is dry, nutty, fruity and malty with light hop notes.

BEER DESTINATIONS

DURHAM, NORTHUMBERLAND, TYNE & WEAR

Tynemouth
Newcastle
Gateshead
Sunderland

CENTRAL
Gateshead, Tyne & Wear
www.theheadofsteam.co.uk/gateshead

Its nickname is 'the coffin' as a result of its unusual wedge-shape. The pub dates from 1856 and is a Grade II-listed building, a four-storey extravaganza of Victorian design. It fell into disrepair but was rescued by the Head of Steam pub group, which also owns pubs in Newcastle, Durham, Huddersfield and Tynemouth. The group spent a fortune restoring the Central, and now you can revel in its full glory, with chandeliers, stained glass windows, intricate plasterwork and friezes. The centrepiece is the stupendous area known as the Buffet, with a carved U-shaped counter and magnificent mahogany back bar. There's a small, intimate snug while upstairs there are function rooms and even a rooftop terrace. Downstairs, 14 handpumps serve beers from Big Lamp, Black Sheep and Wylam, with Harviestoun Bitter & Twisted from north of the border. These are occasionaly supplanted by themed beer festivals. Recent ones include a Yorkshire beer festival and Americana.

CROWN POSADA
Newcastle, Tyne & Wear
www.crownposadanewcastle.co.uk

A jewel in the pantheon of great English pubs, the Crown Posada is recognised by CAMRA as having a nationally important historic pub interior. It's around 250 years old and its curious name stems from the 19th century when a Spanish sea captain installed his mistress here: posada is Spanish for inn or resting place. The road it sits on leads down to the Quayside where ships plied their trade when Newcastle was a flourishing port. You enter the pub through a wrought-iron gate and find yourself in a long, narrow room divided by mahogany and stained glass screens. There's a bench-seated lounge at the rear where you can admire the ornately moulded ceiling. But the pub's main glory lies in two superb stained glass windows, one showing a pre-Raphaelite woman filling a glass, the second a man in Tudor attire raising that glass to the heavens. The walls of the pub are covered in local photos of old Newcastle and cartoons of former customers. Beer comes from rotating local breweries and may include Consett, Tyne Bank and Wylam, with Fyne Ales from Scotland.

MUSEUM VAULTS
Sunderland, Tyne & Wear
0191 565 9443

The Vaults was a beer house – which means it sold neither wine nor spirits – until 1978, and has been run by the same family for more than 40 years. It sells the full range of Maxim brewery beers, which is fitting as the pub stands opposite the site of the demolished, asset-stripped and much-missed Vaux brewery, best known for its Double Maxim brown ale. It's a small, comfortable pub with open fires in winter – it can be bitterly cold in this part of the world – and is home to several local groups. The landlord hosts regular book fairs. It's also a shrine to Sunderland football club and is decked out with red and white mementos. The Maxim beers are complemented by many other ales from breweries in the Northeast.

TYNEMOUTH LODGE HOTEL
Tynemouth, Tyne & Wear
www.tynemouthlodgehotel.co.uk

Dating from 1799, this attractive tiled freehouse is a Tyneside institution, which claims to have the biggest sales of Draught Bass in the area. The U-shaped bar offers just good beer – no TV or canned music. As well as Bass, there's a wide range of cask beers, often from Scotland: Deuchar's IPA is a regular. Mordue beers also feature. They have a policy of stocking fast-selling house beers to ensure that that the cask beer is always fresh. The Tynemouth Lodge Hotel been in every edition of the *Good Beer Guide* for 30 years and landlord Hugh Price was awarded a certificate for this achievement by the local CAMRA branch, which is displayed in the bar. There's a large beer garden on the edge of Northumberland Park and it's a useful watering hole for those tackling the Coast-to-Coast cycle route. In spite of the name, the hotel does not provide accommodation.

The Central in Gateshead is owned by the Head of Steam pub group whose award-winning pubs serve a great range of beers

Orkney: Quoyloo, Orkney

Orkney Isles

Highland: Swannay, Orkney

Aberdeen

Williams Brothers: Alloa, Clackmannanshire

Harviestoun: Alva, Clackmannanshire

Cairndow

Alva Alloa

Glasgow

Edinburgh Loanhead

Livingston

Fyne Ales: Cairndow, Argyll

Stewart: Loanhead, Midlothian

STEWART BREWING

EDINBURGH NO.3

PREMIUM SCOTTISH ALE
4.3% ABV

Alechemy: Livingston, West Lothian

ALECHE

SCOTLAND

Scotland's beer has enjoyed a remarkable renaissance in recent years. For decades brewing was dominated by a duopoly of Scottish & Newcastle and Tennent Caledonian, who concentrated on lager and indifferent keg beer. But the success of Caledonian Deuchars IPA in the late 1980s led to a flowering of new breweries that have brought a choice that includes both traditional and new styles of beer.

The country's brewing heritage is framed by its climate and geography. Rugged terrain, isolated communities, mountains and snow have all played their part in developing a style of beer that has to warm drinkers as well as refresh them. A similar role is played by beer's close cousin, whisky, whose original Gaelic name *uisge beatha* means water of life.

MATURING BEER IN WHISKY CASKS

Both beer and whisky have played a crucial role in sustaining the Scots and it's fitting that in recent years a number of brewers have cemented the link between the two drinks by maturing strong ale in wooden casks supplied by distillers.

Beer and whisky production divided Scotland in two. Beer requires the finest quality malting barley and that grows mainly in the Lowlands, which is where most commercial breweries developed. Whisky on the other hand, as a result of distillation and long ageing, can use poorer grain grown in the north. Scottish beer for centuries was rich and malty, and was less heavily hopped than beers south of the border. Hops were grown for a while in the Borders but as the climate grew

BEER DESTINATIONS
> go to page 280

colder the plant perished, though there are now efforts being made to grow hops again, courtesy of climate change.

The earliest brewers in Scotland were the Picts, who brewed a potent beer made with heather. A recipe for heather ale was discovered in the 1990s and led to the William Brothers brewery in Alloa developing Fraoch, brewed with heather and ginger as well as barley malt and hops. It has become a cult beer in its homeland and is widely exported.

RICH, WARMING AND HEAVY

Exporting beer has played an important role in Scotland. A commercial industry grew in the 18th century and supplied not only the domestic market but also North America, the Caribbean, India and Australasia, where many Scots had settled following the Highland Clearances. The beers were rich, warming and heavy, reflected in the name Heavy for one leading style. The nature of Scottish beer was also influenced by the Auld Alliance with France: many refugees from the French Revolution settled in Edinburgh and Glasgow and drank ale they dubbed 'Scottish Burgundy'. They were beers made with dark roasted grains and oats as well as pale malt and were lightly hopped.

The nature of beer in Scotland started to change in the 19th century. In step with English brewers who were developing India Pale Ale for export, producers in Edinburgh and Alloa harnessed water rich in sulphates to develop their interpretations of paler beer. While the term IPA was used – most notably in Deuchars IPA – many Scottish brewers preferred to call such beers simply Export, a name that has survived. On the reverse side of the brewing coin, Scots who returned from abroad brought with them a taste for the new golden lager beers they had discovered. Lager brewers sprang up in Edinburgh and Glasgow to meet the demand, heightened by the fact that lager made the perfect chaser for a dram of whisky.

SCOTLAND'S NEW BEER SCENE

A spate of mergers in the 1960s saw the near-destruction of Scotland's brewing heritage, and it seemed that Scotland's rich tradition of beer would be lost. But the beer revolution has seen new independent brewers starting up who have not only restored the country's brewing pride but have also innovated and brought a dynamic new beer scene to the country. From the Borders to Orkney, Shetland and the Western Isles, brewers have rediscovered Scotland's rich tapestry of beer and have added their interpretations of 'New World' beers. Alongside traditional Lights and Heavies, drinkers will find golden ales and IPAs while both Harviestoun and Innis & Gunn have had success in export markets with beers aged in whisky and Bourbon casks. Brewing is no longer just an urban activity. Fyne, in a glen by Loch Fyne, has won acclaim for both a modern golden ale, Jarl, and a traditional Scottish beer, Highlander. BrewDog in Ellon has enjoyed phenomenal success at home and abroad with both beer and bars, though the founders have set their faces against cask-conditioned products. WEST's Bavarian-style beerhouse in Glasgow, run by Petra Wetzel from Bamberg in Germany, shows what true lager can taste like.

Caledonian remains by far the biggest Scottish brewery. Its Deuchars IPA is sold throughout Britain and its success prompted a takeover by Scottish & Newcastle in 2004. S&N in turn was bought by Heineken four years later. Rather than dumbing down Deuchars, the Dutch giant encourages its Amsterdam staff to visit Edinburgh to see 'a real brewery'. Small is evidently beautiful.

From the Borders to Orkney, Shetland and the Western Isles, brewers have rediscovered Scotland's rich tapestry of beer

Insider's view...

Catherine Maxwell Stuart
www.traquair.co.uk

In the 1970s we were only brewing a few times a year at Traquair then CAMRA turned up. They did a lot for regional brewers at a time when Scotland was dominated by just two big brewers: Tennent Caledonian and Scottish & Newcastle. When Michael Jackson mentioned Traquair House Ale in his World Guide to Beer, we started to get interest from the United States, Japan and Scandinavia.

Over the past 20 years there's been an extraordinary explosion of new breweries in Scotland. Many of them are brewing English and European styles – there are very few traditional Scottish ales being produced. I hope they will turn their attention to Scottish styles – I'm sure 'provenance' will come to beer as well as wine.

To keep up with demand for our beers, we've had to add a micro plant next to the main brewery. We're producing 1,000 hectos a year – that's 250,000 bottles. House Ale and Jacobite Ale are now brewed in equal amounts and sales of Jacobite have overtaken House Ale in the US.

Today we're exporting to France, Italy, Finland, Brazil and Chile as well as our established markets. We export between 65 to 70 per cent of our production.

Lady Catherine Maxwell Stuart and her family run Traquair House, Scotland's oldest stately home, and the restored historic Traquair House brewery

Established: 2012

Founder: James Davies

Beers: Rhapsody, Ritual, Five Sisters, Bad Day At The Office, Ten Storey Malt Bomb, Black Aye PA, Up & Atom, Starlaw, Citra Burst, Rye O' Rye, Almighty Mofo

Website: www.alechemybrewing.com

ALECHEMY

Livingstone, West Lothian

Alechemy? Sounds like hubble, bubble, toil and trouble with a bunch of cackling witches sitting around a cauldron. 'Perhaps we were too clever for our own good with the name!' laughs the brewery's founder James Davies. 'Basically the name originated because I'm a chemist by training and the turning of base metals into gold is alchemy, so we used the tag line "turning grain into gold", and hence the name Alechemy.'

The brewery's Great Cosmati is a powerful and strong IPA with a strident and robust citrus character and a bitter finish that's like an air raid siren warning of a bombardment of hop cones. However, just in case you were under the impression that Alechemy is a single issue hop-happy brewery, along comes a curve ball in the shape of Davies praising another of his beers, this time Ritual (originally released under the name Cairnpapple IPA).

'It's a good session beer, a nice easy drinking 4.1% pale ale with Challenger and Cascade,' he says.

'I'm quite fortunate in that I like pretty much every style of beer. I obviously veer more to the hoppy and aromatic but you can't beat a good well-made pint of mild either.'

OPEN-MINDED BREWING

Davies oversees an eclectic and open-minded approach to brewing that is one of Alechemy's great strengths. The beers they make cross a spectrum of styles. Many are exciting and exhilarating with hop varieties such as Cascade, Columbus and Galaxy leaping into the brewing kettle and bringing forth fresh, zingy flavours; others are luscious and lubricious in their malt-forward profile: a chocolate stout here, an oatmeal one there and an amber ale made with rye proudly standing up in the centre of the room over there.

James Davies grew up in Mid Calder in West Lothian and then went off into the world to gain a Masters in chemistry. A PhD in protein glycosylation pathways in brewers yeast followed,

The brewing team who turn hops and malt into gold: James and Adam Davies, Lewis Scothern and Iain Couper

which means that if you want you can call him Dr. He also worked for six years as a molecular biologist and in the field of drug metabolism and pharmacokinetics.

However, beer cast a spell upon him. Before he started Alechemy he was already an accomplished home brewer, who had started with extract kits in college – 'diabolical,' he recalls with a smile – before moving onto a full mash system. There were also the beery epiphanies. 'I visited America a lot and got to like Sierra Nevada, Stone, Rogue and Cigar City's beers and so I started playing about with American styles and trying to get as much hops in a beer as possible – but after my early over enthusiastic almost undrinkable hoppy beers I managed to get some balance.'

And in 2011, with his sense of balance in place, Davies returned home to Mid Calder, found a brewery on an industrial estate in neighbouring Livingston and began the process of turning grain into gold.

"I'm quite fortunate in that I like pretty much every style of beer. I obviously veer more to the hoppy and aromatic but you can't beat a good well-made pint of mild either."

Beers to try...

Black Aye PA, 4.8%
Dark moonless night in colour with scatterings of citrus hovering about the creamy nose; in the glass it mashes up roast and creamy chocolate with a background of slight orange. The finish is dry.

Rye O'Rye, 5.6%
Amber ale spiced with rye; a warming, crunchy and crisp mouthfeel, with plenty of citrus to keep the balance, and a long dry finish.

Almighty Mofo, 7.1%
A gold-amber beer with a pungent nose of grapefruit, orange and leafy hops. There is plenty of boozy orange and a bracing grainy backbone. A smooth mouthfeel leads to a bitterness that won't fade.

Superior IPA gets four separate hop additions in the brewing process, building layers of flavour and aroma, and is available bottle-conditioned

Established: 2001

Founder: Jonny and Tuggy Delap

Beers: Jarl, Piper's Gold, Blooming Brew, Chai.P.A, From the Ashes, Nebula, Maverick, Hurricane Jack, Vital Spark, Avalanche, Highlander, Brewer's Fuel, Holly Daze, Bell Rock, Bell Rock 'N' Hop, Fladda Rock, Fladda Rock 'N' Roll, Muckle Flugga, Sanda Black IPA, Sanda Blonde IPA, Start Point, Weavers Point, Landslide, Snotty IPA, Sublime Stout, Zombier, Superior IPA

Website: www.fyneales.com

FYNE ALES

Cairndow, Argyll

You come to drink in the scenery as well as the beer at Fyne. The brewery stands at the head of Loch Fyne in glorious countryside, with deeply-wooded hills rising in the background. It's a sea loch and the area is famous for its oysters and kippers. The name means Loch of the Vine, though as vines don't grow there, the success of the brewery and its hoppy ales suggest the name should be quietly amended to Loch of the Bine.

TRADITIONAL AND MODERN

Fyne blends the old and the new. Firmly traditional dark Heavy ales are accompanied by modern golden ales, all of them booming with hop notes that stress the changing nature of brewing in a country where beers have been best known in the past for their rich roasted malt character.

The brewery was founded in 2001 by Jonny and Tuggy Delap on their farm. At the time there was little good beer in the area and they decided to address the problem with their own small brewery. They launched their first beer, Highlander – a traditional strong ale – on St Andrew's Day, the same day a herd of Highland cattle arrived on the farm. In spite of the success of its golden ales, Highlander remains the beer that has won most awards for the brewery and proves there's still a place for traditional Scottish styles. The 10-barrel plant is in an old milking parlour and it uses the finest Maris Otter malting barley. Crystal-clear soft water comes from a burn behind the brewery and has filtered through peat bogs. Hops are a blend of English and imported varieties. The area is popular with visitors and the brewery draws thousands of them to its annual FyneFest in June with good music and food alongside beer, with the hills resounding to the bibulous jollity. A brewery tap has also been added and visitors can tour the brewery and have a tutored tasting before settling in the courtyard with a glass of the freshest beer possible.

The brewing team at Fyne produce a range of beers from gold to dark, but Jarl is now the biggest seller

Fyne was the first Scottish brewery to use Citra. The head brewer at the time was encouraged to try the hop and was staggered by the intense gooseberry, tropical fruit and lychee character it gives to beer

Tragically, Jonny Delap died in 2010 and didn't live to see the brewery 'go national' when Jarl won the golden ales category in CAMRA's Champion Beer of Britain competition in 2013. Jarl – pronounced 'Yarl' – takes its name from the Norwegian jarls or earls who raided the area in the 12th century. Its big citrus attack on aroma and palate comes from the use of just one hop, American Citra, a variety that dates from 2009.

Tuggy Delap and her son Jamie, who took over as managing director when his father died, think Fyne was the first Scottish brewery to use Citra. The head brewer at the time, Wil Wood – now with Lacons in Great Yarmouth – was encouraged to try the hop and was staggered by the intense gooseberry, tropical fruit and lychee character it

gives to beer. It's now the brewery's biggest-selling brand and has won a number of prestigious awards.

Fyne's large portfolio of beers ranges across the spectrum, from dark stout to golden ales and more traditional Scottish styles. Arguably the most interesting innovation comes in the shape of Superior IPA, which at 7.1% puts it firmly in the camp of the original Victorian style. The beer is not shy on hop character: hops are added four times, including while the beer is aged for a month prior to being casked or bottled. The beer is also kräusened, a rare event in British brewing. It's usually associated with traditional lager production in Germany, when young beer or sugary extract – wort – is added to the conditioning tank to encourage a strong second fermentation. In this case, Jarl is

Fyne is set in ravishing scenery, and the brewery draws visitors eager to drink in the landscape and ales

Beers to try...

Jarl, 3.8%
A robust 40 units of bitterness from Citra hops balance the honey character of the malt. It has a big blast of citrus fruit and tart hops on the aroma, with juicy malt in the mouth and a long, quenching finish that's a fine blend of honey malt, tart hops and tangy fruit.

Highlander, 4.8%
A complex, fiercely traditional Scottish beer but with powerful bitterness from Celeia, Challenger and Mount Hood hops. The beer is bittersweet with dark malt, burnt fruits and floral hops dominating the aroma and palate, but with a late burst of bitter hops in the finish.

Superior IPA, 7.1%
Hopped with Cascade and Citra, it's dominated by fruit: apricot, peaches and grapefruit, with added resinous notes from the hops. Juicy malt, tangy hops and rich fruit coat the tongue while the finish ends dry and bitter but is well balanced by sappy malt and citrus fruits.

blended with the maturing beer, heightening the hop notes. The bottled version contains active yeast and can be laid down for a year or more.

The success of the brewery and beers means growth and Jamie and his team have been busily laying the foundations for a new brewery due to come on stream at the end of 2014. It will quadruple production to 40 barrels a week and will mean that the west coast of Scotland will never be short of good beer again.

Trailblazing brewers...

BREWDOG

BrewDog's brewery is a cavernous, cathedral-like brewing hall with its steel ribs reaching out and holding up the sky; it's a lively animated space on brewing day as rock music plays and brewers mill about: clambering up steel ladders to check brewing vessels and ducking beneath metal pipes through which beer flows. Outside sit the fermenting vessels – silvery, towering cylinders that receive more hops as the beer sleeps, through something called a hop cannon. This feels like a brewery committed to the future.

However, there's one thing missing. BrewDog don't make cask beer: they stopped making it in 2011. They used to make some very good cask beers such as 5AM Saint, Paradox and even their iconic Punk IPA, but that was then this is now. Their beers are sold either in bottle or what is called – for want of a better word – craft keg. Go to any of the brewery's bars in Edinburgh, Bristol, Sheffield or London and you won't find a handpump. You will find friendly bar staff who are exceptionally knowledgeable about beer, but it won't be cask. The brewery has also had a difficult relationship with CAMRA, to say the least.

Yet, BrewDog cannot be ignored. Their craft keg might not be cask but it's neither the tinny-tasting, strained keg of the past, which had as much of a relationship with flavour as processed cheese has with the Slow Food movement. BrewDog is also seen by many drinkers as one of the most significant and exciting developments in the world of beer for many years, and those drinkers would probably include a fair many cask beer aficionados.

So what makes them trailblazing? For a start, without them we probably wouldn't have had the likes of Magic Rock (whose High Wire could be seen as a tribute to Punk IPA), Kernel and Wild Beer. For better or worse they have been an inspiration. BrewDog has brought many young men and women to beer and, in a similar way to how the Sex Pistols broke out of the punk ghetto, they have transcended the beer bubble. They have been heard of by people who rarely drink beer, a recognition factor many breweries would love. Your mum has probably heard of them.

LOVE HOPS AND LIVE THE DREAM

Even though it's not cask, BrewDog brew good beers. A bottle of their flagship Punk IPA has a pungent and arousing nose of ripe peach and apricot skin; lychee, papaya and mango trips off the tongue, while there's a gentle touch on the elbow of white pepper in the dry and grainy finish. Meanwhile Jack Hammer is a big beast of a strong IPA with its bitter finish clanging away like an alarm bell and the even stronger (9.2%) Hardcore IPA has an intense swagger of grapefruit, blue cheese and pine cones on the nose while in the mouth it is fulsome with a concentration of sweet grapefruit alongside a resiny hoppiness – this is a beer able to hold its head high against anything the likes of Stone can produce.

Without them we probably wouldn't have had the likes of Magic Rock (whose High Wire could be seen as a tribute to Punk IPA), Kernel and Wild Beer. For better or worse they have been an inspiration. BrewDog has brought many young men and women to beer

Yes they can be controversial. By and by the world of beer is a relatively cordial one but some of BrewDog's comments on the nature of British brewing not only upturned the apple cart but starting throwing the fruit about. This is something that co-founder James Watt maybe acknowledged when I met him up the north of Scotland, where the brewery have their home, early on in 2014: 'there are things we wouldn't do now.'

That was then, this is now, and the brewery continues to trailblaze, innovate and inspire. Whatever you may think of them, they are certainly never boring, and there might be things they will do in the future: such as returning to cask.

BrewDog's founders James Watt and Martin Dickie are inspiring UK brewers with their hop-forward beers

Established: 1985

Founder: Ken Brooker

Beers: Bitter & Twisted, Broken Dial, Old Engine Oil, Schiehallion, The Ridge, Ola Dubh

Website: www.harviestoun.com

HARVIESTOUN

Alva, Clackmannanshire

Harviestoun has played a pivotal role in the revival of handcrafted beer in Scotland. When Ken Brooker opened his brewery in old cattle byres in Dollar in 1985, the country was dominated by the industrial products of McEwan's and Scottish & Newcastle. Brooker, along with Broughton Ales, brought much-needed relief to parched throats north of the border. He had crossed the border: he's an Essex man who went to work in Scotland for the Ford Motor Company, grew tired of selling cars and turned to his home-brewing hobby to start a new career.

As they say in Essex, the boy done good. Using kit that was either salvaged or scrap, Brooker launched his first beer called, bluntly, Real Ale. Cynics thought it would die a death in a country where handpumped beer was as rare as the famous rocking-horse droppings. But it took off faster than a Ford Fiesta and Brooker was rushing to keep up. To deepen his Scottish credentials, he added both a 70 Shilling and an 80 Shilling, followed by an 85 Shilling with the almost impossible name of Ptarmigan.

Brooker's major creations were Schiehallion, a lager named after a local mountain – brewed, with subtle humour, with German Hersbrucker hops – and Bitter & Twisted, a hoppy golden ale. The name of the latter comes from a speeding fine that made Brooker furious and he took it out on his mash tun and copper by brewing the new ale. Both beers went on to win many British and international awards, including the supreme accolade of Champion Beer of Britain for B&T in 2003.

That was the year Harviestoun moved out of the cattle byres to a new site in nearby Alva with a modern plant capable of producing 10,000 barrels a year. It's on an industrial estate, but one with a difference – smart, modern buildings with a backdrop of the wooded Ochil hills. Stuart Cail, who had brewed with Vaux in Sunderland, joined as head brewer and fashioned new beers for a new century.

TAKEOVER AND INDEPENDENCE

Success is a double-edged sword in brewing. In 2006, Harviestoun was bought by the large Edinburgh brewery, Caledonian, best known for its Deuchars IPA. The takeover proved to be benign and came to a rapid end just two years later when Caledonian was bought by S&N and the

There are three versions, or 'expressions', to use the whisky term: 12, 18 and 30, taken from the age of the whiskies originally in the casks

Harviestoun managers bought themselves free of the deadly embrace. All the while, Stuart Cail was beavering away to produce new beers, of which Old Engine Oil, a dark porter-style beer, proved to be the most successful. Spurred by the success of Innis & Gunn in Edinburgh with its oak-aged beer, Harviestoun entered into a partnership with Highland Park distillery on Orkney, which makes some of the most-prized single malt whiskies in Scotland. While Innis & Gunn uses oak from the American Bourbon industry, Highland Park goes a different route with casks from sherry makers in Spain. Harviestoun fills the casks with a strong, 8% version of Old Engine Oil called Ola Dubh, Gaelic for black oil. There are three versions, or 'expressions', to use the whisky term: 12, 18 and 30, taken from the age of the whiskies originally in the casks. Ola Dubh has been an enormous success, especially in the United States.

Ken Brooker has deservedly retired, content in the knowledge that he helped change the perception and appreciation of Scottish beer.

Brewery staff Mike and Jonny fill Highland Park whisky casks with Ola Dubh to create their oak-aged beer

Beers to try...

Bitter & Twisted, 3.8%
The beer has creamy malt and spicy hops on the nose with a hint of citrus fruit: the fruit builds in the mouth, balanced by floral and grassy hops and honeyed malt. The finish has a lingering fruity character with gentle hop bitterness and juicy malt notes.

Old Engine Oil, 4.5 % cask, 6 % bottle
An intriguing Scottish interpretation of an English Porter. It's brewed with pale and roasted malts with a generous spoonful of oats for a creamy flavour. It has an inviting aroma of roasted grain, burnt fruit, coffee and chocolate, with some cherries lurking underneath. Coffee and dark fruits dominate the palate, with a long, complex finish packed with burnt fruit, coffee, cherries and peppery hops.

Ola Dubh, 8 %
This is Old Engine Oil with knobs on. The beer is aged in Highland Park casks and it's fascinating to taste the difference between 12, 18 and 30-year old casks. There are profound notes of oak, smoke, tannins, vanilla and honeyed malt balancing the coffee and hop character of the beer.

Highland is a newcomer to Orkney, adding to consumer's choice and appreciation

HIGHLAND

Established: 2006

Founder: Rob Hill

Beers: Orkney Best, Island Hopping, Dark Munro, Scapa Special, Sneaky Wee Orkney Stout, Orkney IPA, St Magnus Ale, Strong Northerly, Orkney Blast, Old Norway, Orkney Porter

Website: www. highlandbrewingcompany.co.uk

ORKNEY

Established: 1988

Founder: Roger White

Beers: Raven, Dragonhead, Northern Light, Red MacGregor, Corncrake, Andrews Ale, Clootie Dumpling, No. 1, Norseman Pale Ale, Dark Island, Atlas Blizzard, 1878, Skull Splitter

Website: www. sinclairbreweries.co.uk

HIGHLAND & ORKNEY

Swannay & Quoyloo, Orkney

Orkney is paradise for lovers of good beer and single malt whiskies. There are two distilleries on the islands, Highland Park and Scapa, and they are joined by two breweries, meaning a lot of grain is consumed in the production of two sublime forms of alcohol. The islands used to be a no-go area for beer, with local pubs offering only industrial brands from giant producers, until Roger White arrived and opened Orkney brewery in 1988, the first brewery on the islands for 50 years. An engineer by trade, White is that rare, possibly unique, character: a teetotal brewer, the Beethoven of the beer world, creating great beers he can't taste. Other people did taste his beers, though, and he rapidly built a reputation for quality ales across Scotland and south of the border.

The brewery was first based in an old school house with thick stone walls ideal for keeping beer at the right temperature during the production cycle. The brewing process is conducted along strict ecological lines, with waste water treated in two lakes to support fish and mallard ducks. A recent addition to the range, Corncrake Ale, helps support the work of the Royal Society for the Protection of Birds in Scotland.

Roger White retired after a long slog building up such revered beers as Raven, Dragonhead Stout and multi-award-winning Red MacGregor, Dark Island and Skull Splitter. His legacy is built on his great skill at blending traditional Scottish brewing practice with a modern twist to give his beers the flavours demanded by today's drinkers.

Highland brewery brew most of their beers on a 20-barrel kit, but they retain their original brewing equipment for creating special short-run beers

A NEW START

When Orkney was bought by the Atlas brewery on the Scottish mainland, brewer Rob Hill was made redundant. He's a tough Lancastrian who earned his brewing spurs with Moorhouse's in Burnley. Instead of sulking, he looked around for suitable premises to open his own plant and found them in buildings on an old farm in Swannay. He launched Highland Brewing in 2006 with a five-barrel kit made up of bits and pieces begged and borrowed from previous owners. His success was rapid with such beers as

Dark Munro and Scapa Special and he was forced to add a second 20-barrel plant to keep pace with demand from some 300 outlets in Scotland. He has retained the original kit for special short-run beers, such as a 9% Vintage Porter.

Both breweries have prospered. Orkney has moved into new premises at Quoyloo that has allowed it to double production and both companies have added visitor centres, with Orkney offering not only tours of the brewery but also a tasting room and café. Awards have come thick and fast, with

Orkney winning major prizes from CAMRA and SIBA nationally and, in Scotland, for Dark Island, Red MacGregor and Skull Splitter, while Highland has picked up prizes in the prestigious International Brewing Awards for Blast and IPA.

Orkney also made headlines in 2008 when it became embroiled in an absurd controversy surrounding Skull Splitter. A complaint was made to the Portman Group, which is funded by the brewing industry and monitors the way in which beer is promoted to the public. The complainant said the name encouraged people to drink strong beer to excess. Norman Sinclair, owner of Orkney, mounted a strong defence, pointing out that several of his beers commemorated figures from Orkney's past. In particular, Skull Splitter was the nickname given to Thorfinn Einarsson, the seventh earl of Orkney: the Vikings invaded the islands in the eight century and took control of them in the following century. Fortunately common sense prevailed, the complainant went away, allowing drinkers to revel in the flavours of the beer that celebrates the islands' rich history.

Orkney has added to its portfolio a highly praised 10% version of Dark Island that is aged in local whisky casks for three months and which cements the close relationship between the two barley-based drinks on the islands.

Skull Splitter was the nickname given to Thorfinn Einarsson, the seventh earl of Orkney: the Vikings invaded the islands in the eight century and took control of them in the following century

Beers to try ...

Dark Munro, 4%

A dark beer based on Rob Hill's experience of brewing award-winning mild at Moorhouse's. It's brewed with pale, chocolate and crystal malts and hopped with Fuggles and has a luscious aroma and palate of chocolate, vinous fruit, cocoa beans and spicy hops.

Dark Island, 4.6%

A true ruby-red Scottish Heavy brewed with Maris Otter pale, chocolate and crystal malts and is hopped with Goldings and Omega varieties. It has a fruity, blackcurrant aroma with roasted grain and earthy hop resins, with tart fruit developing in the mouth and finish.

Skull Splitter 8.5%

A powerful beer that recalls an ancient Scottish style known as Wee Heavy, a type of barley wine. It's brewed with pale, chocolate and crystal malts and hopped with East Kent Goldings. The deep amber beer has a massive aroma and palate of creamy malt, berry fruits, molasses, caramel and peppery hops, with hints of dates and figs.

Beer trends...
BEER AND FOOD MATCHING

In July 2014 a top wine expert astonished polite society by suggesting beer had a place on the dining table.

Christian Holthausen, a sommelier who specialises in Champagne, wrote in the *Guardian* newspaper: 'I explored the idea of selecting a wine that is tailored to the moment, but sometimes a beer could be more appropriate. The truth is that beer can be very complicated. Many sommeliers have told me – in hushed tones – that beer has a larger range of flavours than wine.' Warming to his theme, Holthausen added: 'Brewers play with more than just grapes, tanks and barrels. They can use barley or wheat (for sweetness) and hops (bitterness), as well as spices, fruits and chocolate.'

His thoughts underscored what beer writers have been arguing for years: that beer shouldn't be treated as an also-ran at the dining table – whether in the home or the pub – or thought of as just a fizzy fire extinguisher with a late-night curry. Beer comes in all colours and flavours, from pale gold to jet black, and offers rich malt and spicy, fruity and peppery notes. It's often the ideal companion for food and in some cases is a more suitable match than wine.

Pub chefs are warming to the idea of beer-and-food matching. Two top chefs in Yorkshire, James Mackenzie of the Pipe & Glass near Beverley and Andrew Pern of the Star at Harome, have joined forces with the Great Yorkshire Brewing Company to produce a 5% Honey Beer they serve with such dishes as tagliatelle of corn-fed guinea fowl, battered oyster and lemon balm fritters, goats cheese soufflé, Barnsley chop, East Coast lemon sole, and risotto of wild garlic with broad beans.

The George & Dragon in Acton, West London, re-opened in 2014 with its own small brewery and

a policy of matching beer and food. Best Bitter, Pale Ale, Wheat Beer and Dark Matter Dry Stout are served alongside the chef's pork pie and chilli; sausages and English mustard; black pudding fritters with beetroot ketchup; Dark Matter rarebit; beer fondue with garlic soldiers; and sweet potato and pulled pork hash. Tantalising and tempting food. Forget the corkscrew and reach for the beer glass.

Pub chefs Andrew Pern and James Mackenzie joined forces with the Great Yorkshire Brewing Company to develop Honey Beer for their pub restaurants

Spicy food

India Pale Ale was developed to match hot and spicy food and its quenching and bitter character cuts the pungent flavours of curry. IPA and pale ale are also a good match for Thai cuisine. There are as many beers as there are varieties of pizza: depending on the topping, amber or strong brown ale, with good hop notes, go well, with paler and bitterer beers reserved for spicier pizzas.

Fish

The Czechs, who know a bit about beer, match Pilsner or other golden lagers with carp. In general white fish and blond beers – golden ales and pale ales – are ideal companions. Trout goes well with a robust brown ale or porter while it's a good idea to follow the Irish and drink stout with shellfish: there are many stout and oyster festivals in the Emerald Isle.

Desserts

Fruity beers – either those using citrus-strong hops or actual fruit – cut the sweetness of creamy desserts. With chocolate desserts, the acidity of stout tackles the sweetness of the dish.

Cheese

Beer is the perfect partner for cheese: it's no accident that the Trappist breweries in Belgium make cheese as well as beer. Pale Ale in particular goes well with the salty, tangy nature of blue cheese, while softer and creamier cheeses should be accompanied by a strong amber or dark beer offering roasted malt and spicy hops.

Established: 2004

Founder: Steve Stewart

Beers: Zymic, Pentland IPA, Copper Cascade, Edinburgh No.3, 80/-, Coconut Porter, Edinburgh Gold, Black IPA, Embra, Hollyrood, St. Giles, Hefewiezen, Pilsen, Cauld Reekie, Radical Road, Doppelbock

Website: www.stewartbrewing.co.uk

STEWART

Loanhead, Midlothian

Steve Stewart's approach to putting something back into the community is to pay homage to his alma mater. Alongside his main brewery, he has built a smaller pilot plant called the Craft Beer Kitchen where students from Heriot-Watt University in Edinburgh can hone their brewing skills. The university has an acclaimed International Centre for Brewing and Distilling and it was there that Steve moved up a gear from home brewing to commercial production. Now he encourages students to turn theory into practice by using his equipment.

In 2014, with a fanfare of publicity, four of them – called the Natural Selection Brewing Team, in deference to the work of Charles Darwin – launched Mutiny on the Beagle. *Beagle* was the name of Darwin's ship when he toured the world to refine his theory of the origin of species and the beer is a classic English-style India Pale Ale that uses only

The beers can be both weird and wonderful, including Hopricot made with the addition of apricots

home-grown hops: Admiral, First Gold, Pilgrim and a new hop currently under development.

Steve Stewart is delighted to welcome the students as part of his dedication to producing full-flavoured beers that reflect ancient and modern brewing practice in Scotland. When he left Heriot-Watt he studied for a Masters in energy and the environment, where he met his wife, Jo, who is now shoulder to shoulder with him at the brewery and takes charge of sales.

US INSPIRATION

When he finished his studies, Steve spent useful time working for the major British brewing group Bass, where he learnt just about everything there is to know about making beer and retailing it. But it was when he brewed at the small craft Harpoon plant in Boston, Massachusetts, where an acclaimed IPA is brewed, that he finally got the inspiration to go back home and launch his own company.

With the help of Jo's father, he assembled a 10-barrel plant and opened for business in 2004. Two of the three beers that formed the early portfolio made a deep bow in the direction of traditional Scottish brewing. Edinburgh No 3 recalls Younger's No 3, a style known as Export that was Scotland's interpretation of English IPA. 80/- helps restore one of the most famous Scottish styles, a true Heavy brewed with several dark malts and only lightly hopped. Edinburgh Gold is a beer with a modern twist: unlike the 80/-, it's a heavily hopped beer and has the tart, citrus character demanded by many younger drinkers.

Within a decade, the Stewarts had burst out of their first home and moved to a new site where they built a larger brewery. The modern kit comes from Bavaria and is based on the Continental system of mash mixer, lauter or filtration vessel, and copper whirlpool. Production has been expanded as has the beer range, which now includes Pentland IPA and Copper Cascade. The large brewery complex employs some two dozen people.

The Craft Beer Kitchen is not just for the use of Heriot-Watt students. Members of the public, home brewers and publicans can descend on the brewery at weekends and design and brew their own recipes. The beers can be both weird and wonderful,

including Hopricot made with the addition of apricots, Popcorn Pilsner and the sour Berliner Weisse style of wheat beer brewed with the addition of blackcurrants. When you visit Stewart, fasten your seat belt and prepare for an exhilarating ride.

Beers to try...

Edinburgh No.3, 4.3%
Brewed with Maris Otter pale, chocolate and crystal malts and hopped with just English Challenger. It has a toasted malt aroma and palate, with chocolate and cobnuts, balanced by spicy hops.

80/-, 4.4%
In sharp contrast to No 3, this beer has a complex hop make-up of Challenger, German Magnum and Tettnanger, and Styrian Goldings. The auburn-coloured beer has a bready/malty aroma of roast, chocolate and Ovaltine, with sultana fruit and spicy hops building in the mouth. The finish is bittersweet to start but ends dry with rich malt, dark fruits, chocolate and hop resins.

Edinburgh Gold, 4.8%
Brewed with pale, cara pils and wheat malts and generously hopped with Challenger, Magnum, Tettnanger and Styrian Goldings. Citrus fruit bursts from the glass with juicy malt and grassy hops. Tart and tangy hops dominate the palate but are balanced by sappy malt and herbal hops. The long, lingering finish is packed with tart fruit, spicy hops and juicy malt.

Established: 1998

Founder: Bruce and Scott Williams

Beers: Harvest Sun, Gold, Fraoch Heather Ale, 80/-, Black, Roisin, September Song, Birds & Bees, Cock O' the Walk, Kelpie, Red, Movember Foxtrot Whisky, Yule Smile, Good Times, Grozet, Joker IPA, Seven Giraffes, October Zest, Midnight Sun, Ebulum, Profanity Stout, Alba Scots Pine Ale

Website: www.williamsbrosbrew.com

WILLIAMS BROTHERS

Alloa, Clackmannanshire

Bruce and Scott Williams have a great passion for Scottish brewing and its historic roots, which they've brought to bear on a range of beers that have won world-wide acclaim. Their most famous beer, Fraoch, is a beer made with heather and has helped create an interest in brewing with ingredients that reach beyond barley and hops. The story begins in the Williams family's home-brew shop in Glasgow in 1988. A Gaelic-speaking woman from the Western Isles came to the shop with the translation of a recipe for a beer called Leanne Fraoch – Heather Ale. The origins of the beer were lost in the mists of time, brewed not by Celts but by Picts, a cave-dwelling race that was brutally exterminated by Irish raiders in the fourth century.

According to legend, the last Pict threw himself from the cliffs into the sea rather than pass on the secret of heather ale to the King of Ireland.

But heather ale lingered on in remote parts of the Highlands and Islands. A visitor to Islay in 1744 noted that beer there was made from malt, hops and 'heath'. Ancient Pictish kilns have been discovered in Galloway and in his 19th-century book Curiosities of Ale and Beer, John Bickerdyke described the way in which heather was used to brew: 'The blossoms of the heather are carefully gathered and cleansed, then placed in the bottom of the vessels. Wort of the ordinary kind is allowed to drain through the blossoms and gains in its passage the peculiar flavour known to all familiar with

According to legend, the last Pict threw himself from the cliffs into the sea rather than pass on the secret of heather ale to the King of Ireland

Williams Brothers have had great success in export markets with Fraoch but they've added a range of conventional beers for domestic sale

heather honey.' The beer has close connections to the *sahti* beers made in Nordic countries where the beer is filtered through juniper twigs.

Bruce Williams was fascinated with the recipe he'd been given and he brewed his interpretation of Fraoch – pronounced 'frook' – at several Scottish breweries until he was joined by his brother Scott in 2004 and they moved in to the former bottling hall of George Younger's brewery in Alloa. It was a good town to choose for Alloa was once called the 'Capital of Brewing in Scotland' due to the fine water that percolates down from the mountains and, in common with Burton upon Trent in England, is ideal for producing distinctive ales. Fraoch has become an international cult beer and is in such demand in cask and bottled forms that the brothers and their staff have to refrigerate heather when it's

The beers include Alba made with sprigs of Scottish spruce and pine, and based on a Viking recipe

The brewery changed its name to Williams Brothers when it decided to add more conventional cask beers to the range

harvested in order to have sufficient supplies to brew the beer all year round.

The brothers started with a 10-barrel plant but have expanded dramatically and now have 25 recipes that are produced on a regular or seasonal basis. Delving into Scottish brewing history, the beers include Alba made with sprigs of Scottish spruce and pine, and based on a Viking recipe – another connection to *sahti* – Grozet brewed with gooseberries from a 16th-century monks' recipe, Ebulum, an elderberry black ale first brewed by Welsh Druids who brought their recipe to Scotland, and Kelpie made with seaweed. Nollaig is brewed with spruce for Christmas and Hogmanay and is the ideal companion when kissing under the mistletoe.

BEERS MADE WITH SEVEN GRAINS

Bruce and Scott decided to change the name of the brewery from Fraoch to Williams Brothers when they added a range of more conventional cask beers that could be sold in pubs and bars across Scotland. They include a traditional 80/-, a red ale, several golden beers and the mighty 7% Profanity Stout. One of the brothers' most popular beers is Seven Giraffes, an India Pale Ale that is infused with citrus and elderflower. It's brewed with seven grains – lager malt, ale malt, wheat, Vienna, Munich, pale rye and pale crystal malts, and is hopped with Amarillo, Cascade and First Gold varieties. The curious name comes courtesy of Scott's young daughter. She heard him talking about seven grains but thought he'd said seven giraffes: her toy giraffe graces the label.

The finest version of Fraoch is an 11 % beer that has been aged for a year in oak casks obtained from the Auchentoshan single malt whisky distillery. The casks, originally used to make sherry in Spain, deliver an added layer of oak, smoke, vanilla and sweet wine to the already complex flavours of the beer. There's never a dull moment but plenty of surprises at the brothers' brewery.

Unusual ingredients, including heather, gooseberry, spruce and pine, are added to malt and hops to create the beers

Beers to try ...

Kelpie, 4.4%

Brewed with bladderwrack seaweed along with pale malt and First Gold hops. The pale beer has an iron-like aroma and palate, balanced by sappy malt and spicy hops. The finish is tart and tangy with a herbal and fruity intensity.

Fraoch Heather Ale, 5%

Brewed with pale malt, carapils, flowering heather and bog myrtle, and hopped with First Gold. The beer has a delicate flowery, fruity bouquet with minty notes on the palate, balanced by gentle hop resins and juicy malt. The finish is dry, earthy, minty, floral and quenching.

Seven Giraffes, 5.1%

Honeyed malt and citrus fruit from the hops are joined by the earthy, fruity, minty notes of elderflower. There's a hint of toffee on the palate and the finish is lingering, quenching, hoppy and fruity.

BEER DESTINATIONS

PRINCE OF WALES
Aberdeen
www.princeofwales-aberdeen.co.uk

This ancient ale house, tucked away down an alley off the main Union Street, is an Aberdeen institution: a pub that served good beer when all around offered nothing but fizz. Inside, this heritage pub has the longest bar in the Granite City, with flagstone floors, pews and side booths. At the bar, chefs work in an open kitchen to supply full meals and snacks: the pub is open for breakfast. It's now part of the Belhaven group, owned by Greene King in England, and you will find their beers on the bar, but there's a tremendous range of beers from smaller independent breweries, including Kelham Island Pale Rider and Theakston Old Peculier from Yorkshire and Hop Back Summer Lightning from the deep south. There are folk and quiz nights.

CAFÉ ROYAL
Edinburgh, Midlothian
www.caferoyaledinburgh.co.uk

Nothing can quite prepare you for this: the marble floor, the leather bench seats, the ornate moulded ceiling, the tiled fireplace, the chandeliers and the vast central bar with a magnificent mahogany gantry. It pays homage to the pomp and pride of Victorian Britain, a pride underscored by its most famous feature of all, six tiled murals depicting inventors and innovators: Benjamin Franklin, William Caxton, James Watt, George Stephenson, Robert Peel and Michael Faraday. Etched glass doors lead to the Oyster Bar that serves fish and seafood in surroundings every bit as elegant as the main bar: there's wood panelling, more tiled murals and a series of stained glass windows illustrating archery, tennis, rugby and even cricket. Deuchars IPA is always on the bar with guest ales from several other Scottish breweries. Go and marvel.

OXFORD BAR
Edinburgh, Midlothian
www.oxfordbar.co.uk

'The Ox' is penny plain compared to the Café Royal's grandeur, but it's been a New Town institution since the late 19th century. It sprang to national and even international fame as the preferred drinking place for Inspector Rebus, the hard-drinking cop in Ian Rankin's novels. The author himself can occasionally be spotted sampling a glass of Deuchars IPA. The front bar is tiny, dominated by its counter, but there's a more spacious room up a few steps to the side, with wooden tables and chairs. It's popular with rugby fans on match days and attracts a wide clientele of what used to be called the demi monde of writers, artists and the kind of people who would pass on information to Rebus in return for a pint. It's an arresting place.

BABBITY BOWSTER
Glasgow
www.babbitybowster.com

A pub, restaurant and hotel, it takes its name from a Scottish dance and theme is stressed by drawings of musicians on the walls. It's a brilliant recreation of an 18th-century coffee house, based in a tall and elegant building in the Merchant City area of Glasgow. The ground-floor bar is spacious and well lit from large windows, with plenty of standing room as well as wooden tables on stripped wood floors. There's a welcome open fire, fuelled by peat, on colder days. The Bowster has a deserved reputation for the quality of its food, with a French chef serving the upstairs restaurant, which concentrates on local Scottish ingredients, including fish and seafood. Meals are also served in the downstairs bar. Deuchars IPA is a regular beer with Jarl from Fyne Ales and regular guest beers, all served by Scottish tall founts. The pub even boasts a beer garden: a rarity in Glasgow.

THREE JUDGES
Glasgow
www.threejudges.co.uk

This was where the good beer flag was unfurled and proudly displayed during the dog days of Scottish brewing. Away from the city centre and over the road from Kelvinhall Underground station, a passionate and revered landlord called Charles Rennie served cask ales from near and far and inspired other publicans to follow his lead and prove there was more to beer than the keg offerings of S&N and Tennents. His success can be measured by the number of framed awards from the local branch of CAMRA and the display of beer mats stuck to walls and ceilings. The Three Judges has a large bar with a brass rail and foot rest, with eight handpumps serving beer from throughout Britain: one pump is reserved for cider. Deuchars IPA is a regular. Go and pay homage: there's no food but customers are welcome to take their own.

Aberdeen

Glasgow

Edinburgh

The Oxford Blue is an Edinburgh institution, and has been immortalised by crime writer Ian Rankin as the local of his most famous character Inspector Rebus

INDEX

BOOKS FOR BEER LOVERS

CAMRA Books, the publishing arm of the Campaign for Real Ale, is the leading publisher of books on beer and pubs. Key titles include:

Good Beer Guide 2015
Editor: Roger Protz

The original independent guide to good beer and good pubs. You're never far from a great pint with the *Good Beer Guide* to hand. Now in its 42nd edition, the fully revised and updated Guide recommends pubs in England, Wales, Scotland, Northern Ireland and offshore islands that serve the best real ale. From country inns through urban style bars to backstreet boozers – if you love pubs, don't leave home without the Good Beer Guide.
£15.99 ISBN 978-1-85249-320-2

300 More Beers to Try Before You Die!
Roger Protz

300 More Beers to Try Before You Die! takes beer lovers on an exciting new odyssey through 300 of the best beers from around the world. A companion volume to the best-selling *300 Beers to Try Before You Die!*, award-winning beer writer Roger Protz selects 300 more beers that represent the most interesting products of the brewer's art available today. The book charts the world-wide beer revival and features new ales from America, rediscovered classics like English abbey beer and inventive new twists on age-old recipes from experimental brewers in Europe and beyond, plus much, much more.
£14.99 ISBN 978-1-85249-295-3

Great British Pubs
Adrian Tierney-Jones

Great British Pubs is a practical guide that takes you around the very best public houses in Britain and celebrates the pub as a national institution. Every kind of pub is represented in these pages with categorised listings featuring full-colour photography illustrating a host of excellent pubs from the seaside to the city and from the historic to the ultra-modern. Articles on beer brewing, cider making, classic pub food recipes and traditional pub games are included to help the reader fully understand what makes a pub 'Great'.
£14.99 ISBN 987-1-85249-265-6

The Beer Select-O-Pedia
Michael Larson

The Beer Select-O-Pedia is an enthusiast's guide through the delicious world of beer, demystifying scores of traditional and innovative new styles from Britain & Ireland, Continental Europe and America. Organised into families of beer styles according to their origins, it is easy to look up the style of beer you are drinking and discover more. Much more than a list of recommended brews and breweries, this book gives beer lovers all the information they need to navigate the ever-expanding world of beer and find new brews to excite their tastebuds.
£12.99 ISBN 978-1-85249-318-9

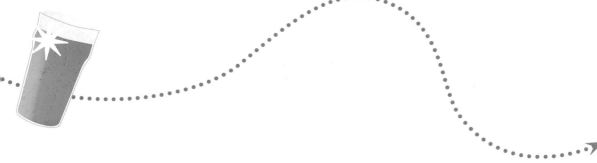

Good Bottled Beer Guide
Jeff Evans

A pocket-sized guide for discerning drinkers looking to buy bottled real ales and enjoy a fresh glass of their favourite beers at home. The 8th edition of the *Good Bottled Beer Guide* is completely revised, updated and redesigned to showcase the very best bottled British real ales now being produced, and detail where they can be bought. Everything you need to know about bottled beers; tasting notes, ingredients, brewery details, and a glossary to help the reader understand more about them.
£12.99 ISBN 978-1-85249-309-7

Good Beer Guide Belgium
Tim Webb & Joe Stange

The Good Beer Guide Belgium is CAMRA's iconic guide to the world-renowned home of serious beers. Completely revised and updated, this is the indispensible work for all Belgian beer lovers, even in Belgium itself. The definitive, totally independent guide to understanding and finding the best that Belgian brewing has to offer. The Guide is an essential companion for any visit to Belgium or for seeking out quality Belgian beer around the world.
£14.99 ISBN 978-1-85249-311-0

Brew Your Own British Real Ale
Graham Wheeler

The perennial favourite of home-brewers, *Brew Your Own British Real Ale* is a CAMRA classic. This new edition is enhanced and illustrated. Written by homebrewing authority Graham Wheeler, *Brew Your Own British Real Ale* includes detailed brewing instructions for both novice and more advanced home-brewers, as well as comprehensive recipes for recreating some of Britain's best-loved beers at home.
£14.99 ISBN 978-1-85249-319-6

101 Beer Days Out
Tim Hampson

101 Beer Days Out is the perfect handbook for the beer tourist wanting to explore beer and brewing culture in their local area and around the UK. From historic city pubs to beer festivals; idyllic country pub walks to rail ale trails; tourist brewery tours to serious brewing courses – Britain has beer and brewing experiences to rival any in the world. *101 Beer Days Out* brings together for the first time the best of these experiences, ordered geographically and with full visitor information, maps and colour photography – the best way to celebrate Britain's national drink.
£12.99 ISBN 978-1-85249-288-5

Order these and other CAMRA books online at www.camra.org.uk/books, ask at your local bookstore, or contact: CAMRA, 230 Hatfield Road, St Albans, AL1 4LW. Telephone 01727 867201

A CAMPAIGN OF TWO HALVES

Campaigning for Pub Goers & Beer Drinkers

CAMRA, the Campaign for Real Ale, is the not-for-profit independent voice of real ale drinkers and pub goers. CAMRA's vision is to have quality real ale and thriving pubs in every community. We campaign tirelessly to achieve this goal, as well as lobbying government to champion drinkers' rights. As a CAMRA member you will have the opportunity to campaign to save pubs under threat of closure, for pubs to be free to serve a range of real ales at fair prices and for a long term freeze in beer duty that will help Britain's brewing industry survive.

Enjoying Real Ale & Pubs

CAMRA has over 165,000 members from all ages and backgrounds, brought together by a common belief in the issues that CAMRA deals with and their love of good quality British beer. From just £23* a year – that's less than a pint a month – you can join CAMRA and enjoy the following benefits:

Subscription to *What's Brewing*, our monthly colour newspaper, and *Beer*, our quarterly magazine, informing you about beer and pub news and detailing events and beer festivals around the country.

Free or reduced entry to over 160 national, regional and local beer festivals.

Money off many of our publications including the *Good Beer Guide,* the *Good Bottled Beer Guide* and *Great British Pubs.*

Access to a members-only section of our national website, www.camra.org.uk, which gives up-to-the-minute news stories and includes a special offer section with regular features.

Special discounts with numerous partner organisations and money off real ale in your participating local pubs as part of our Pubs Discount Scheme.

Log onto **www.camra.org.uk/join** for CAMRA membership information.

CAMPAIGN
FOR
REAL ALE

*£23 membership cost stated is only available via Direct Debit, other concessionary rates available. Please note membership rates stated are correct at the time of printing but are subject to change. Full details of all membership rates can be found at: www.camra.org.uk/membershiprates